汉英对照针灸美容

Chinese-English Edition
of Acupuncture Cosmetology

主编 郑美凤
Chief Compiler   Zheng Mei-feng

主译 韩丑萍
Chief Translator   Han Chou-ping

上海科学技术出版社
Shanghai Scientific and Technical Publishers

Shanghai Scientific and Technical Publishers
71 Qinzhou Road(South), Shanghai, 200235, China

Chinese-English Edition of Acupuncture Cosmetology
Chief Compiler Zheng Mei-feng Chief Translator Han Chou-ping

ISBN 978－7－5323－8908－7   paperback

图书在版编目（CIP）数据

汉英对照针灸美容 = Chinese-English Edition of Acupuncture Cosmetology／郑美凤主编;韩丑萍主译.—上海：上海科学技术出版社,2007.9
　ISBN 978－7－5323－8908－7

　Ⅰ.汉…　Ⅱ.①郑…②韩…　Ⅲ.美容-针灸疗法-汉、英
Ⅳ.R246.7

　中国版本图书馆 CIP 数据核字(2007)第 053803 号

上海世纪出版股份有限公司
上 海 科 学 技 术 出 版 社　出版发行
（上海钦州南路 71 号　邮政编码 200235）
苏州望电印刷有限公司印刷　新华书店上海发行所经销
开本 889×1194　1/32　印张 10.5　字数 268 千
2007 年 9 月第 1 版　2007 年 9 月第 1 次印刷
定价：28.00 元

本书如有缺页、错装或坏损等严重质量问题，
请向印刷厂联系调换

内容提要

　　针灸美容从中医学的整体观念出发,充分调动人体自身的积极因素,具有简便易行、安全可靠、效果显著、无不良反应等特点,力求从根本上使人变美,为人体美容提供了一条行之有效的途径。

　　本书共分上、中、下三篇。上篇为针灸美容基础理论,介绍针灸美容的概述、解剖学基础、常用穴位和常用方法,其中针灸美容的常用方法包括体针、耳针、三棱针、皮肤针、火针、电针、穴位埋线、穴位注射、艾灸和拔罐。中篇为针灸美容治疗,介绍皮肤科、五官科及其他损美性病证的治疗和针灸保健美容。下篇为针灸美容典型验案介绍。

　　本书内容丰富,通俗易懂,可作为海内外广大临床医生、医学院校学生、留学生、美容院美容师的参考用书,亦可作为广大美容爱好者的学习用书。

汉英对照

Chinese-English
Edition of
Acupuncture
Cosmetology

针灸美容

Synopsis of Contents

汉英对照

Chinese-English
Edition of
Acupuncture
Cosmetology

针灸美容

Based on the holistic view of traditional Chinese medicine, acupuncture cosmetology acts to bring all active factors of the human body into play. It is easy, safe and reliable with remarkable effects but without adverse reactions, and therefore it provides an effective means for human cosmetology.

This book consists of three parts. The first part contains the basic theory, the outlines, anatomy basis, common acupoints and common methods of acupuncture cosmetology. The common methods include body needles, auricular needles, three-edged needle, dermal needle, fire needle, electric acupuncture, catgut implantation on acupoints, acupoint injection, moxibustion and cupping. The second part is the treatment and acupuncture health-preservation cosmetology involving dermatology, ENT and other beauty-impairing conditions. The third part collects typical case reports of acupuncture cosmetology.

With rich contents and easy-to-understand words, this book can serve as a good reference book for clinicians, medical students, international students and beauty salon workers as well as those who are interested in facial beautification.

前　言

　　随着社会发展和人民生活水平的提高，人们已经逐步形成了不仅要长寿，而且要健康美貌的理念，追求美已成为一种时尚，美容已成为目前人们的热门话题之一。中国针灸具有悠久的历史，不仅有公认的临床治疗效果，更有卓著的强身健体、美容养颜的功效，适合当今社会的需求。针灸美容从中医学的整体观念出发，充分调动人体自身的积极因素，具有简便易行、安全可靠、效果显著、无不良反应等特点，从根本上使人变美，为人体美容提供了一条行之有效的途径。目前，已引起了国内外不少美容专家的重视，越来越受到美容医师和广大患者的青睐。

　　本书共分上、中、下三篇。上篇为针灸美容基础理论，介绍针灸美容的概述、解剖学基础、常用穴位和常用方法，其中针灸美容的常用方法包括体针、耳针、三棱针、皮肤针、火针、电针、穴位埋线、穴位注射、艾灸和拔罐。中篇为针灸美容治疗，介绍皮肤科、五官科及其他损美性病证的治疗和针灸保健美容。下篇为针灸美容典型验案介绍。全书图文并茂，内容丰富，通俗易懂，汉英对照，可作为海内外广大临床医生、医学院校学生、留学生、美容院美容师的参考用书，亦可作为广大美容爱好者的学习用书。

汉英对照

Chinese-English
Edition of
Acupuncture
Cosmetology

针灸美容

本书承蒙上海科学技术出版社单宝枝女士的指导和大力支持,在此表示衷心的感谢!

在编写过程中参考了大量公开出版的文献资料,由于时间仓促,未能与相关作者一一联系,在此一并致呈谢意,并于书末列出了参考文献名称。由于编者水平有限,书中错误纰漏、欠妥之处在所难免,敬希广大读者批评指正。

编　者

2006 年 12 月于中国福州

Preface

With social advances and improvement of living conditions, people started to pursue not only longevity but also health and beauty. The pursuit of beauty or cosmetology has now become a hot and fashionable topic. Owing to its long history, Chinese acupuncture can obtain recognized therapeutic efficacy as well as functions in health-building and facial beauty. Based on the holistic view of traditional Chinese medicine, acupuncture cosmetology acts to bring all active factors of the human body into play. It is easy, safe and reliable with remarkable effects but without adverse reactions, and therefore it provides an effective means for human cosmetology. Currently acupuncture cosmetology has attracted attention from cosmetology experts from both home and abroad and become popular among cosmetology workers and varieties of customers.

This book consists of three parts. The first part contains the basic theory, the outlines, anatomy basis, common acupoints and common methods of acupuncture cosmetology. The common methods include body needles, auricular needles, three-edged needle, dermal needle, fire needle, electric acupuncture, catgut implantation on acupoints, acupoint injection, moxibustion and cupping. The second part is the

汉英对照
Chinese-English
Edition of
Acupuncture
Cosmetology

针灸美容

汉英对照

Chinese-English
Edition of
Acupuncture
Cosmetology

针灸美容

treatment and acupuncture health-preservation cosmetology involving dermatology, ENT and other beauty-impairing conditions. The third part collects typical case reports of acupuncture cosmetology. With illustrations, rich contents and easy-to-understand words, this book can serve as a good reference book for clinicians, medical students, international students and beauty salon workers as well as those who are interested in facial beautification.

I'd like to extend my sincere thanks here to Madame Shan Bao-zhi from Shanghai Scientific & Technical Publishers for her instructions and support!

Due to the tight schedule, I failed to contact all the authors concerned during quoting the relevant published literature, books and data and I'd like to extend my thanks to all of them here as well and have listed references at the end of the book. For the possible careless omissions or inappropriate expressions, any suggestions from the readers are welcome for the future improvement.

Zheng Mei-feng

December 2006, Fuzhou, China

目　录

汉英对照

Chinese-English
Edition of
Acupuncture
Cosmetology

针灸美容

中篇

针灸美容治疗

下篇

针灸美容典型验案

汉英对照

Chinese-English
Edition of
Acupuncture
Cosmetology

针灸美容

Contents

汉英对照
Chinese-English
Edition of
Acupuncture
Cosmetology

针灸美容

Part 2

The Treatment of Acupuncture Cosmetology

Part 3

The Typical Case Reports of Acupuncture Cosmetology

汉英对照

Chinese-English
Edition of
Acupuncture
Cosmetology

针灸美容

汉英对照

Chinese-English
Edition of
Acupuncture
Cosmetology

针灸美容

上篇
针灸美容基础理论

Part 1
The Basic Theory of Acupuncture Cosmetology

第一章　针灸美容的概述

汉英对照

Chinese-English
Edition of
Acupuncture
Cosmetology

针灸美容

上篇 ◉ 针灸美容基础理论

　　针灸美容就是从中国传统医学的整体观念出发，以针灸方法为手段，通过对局部皮肤及穴位的刺激，达到疏通经络、调理脏腑、和顺气血、消肿散结，从而减轻或消除影响容貌的某些生理性变化或病理性疾患，获得强身健体、美化容颜、延缓衰老目的的一种方法。具有简便易行、无毒无害、安全可靠、效果迅速、疗效持久、不易复发、适应证广等特点。

　　中医学认为：外表容貌只是人体这个有机整体的一部分，它的荣衰与机体内在脏腑、经络、气血有密切联系。《灵枢·邪气藏府病形》中有："十二经脉，三百六十五络，其血气皆上于面，而走空窍，其气之津液，皆上熏于面。"指出了气血津液，水谷精微通过经络上循于面，才能使其红润光泽，富有弹性。可见，只有脏腑功能正常，气血旺盛，才能青春常驻。因此，美容应当从调理脏腑、经络气血着手，从根本上解决、改善外表容貌的问题，这才是真正的、治本的美容方法。而针灸美容就是从中医的这个整体观念出发，达到调和脏腑气血、强身健体、美容养生的目的。

Chapter 1
The outlines of acupuncture cosmetology

Acupuncture cosmetology refers to an approach to keep fit, beautify appearance and delay the aging process through acupuncture. This approach is based on the holistic view of traditional Chinese medicine and acts to dredge meridians, regulate zang-fu organs, harmonize qi and blood, remove swelling, dissipate masses and thus relieve or remove some physiological or pathological beauty-impairing conditions through stimulating local skin and acupoints. Also, this approach is simple, safe and reliable with fast or persistent effect, extensive indications and slim chance of recurrence but without harmful side effects.

TCM holds that a person's appearance is just one part of the whole body and closely related to the internal organs, meridians, qi and blood. The *Ling Shu · Xie Qi Zang Fu Bing Xing* (the 4th chapter of *Huang Di Nei Jing · Ling Shu*) states that "the qi and blood of 12 regular meridians and 365 collaterals all ascend to the face and the fluids of qi are also carried to the face", indicating that qi, blood, body fluids and nutrients transformed from water and food ascend to the face through meridians and make the face red, moistening, lustrous and elastic. Therefore only with normal functions of zang-fu organs and abundant qi and blood, can youth and beauty remain forever. As a result, regulation on zang-fu organs, meridians, qi and blood is the true and primary cosmetic approach for facial appearance. Based on the holistic view of traditional Chinese medicine, acupuncture cosmetology aims to regulate

汉英对照

Chinese-English
Edition of
Acupuncture
Cosmetology

针灸美容

上篇 ● 针灸美容基础理论

实践证明,针灸美容具有其他美容方法不可比拟的持久疗效。对于治疗肥胖症、黄褐斑、痤疮、扁平疣、老年斑、脱发及其他损容性病证等都有显著的效果。现在开展较多的有针灸瘦脸、针灸瘦身、针灸祛斑、针灸祛痤疮、针灸祛黑眼圈、针灸祛眼袋、针灸改变肤色、针灸丰胸等等,并不断扩大它的应用范围。通过针灸改善局部乃至全身的血液循环、皮肤与皮脂的新陈代谢、提高机体内外的免疫能力。

针灸美容没有绝对禁忌证,同任何疗法适当配合都能提高疗效。而且针灸美容较之于仅注重局部皮肤营养而达到美化容颜的西方美容方法,效果更加稳定、持久,这也是针灸美容越来越引起人们重视和关注的一个重要原因。针灸通过内调外治、标本兼治来调整机体,针灸美容既重视局部,更重视整体,从整体观念出发,标本兼治,由内而外,达到美容的效果。且在针灸美容的同时还可兼治体内许多疾病。可以断言,在新世纪里针灸美容将有一个突飞猛进的发展。

functions of zang-fu organs, qi and blood, consolidate body resistance, beautify the appearance and preserve health.

It's been proved that acupuncture can produce persistent cosmetic effect that can never be obtained by other cosmetic methods. Acupuncture has marked effect in the treatment of obesity, chloasma, acne, flat wart, senile plaque, loss of hair and other beauty-impairing conditions. The current acupuncture cosmetic items mainly include shaping facial lift, weight loss, chloasma, acne, panda eyes, baggy eyelids, beautification of skin colors and breast augmentation. Actually the application scope of cosmetic acupuncture has been spreading all the time. Acupuncture can improve local or even general blood circulation, metabolism of skin and sebum and immunity of the organism.

Acupuncture has no absolute contraindications and can work together with any other therapies to improve the result. In addition, acupuncture cosmetology can produce more stable and persistent effect than western cosmetic methods that only target on local skin nutrition; and that is also why it is now attracting more and more attention. Acupuncture aims to regulate the whole body through actions on both internal organs and external symptoms. Acupuncture cosmetology attaches emphasis on local area but more on the whole body. What's more, in addition to cosmetology, acupuncture can also work well for varieties of diseases. Consequently it can be concluded that acupuncture cosmetology will have a dramatic breakthrough in the new century.

汉英对照

Chinese-English
Edition of
Acupuncture
Cosmetology

针灸美容

上篇 ◉ 针灸美容基础理论

第二章　针灸美容的解剖学基础

第一节　针灸美容与经络的关系

中医学认为,人体以五脏为中心,通过经络系统将脏腑、四肢百骸、五官九窍、皮肉筋骨等将全身各组织器官联系成有机的整体;又通过经络运行精、气、血、津液的营养作用,维持着各自不同的生命活动。人体各部既有着不同的生理功能,但又共同进行着有机的整体活动,通过经络系统的联络、沟通的架构使机体的内外上下保持着协调统一,构成一个有机的整体。

经络系统由经脉与络脉构成。经脉是经络系统的主干,包括十二经脉及其相连属的部分(十二经别、十二经筋、十二皮部)以及奇经八脉;络脉主要是十五络脉以及孙络、浮络等。《灵枢·海论》说:"夫十二经脉者,内属于府藏,外络于肢节。"由于十二经脉及其分支纵横交错、入里出表、通达上下,联系了脏腑器官;奇经八脉沟通于十二经之间,经别打通了经脉体表与内脏、肢末与头胸腹的联系;经筋、皮部联结了肢体筋肉皮肤。经络于人体无处不在,贯穿上下内外,起到运行气血,濡养周身,抗御外邪,保卫机体,联系内外,反映证候的作用。当某一脏器或局部发生病症时,可以通过经络系统反映到体表或全身,同样,全身的疾病也可反映在某一局部,形成具有一定规律的经络证候,医生就可以依据这个规律做出临床辨证,提供治疗的基础。

Chapter 2
The anatomy basis of acupuncture cosmetology

Section 1
The relationship between acupuncture cosmetology and meridians

TCM holds that the human body is centered on five zang-organs and connects general tissues and organs (including zang-fu organs, limbs, bones, five sense organs, nine orifices, skin, muscle and tendons) into an organic whole through meridian system; in addition, the human body maintains respective life activities also through distributing essence, qi, blood and body fluids by meridians. Different parts of the body have different physiological functions but they share the common organic activities and keep perfect harmony and unity through connection of meridians.

The meridian system consists of meridians and collaterals; the former constitutes the main trunks of meridian system and includes the 12 regular meridians and their attachments (12 divergent meridians, 12 muscle regions and 12 cutaneous regions) as well as eight extraordinary meridians, while the latter mainly refers to 15 collaterals, minute collaterals and superficial collaterals. The *Ling Shu* · *Hai Lun* (the 33rd chapter of *Ling Shu*) states that "internally, the 12 regular meridians connect with the zang-fu organs, and externally with the joints, limbs and other superficial tissues of the body". As the 12 regular meridians and their branches connect zang-fu organs through relationship of interior and exterior, and upper body and lower body; the eight extraordinary meridians link all

汉英对照
Chinese-English
Edition of
Acupuncture
Cosmetology

针灸美容

Part 1 The Basic Theory of Acupuncture Cosmetology

气血是经经络系统传注、输布周身以温养、濡润人体的各个脏腑组织器官并维持其功能正常的物质基础；也是脏腑经络功能正常的产物。人的面部皮肤红润光泽、细腻滑润、富有弹性；毛发浓密光亮、乌黑柔顺；身体的匀称健美等等，都有赖于充足的阳气、阴血、津液通过经络源源不断地输送。同时，经络也将不利于人体的代谢产物及时排出，从而避免了损容性疾病的发生。可见脏腑、经络的功能正常，人体才能表现为健康的美。如果某一脏腑发生病变或某一经络功能障碍，导致气血不足或气血失调；或导致护卫机体的功能减弱，外邪侵袭于内，邪毒内蕴，代谢异常，也必然会通过经络、脏腑、体表之间的复杂联系反映出来，表现为面色萎黄或苍白，面容憔悴，皱纹满布，皮肤苍老晦暗，弹性减弱，毛发干枯早白、稀疏脱落等多种损容性疾病或形体不匀称等多种损形性疾病。自古《素问·上古天真论》就有记载："女子……五七阳明脉衰，面始焦，发始堕；六七三阳脉衰于上，面皆焦，发始白；丈夫……六八阳气衰竭于上，面焦，发鬓颁白。"

汉英对照

Chinese-English
Edition of
Acupuncture
Cosmetology

针灸美容

上篇 ◉ 针灸美容基础理论

the 12 regular meridians; the divergent meridians connect the body surface and internal organs, and extremities and head, chest and abdomen; and muscle and cutaneous regions connect the limbs, muscles, tendons and skin. The meridians and collaterals are distributed both interiorly and exteriorly over the body, transporting qi and blood to nourish the whole body, defend pathogenic factors, protect the body, connect interior and exterior and reflect body conditions. Disorders of a certain organ or local area may manifest in body surface or whole body through meridian system, likewise, the general condition may also manifest in a specific area with a group of symptoms and signs with certain laws, which can provide basis for syndrome differentiation as well as therapeutic approaches.

Qi and blood are fundamental substances of meridian system to be transported and distributed to all over the body to warm, nourish, moisten and maintain the normal functions of zang-fu organs and tissues. Qi and blood are also products of normal functions of zang-fu organs and meridians. A red, moist, lustrous and elastic face, dense, bright, and dark hair as well as body fitness all depends on incessant transportation of yang-qi, yin-blood and body fluids through meridians. In the meanwhile, timely discharge of metabolic wastes through meridians can prevent occurrence of beauty-impairing diseases. Therefore only with normal functions of zang-fu organs and meridians, can human body be healthy and beautiful. Pathologic changes of one certain zang-fu organ or dysfunction of one certain meridian may result in deficiency or disorder of qi and blood or weakness in protecting the body, and subsequently exogenous pathogenic factors attacking the interior and abnormal metabolism will definitely show externally

汉英对照

Chinese-English
Edition of
Acupuncture
Cosmetology

针灸美容

Part 1 The Basic Theory of Acupuncture Cosmetology

正因为经络的这种生理功能作用与病理变化反映，所以当人的外在容貌形体出现问题时，应探求其相应的内在原因，有的放矢地进行调整，达到真正恢复健康美的目的。针灸美容，就是从人的整体出发，通过调整经络，充分调动人体自身的积极因素，而达到扶正祛邪，恢复脏腑、气血的功能，强身健体，延缓人体衰老的效果。可见针灸美容利用经络的调整作用来达到治本为主、治标为辅的目的，其疗效持久稳定。

第二节　针灸美容与腧穴的关系

腧穴是人体脏腑经络之气输注于体表的部位。古代医籍中有"砭灸处"、"节"、"会"、"骨孔"、"气穴"、"穴位"等不同名称。人体的腧穴大部分归属于各经络，而经络又隶属、联络于一定的脏腑，这样就使腧穴——经络——脏腑间的相互联系成为不可分割的关系。腧穴是针灸治疗的施术部位，也往往是内在情况的反应点。

汉英对照

Chinese-English
Edition of
Acupuncture
Cosmetology

针灸美容

上篇 ◉ 针灸美容基础理论

through the complex relationship among meridians, zang-fu organs and body surface, manifesting such beauty-impairing conditions as a sallow or pale complex, scythropasmus, wrinkles, rough skin in dark color and less elasticity, dry and premature gray hair and loss of hair. The *Su Wen* • *Shang Gu Tian Zhen Lun* (the 1st chapter of *Su Wen*) states that "due to failure of Yangming meridians, women after 35 start to have dry faces and their hairs start to fall down; due to failure of three yang meridians, women after 42 start to have more dry faces and their hairs start to turn gray; and due to exhaustion of yang-qi, men after 48 start to have dry faces and their hairs on temples start to turn gray".

Just because of this physiological function and manifestations of pathological changes of meridians, problems involving external appearance and figure shall be managed by regulating the corresponding internal reasons. Acupuncture cosmetology is based on holistic view and aims to strengthen the body resistance, remove pathogenic factors, restore functions of zang-fu organs, qi and blood as well as delay aging process through stimulating meridians and active factors of the body itself. Consequently acupuncture can produce stable and persistent cosmetic effects by targeting more on the primary cause than external symptoms.

Section 2
The relationship between acupuncture cosmetology and acupoints

Acupoints are the specific sites through which the qi of zang-fu organs and meridians is transported to the body surface. Acupoints have been called different names in ancient literature including "Bian Jiu Chu — a spot for Bian-stone needle and

分布在人体的腧穴很多，现代针灸学将腧穴大体分为十四经穴、经外奇穴、阿是穴三类。分布于十二经脉及任、督二脉上的腧穴，称为"十四经穴"，简称"经穴"，具有主治本经病症的共同作用，是腧穴的主要部分；尚未列入十四经系统，却有一定的穴名又有明确位置的腧穴，称为"经外奇穴"，简称"奇穴"，具有对某些病症的特殊治疗作用；以压痛点或其他反应点作为针刺部位，无具体名称，又无固定位置，多在病变附近的腧穴，称为"阿是穴"，又称"压痛点"、"天应穴"、"不定穴"等。

腧穴具有近治、远治及特殊的治疗作用，是针灸美容的施术部位和作用基础。一切腧穴都具有近治作用，可以治疗该穴所在及邻近部位的脏腑、组织、器官的损容性疾病，总之，身体各部位的腧穴都能治疗邻近部位的病症，针灸美容尤其多用面部的腧穴；肢体远端的腧穴善于调整经络，躯干部位的腧穴善于调整脏腑，这些穴位的应用，能够使针灸美容实现健康的美，达到持久的效果；有些腧穴对某些病症有特殊的治疗作用。针灸美容临床充分灵活地利用了这些作用，根据各种损容性疾病的特点，结合辨证分型，恰到好处地应用这些腧穴，取得预期的结果，并可大大提高某些难治性损容性疾病的治疗效果。

moxibustion", "Jie-joints", "Hui-convergence", "Gu Kong-bone aperture", "Qi Xue-qi point" and "Xue Wei-acupuncture point". Most acupoints of the body are ascribed to different meridians, which in turn connect with zang-fu organs and thus form the inseparable relationship among acupoints, meridians and zang-fu organs. Acupoints are the sites for needling and also the reactive points of internal conditions.

There are numerous acupoints distributed over the human body. Modern acupuncture generally classifies acupoints into three types: acupoints of 14 meridians, extraordinary acupoints and Ashi points. The first type of acupoints distributed in the 12 regular meridians, Governor Vessel and Conception Vessel, which are sometimes abbreviated as "regular acupoints". These acupoints share the common actions of treating diseases of respective meridians and are the major parts of acupoints; the second type of acupoints with specific names and definite locations but are not attributed to the fourteen meridians, which are sometimes abbreviated as "extra acupoints". These acupoints have special effect on certain problems; and the third type of acupoints, also called "tender spots", "reflexing points" and "unfixed points", have no specific names or definite locations but are usually close to the area with pathological changes.

With local, distal and special therapeutic actions, acupoints are the needling sites and action basis for acupuncture cosmetology. All acupoints have local therapeutic actions and can be used for disorders of their locations as well as their adjacent zang-fu organs and tissues. In short, the acupoints in each part of the body can be used for disorders of the nearby areas. The facial acupoints are especially selected for acupuncture cosmetology. Acupoints located in extremities are

第三节　针灸美容与皮肤皮部经筋的关系

皮肤是求美者最关注的部分,分布有丰富的血管、神经。因而健康的皮肤需要充足的气血供养。皮部、经筋是经络系统中主管皮肤、筋骨、关节感觉、运动的部分,具有抗御外来的病邪、维持皮肤正常感觉、温度,同时也反映体内异常状况的重要部位。而经筋则维持了我们骨骼、关节的柔韧、松弛有力的运动中枢。其功能正常,是确保皮肤健美、活动自如、富有弹性而不松弛下垂的关键。机体通过皮部筋骨—经络—脏腑,将内在的气血源源不断输送到体表。同样,针灸美容的浅针、皮肤针、刮痧、拔罐等也是作用于皮肤、筋骨,并通过它们而调整内在的脏腑,从而达到彻底、持久改善外在皮肤的病况的作用。

always good for regulation of meridians; and acupoints located in torso are always good for regulation of zang-fu organs. These acupoints can help to obtain healthy beauty with a persistent effect. Some acupoints have special therapeutic actions on certain diseases. By making advantage of these actions and combining syndrome differentiation according to characteristics of beauty-impairing disorders, acupuncture cosmetology can surely obtain the expected result and greatly improve the therapeutic effect on certain intractable beauty-impairing diseases.

Section 3
The relationship between acupuncture cosmetology and cutaneous and muscular regions of skin

As blood vessels and nerves are distributed in the body skin — the most concerned part of those who pursue beauty — healthy skin requires abundant supply of qi and blood. The cutaneous and muscle regions are parts of the meridians system responsible for skin, muscles, tendons, bones, articular sensation and motion. They can defend exogenous pathogenic factors, maintain normal sensation and temperature of the skin and reflect abnormal changes of internal organs. In addition, the muscle regions also help to maintain the tenacity of bones and joints and relax but powerful motor center. The normal function of cutaneous and muscle regions are keys to healthy, flexible, and elastic skin. Qi and blood of the body are incessantly transported to the body surface through cutaneous muscles and bones — meridians — internal organs. Likewise, such cosmetic acupuncture techniques as shallow needle, dermal needle, Guasha (scraping) and cupping also regulate internal organs through skins, muscles and tendons and eventually improve the external skin conditions.

汉英对照

Chinese-English
Edition of
Acupuncture
Cosmetology

针灸美容

Part 1 The Basic Theory of Acupuncture Cosmetology

第三章 针灸美容的作用原理

针灸美容是通过针灸调整经络脏腑,达到养生保健和治疗损容性、损形性等影响美容的相关疾病的双方面作用的结果。具体来说,它是通过以下几个方面来达到美容的目的的。

一、调理经络以调气养气

用针灸方法疏通经络,行气以活血,维持人体各部分功能活动的协调和相对平衡,使人体气机升降出入有序。而气机是气的根本运动形式,气机正常,人的生命活动就正常。

二、调理脏腑功能以调精养精

中医学认为,五脏藏精而不泻,六腑传化而不藏,通过经络、腧穴调理脏腑功能,做到收藏有节、传导有序,使精血各有所藏,精足而养,才能化气充身。

三、调理性情以调神养神

《红炉点雪》中说:"颜色憔悴,良由心思过度。"故中医理

Chapter 3
The action mechanism of acupuncture cosmetology

Acupuncture cosmetology aims to preserve health and treat relevant beauty-impairing or figure-impairing diseases through regulating meridians and zang-fu organs. More specifically, it works through the following aspects:

1. Regulates and supplements qi through action on meridians

Acupuncture can dredge meridians and circulate qi to promote blood circulation and maintain the coordination and relative balance of functional activities of the human body, which enables qi to ascend and descend in a regular order. As qi activity is the essential motion mode of qi, a normal qi activity guarantees normal life activities.

2. Regulates and supplements essence through action on zang-fu organs

TCM holds that the five zang-organs store essence but do not discharge and the six fu-organs transport and transform but do not store. Acupuncture can regulate functions of zang-fu organs to maintain adequate storage of essence and blood and transform into qi to spread to the body through meridians and acupoints.

3. Regulates and benefits the heart-mind through action on emotions

The *Hong Lu Dian Xue* by Gong Ju-zhong in the Ming dynasty states that "a dry and sallow complexion always results from too much mental stress", indicating that TCM theory

汉英对照

Chinese-English Edition of Acupuncture Cosmetology

针灸美容 Part 1 The Basic Theory of Acupuncture Cosmetology

论把颜面气色、性格情志和脏俯功能做为一个整体来看待，即面色本身可以反映人体脏俯功能以及性格特征，这也是中医针灸美容的深刻原理所在。

汉英对照

Chinese-English
Edition of
Acupuncture
Cosmetology

针灸美容

上篇 ⊙ 针灸美容基础理论

regards facial complexion, emotions and functions of zang-fu organs as a whole, i. e. , the facial complexion can reflect functions of zang-fu organs and emotions, and that is the real principle of acupuncture cosmetology.

第四章　针灸美容的常用穴位

人体常用的经穴有 360 多个,每个穴位都有各自的功效和主治,其中许多穴位都具有美容健身的作用,常选取的穴位介绍如下。

第一节　具有分部作用的穴位

所有腧穴具有治疗该穴所在部位及邻近部位的脏腑、组织、器官的病症,这是一切腧穴作用的共性,也是针灸美容选穴的基础。

一、头部穴位

本处穴位常可用于治疗斑秃、脱发、头皮瘙痒、脱屑等。对目赤痛、迎风流泪、耳鸣、荨麻疹等有效。

1. 前顶:百会前 1.5 寸。

2. 百会:两耳尖直上与前后正中线的交点处。

3. 后顶:百会后 1.5 寸。

4. 四神聪:百会前、后、左、右各旁开 1 寸。

5. 上星:前发际正中,入发际 0.5 寸。

Chapter 4
The common acupoints for acupuncture cosmetology

There are more than 360 common acupoints in the human body. Each acupoint has its own actions and indications, and many of them can be used for facial beauty and health-protection. The introductions of commonly-selected acupoints are as follows:

Section 1　The local acupoints

All acupoints can be used for treating disorders of their locations as well as adjacent zang-fu organs and tissues. That is the common action of all acupoints and also the basis for selection of acupoints in acupuncture cosmetology.

Ⅰ. The head acupoints

The head acupoints can all be used for alopecia areata, loss of hair, scalp itching, and desquamation; they are also effective for red and painful eyes, lacrimation with wind, tinnitus, and urticaria.

1. Qianding (GV 21): 1.5 cun anterior to Baihui (GV 20).

2. Baihui (GV 20): on the crossing point of apex of two auricles and anterior-posterior midline.

3. Houding (GV 19): 1.5 cun posterior to Baihui (GV 20).

4. Sishencong (EX-HN 1): 1 cun respectively posterior, anterior and bilateral to Baihui (GV 20).

5. Shangxing (GV 23): on the midpoint of anterior

汉英对照

Chinese-English
Edition of
Acupuncture
Cosmetology

针灸美容 Part 1 The Basic Theory of Acupuncture Cosmetology

汉英对照

Chinese-English
Edition of
Acupuncture
Cosmetology

针灸美容

上篇 ◉ 针灸美容基础理论

6. 头维：在额角发际直上 0.5 处。

7. 风池：位于胸锁乳突肌和斜方肌之间,取穴时,须俯伏或正坐,于项后枕骨下两侧凹陷中、当胸锁乳突肌与斜方肌之间凹陷处取穴。

（见图 1、图 2）

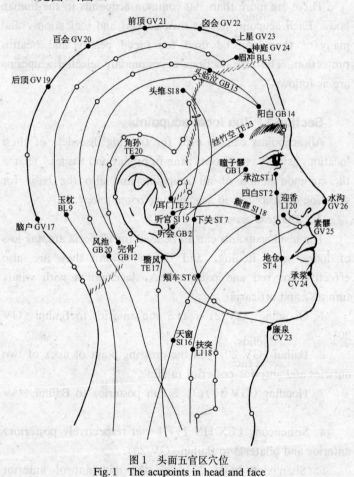

图 1　头面五官区穴位
Fig. 1　The acupoints in head and face

hairline and 0.5 cun within the hairline.

6. Touwei (ST 8): 0.5 cun within the hairline on the corner of the forehead.

7. Fengchi (GB 20): in the depression of bilateral occipital bones between sternocleidomastoid muscle and trapezius muscle. When locating this acupoint, the patients are always asked to take prone or upright sitting position.

(See Fig. 1 and Fig. 2)

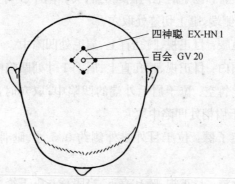

四神聪 EX-HN 1

百会 GV 20

图 2 四神聪
Fig. 2 Sishencong (EX-HN 1)

II. The acupoints around eyes

The acupoints around eyes can be used for myopia, strabismus, red, swelling and painful eyes, eyelid twitching, prolapse of eyelids, trichiasis and other beauty-impairing symptoms such as facial wrinkles (forehead wrinkles and crow's feet).

1. Jingming (BL 1): in the depression of the upper portion of the inner canthus. The patients are always asked to take upright sitting or supine position and the acupoint is located at 0.1 cun superior to inner canthus and close to medial border of

汉英对照

Chinese-English
Edition of
Acupuncture
Cosmetology

针灸美容 Part 1 The Basic Theory of Acupuncture Cosmetology

二、 眼区穴位

本处穴位可调治近视、斜视、目赤肿痛、眼皮跳动、眼睑下垂、倒睫等眼病或眼周损容性症候，如面部皱纹（额皱纹、眼尾纹等）。

1. 睛明：位于目内眦上方的凹陷中。取穴时，正坐或仰卧，于目内眦内上方 0.1 寸，靠近目眶骨内缘处取穴。

2. 攒竹：位于眉毛内侧端的眉头凹陷中。可正坐仰卧；于眉毛内侧端，眶上切迹处取穴。

3. 鱼腰：目正视、瞳孔直上、眉毛处凹陷中。

4. 阳白：目正视、瞳孔直上、眉上 1 寸处凹陷中。

5. 丝竹空：位于眉毛外端的凹陷中；取穴时，正坐仰靠或侧伏，于眉梢处凹陷中取穴。

6. 瞳子髎：位于目外眦外侧约 0.5 寸、眶骨外缘的凹陷中。

7. 承泣：目正视，瞳孔直下，当眼球与眶下缘之间。

8. 四白：位于目正视时瞳孔直下、当眶下孔的凹陷中。

9. 太阳：位于眉梢与目外眦之间向后约 1 寸处的凹陷中。

（见图 1、图 3）

the orbit bone.

2. Cuanzhu (BL 2): on the medial extremity of the eyebrow. The patients are always asked to take upright sitting or supine position and the acupoint is located at medical extremity of eyebrow and on the supraorbital notch.

3. Yuyao (EX-HN 4): in the depression of the eyebrow directly above the pupils with eyes looking straight forward.

4. Yangbai (GB 14): in the depression 1 cun above the eyebrow directly above the pupils with eyes looking straight forward.

5. Sizhukong (TE 23): in the depression at the lateral end of the eyebrow. The patients are always asked to take leaning sitting or lateral lying position and the acupoint is located at the depression of eyebrow end.

6. Tongziliao (GB 1): about 0.5 cun lateral to outer canthus and in the depression on the lateral ridge of the orbit.

7. Chengqi (ST 1): with eyes looking straight forward, the acupoint is directly below the pupil, between the eyeball and infraorbital ridge.

8. Sibai (ST 2): with eyes looking straight forward, the point is directly below the pupil and in the depression of the infraorbital foramen.

9. Taiyang (EX-HN 5): in the depression about 1 cun posterior to the midpoint between the lateral end of the eyebrow and the outer canthus.

(See Fig. 1 and Fig. 3)

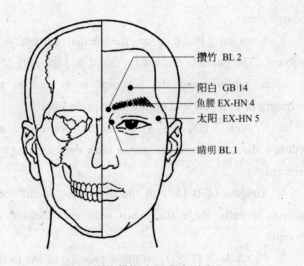

攒竹 BL 2

阳白 GB 14

鱼腰 EX-HN 4

太阳 EX-HN 5

睛明 BL 1

图 3 睛明、攒竹、鱼腰、阳白、太阳
Fig. 3 Jingming（BL 1）, Cuanzhu（BL 2）, Yuyao（EX-HN 4）,
Yangbai（GB 14）and Taiyang（EX-HN 5）

三、 鼻区穴位

本处穴位可调治酒皶鼻、鼻炎等鼻病以及痤疮、口眼歪斜、口疮、唇肿、面痒浮肿、面部皱纹、颜面疔疮等。

1. 素髎：鼻尖正中。

2. 迎香：位于鼻翼外缘中点旁开 0.5 寸处；取穴时，须正坐仰靠或仰卧，于鼻翼外缘中点、旁开约 0.5 寸，当鼻唇沟中取穴。

3. 印堂：前额部，两眉头连线中点。

4. 水沟：人中沟上 1/3 和下 2/3 交点处。

（见图 1、图 4）

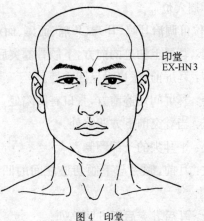

印堂
EX-HN3

图 4　印堂
Fig. 4　Yintang（EX-HN 3）

汉英对照
Chinese-English
Edition of
Acupuncture
Cosmetology

针灸美容 Part 1 The Basic Theory of Acupuncture Cosmetology

Ⅲ．The acupoints around the nasal area

The acupoints around the nasal area can be used for brandy nose, rhinitis and such problems as acne, deviation of the eyes or mouth, aphtha, lip swelling, facial itching and puffiness, facial wrinkles and facial furuncles.

1. Suliao（GV 25）：on the tip of the nose.

2. Yingxiang（LI 20）：0.5 cun lateral to the midpoint of the lateral border of ala nasi. The patients are always asked to take leaning sitting or supine position and the acupoint is located in the nasolabial groove and about 0.5 cun lateral to the midpoint of the lateral border of ala nasi.

3. Yintang（EX-HN 3）：midway between the medial ends of the two eyebrows.

4. Shuigou（GV 26）：the crossing point of the 1/2 and 2/3 of the philtrum.

四、 耳周穴位

本处穴位可调治耳鸣、耳聋、牙痛、面瘫、面痛等耳病。

1. 耳门：耳屏上切迹的前方，下颌骨髁突后缘凹陷处。

2. 听宫：耳屏前，张口时呈凹陷处。

3. 听会：耳屏间切迹前方，张口有凹陷处。

4. 翳风：当乳突前下方凹陷处。

5. 角孙：平耳尖的头部颞侧。

6. 下关：耳前，颧弓与下颌切迹之间的凹陷处，闭口有孔，张口即闭。

7. 完骨：耳后乳突后下方凹陷处。

（见图1）

五、 口周穴位

本处穴位可调治口歪、口角流涎、唇颊部痤疮等，对牙痛、颊肿、口噤不语、面瘫、三叉神经痛，有一定效果。

1. 地仓：位于口角外侧旁开 0.4 寸。于口角水平外侧直线与正视瞳孔垂线之交点处取穴。

(See Fig. 1 and Fig. 4)

Ⅳ. The acupoints around ears

The acupoints around ears can be used for tinnitus, deafness, toothache, facial paralysis and facial pain.

1. Ermen (TE 21): in the depression anterior to the supratragic notch and at the posterior border of the condyloid process of mandible.

2. Tinggong (SI 19): anterior to the tragus and in the depression with mouth open.

3. Tinghui (GB 2): anterior to the intertragic notch and in the depression with mouth open.

4. Yifeng (TE 17): in the depression anterior and inferior to the mastoid process.

5. Jiaosun (TE 20): at the temple side of the same level of ear apex.

6. Xiaguan (ST 7): anterior to the ears and in the depression between zygomatic notch and mandible notch with mouth closed.

7. Wangu (GB 12): in the depression posterior and inferior to the mastoid process.

(See Fig. 1)

Ⅴ. The acupoints around the mouth

The acupoints around the mouth can be used for deviation of the mouth, salivation, acne around lips and cheeks as well as such problems as toothache, cheek swelling, locked jaw, facial palsy, and trigeminal neuralgia.

1. Dicang (ST 4): 0.4 cun lateral to the lateral aspect of the mouth corner, and at the crossing point of lateral straight

汉英对照
Chinese-English Edition of Acupuncture Cosmetology

针灸美容 Part 1 The Basic Theory of Acupuncture Cosmetology

汉英对照

Chinese-English
Edition of
Acupuncture
Cosmetology

针灸美容

上篇 ◉ 针灸美容基础理论

2. 承浆：颏唇沟中点凹陷中。

3. 颊车：位于下颌角前上方一横指的咬肌隆起处。

（见图 1）

六、 胸、腹部穴位

本处穴位可调治胸腹部疼痛、肥胖、面色不华、面部皱纹、荨麻疹、酒皶鼻等。

1. 中脘：腹部正中线上，脐上 4 寸处。

2. 气海：前正中线上，脐下方 1.5 寸处。

3. 关元：前正中线上，脐下方 3 寸处。

4. 天枢：肚脐旁开 2 寸处。

5. 大横：肚脐旁开 4 寸处。

6. 期门：位于乳头直下，第六肋间隙。

（见图 5）

七、 腰、背部穴位

本处穴位具有调治头项腰背强痛、肩背痛、风疹、湿疹、肥胖症、口臭、消瘦、颜面疔疮、痤疮、色素沉着、浮肿、脱发、少白头、黄褐斑以及调整相应脏腑的作用。

1. 大椎：后正中线上，第七颈椎棘突下凹陷中。

2. 肺俞：俯伏，于第二胸椎棘突下，后正中线旁开 1.5 寸处。

line of the mouth corner and vertical line of pupil with eyes looking straight forward.

2. Chengjiang (CV 24): in the depression of the center of mentolabial groove.

3. Jiache (ST 6): one finger-breadth anterior and superior to the prominence of masseter muscle.

(See Fig. 1)

Ⅵ. The acupoints on chest and abdomen

The acupoints on chest and abdomen can be used for chest or abdominal pain, obesity, lusterless complexion, facial wrinkles, urticaria, and brandy nose.

1. Zhongwan (CV 12): on the midline of the abdomen, 4 cun above the umbilicus.

2. Qihai (CV 6): on the anterior midline, 1.5 cun below the umbilicus.

3. Guanquan (CV 4): on the anterior midline, 3 cun below the umbilicus.

4. Tianshu (ST 25): 2 cun lateral to the umbilicus.

5. Daheng (SP 15): 4 cun lateral to the umbilicus.

6. Qimen (LR 14): directly below the nipple, in the 6th intercostal space.

(See Fig. 5)

Ⅶ. The acupoints on lower back and back

The acupoints on lower back and back can be used for stiffness and pain of head, nape, lumbus, back and shoulder, rubella (German measles), eczema, obesity, foul breath, emaciation, facial furuncles, acne, pigmentation, edema, loss

汉英对照

Chinese-English
Edition of
Acupuncture
Cosmetology

针灸美容 Part 1 The Basic Theory of Acupuncture Cosmetology

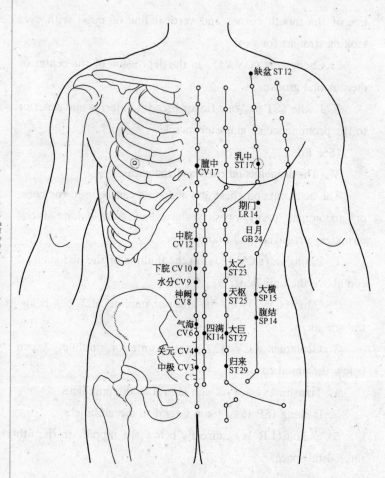

缺盆 ST 12

乳中
ST 17

膻中
CV 17

期门
LR 14

日月
GB 24

中脘
CV 12

太乙
ST 23

下脘 CV 10

水分 CV 9

天枢
ST 25

大横
SP 15

神阙
CV 8

腹结
SP 14

气海
CV 6

四满
KI 14

大巨
ST 27

关元 CV 4

归来
ST 29

中极 CV 3

图 5　胸腹部穴位
Fig. 5　The acupoints on chest and abdomen

　　3. 心俞：俯伏，于第五胸椎棘突下，后正中线旁开 1.5
寸处。

　　4. 督俞：俯伏，于第六胸椎棘突下，后正中线旁开 1.5

of hair, premature gray hair, chloasma and regulation of corresponding zang-fu organs.

1. Dazhui (GV 14): on the posterior midline, in the depression below the spinous process of C_7.

2. Feishu (BL 13): below the spinous process of T_3 and 1.5 cun lateral to the posterior midline with prone position.

3. Xinshu (BL 15): below the spinous process of T_5 and 1.5 cun lateral to the posterior midline with prone position.

4. Dushu (BL 16): below the spinous process of T_6 and 1.5 cun lateral to the posterior midline with prone position.

5. Ganshu (BL 18): below the spinous process of T_9 and 1.5 cun lateral to the posterior midline with prone position.

6. Pishu (BL 20): below the spinous process of T_{11} and 1.5 cun lateral to the posterior midline with prone position.

7. Shenshu (BL 23): below the spinous process of L_2 and 1.5 cun lateral to the posterior midline with prone position.

8. Weishu (BL 21): below the spinous process of T_{12} and 1.5 cun lateral to the posterior midline with prone position. (See Fig. 6)

VIII. The acupoints on four limbs

The acupoints on four limbs can be used for problems in head and face, hidden rashes seborrheic dermatitis, acne, chloasma, redness of the face, facial pigmentation, exophthalmus, urticaria, rubella (German measles), alopecia areata, obesity and constipation.

1. Hegu (LI 4): on the dorsum of the hand, between the 1st and 2nd metacarpal bones, approximately in the middle of the 2nd

汉英对照
Chinese-English
Edition of
Acupuncture
Cosmetology
针灸美容
Part 1 The Basic Theory of Acupuncture Cosmetology

汉英对照

Chinese-English
Edition of
Acupuncture
Cosmetology

针灸美容

上篇 ◉ 针灸美容基础理论

寸处。

5. 肝俞：俯卧，于第九胸椎棘突下，后正中线旁开 1.5 寸处。

6. 脾俞：俯卧，于第十一胸椎棘突下，后正中线旁开 1.5 寸处。

7. 肾俞：俯卧，于第二腰椎棘突下，后正中线旁开 1.5 寸处。

8. 胃俞：俯卧或俯伏，于第十二胸椎棘突下，后正中线旁开 1.5 寸处。

（见图 6）

八、四肢部穴位

本处穴位对调治头面五官疾患、瘾疹、脂溢性皮炎、痤疮、蝴蝶斑、面目红赤、面部色素沉着、突眼、荨麻疹、风疹、斑秃、肥胖、便秘有效。

1. 合谷：手背第一、第二掌骨之间，约平第二掌骨中点处；或以一手的拇指指骨关节横纹放在另一手示指之间的指蹼缘上，当拇指尖下取穴。

2. 内关：腕横纹上 2 寸，两筋之间。

3. 外关：腕背横纹上 2 寸，尺骨、桡骨之间。

4. 曲池：肘横纹外端与肱骨外髁连线的中点处。

5. 尺泽：肘横纹上，肱二头肌腱桡侧缘。

6. 曲泽：肘横纹上，肱二头肌腱尺侧缘。

7. 列缺：桡骨茎突上方，距腕横纹 1.5 寸处。

8. 血海：髌骨内上缘上方 2 寸处。

9. 足三里：犊鼻穴下 3 寸，胫骨前嵴处旁开外一横指。

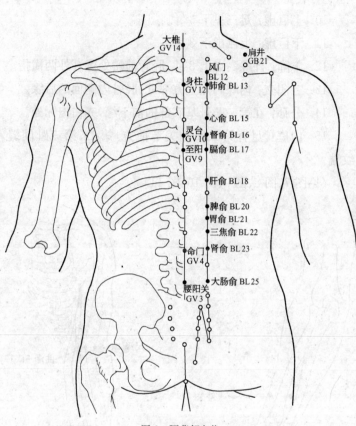

图 6　腰背部穴位
Fig. 6　The acupoints on lumbus and back

metacarpal bone; or, place the coincident position the transverse crease of the interphalangeal joint of the thumb with the margin of the web between the thumb and index finger of the other hand, and the acupoint is where the tip of the thumb touches.

2. Neiguan (PC 6): 2 cun above the transverse crease of the wrist and between the two tendons (m. palmaris longus and

汉英对照
Chinese-English
Edition of
Acupuncture
Cosmetology

针灸美容

Part 1 The Basic Theory of Acupuncture Cosmetology

10. 上巨虚：足三里下 3 寸。

11. 下巨虚：上巨虚下 3 寸。

12. 丰隆：外踝高点上 8 寸，胫骨前嵴处旁开外两横指。

13. 三阴交：内踝高点上方 3 寸、胫骨内侧面的后缘。

14. 公孙：在第一跖骨基底部的前下缘，赤白肉际处。

15. 内庭：足背第二跖趾关节前方，第二、第三趾间缝纹端。

（见图 7、图 8、图 9、图 10、图 11）

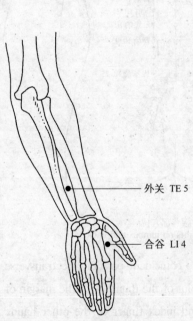

图 7　合谷、外关
Fig. 7　Hegu (LI 4) and
Waiguan (TE 5)

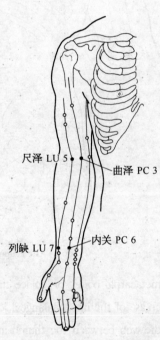

尺泽 LU 5
曲泽 PC 3
列缺 LU 7
内关 PC 6

图 8　内关、尺泽、曲泽、列缺
Fig. 8　Neiguan (PC 6), Chize
(LU 5), Quze (PC 3)
and Lieque (LU 7)

外关 TE 5
合谷 LI 4

m. flexor radialis).

3. Waiguan (TE 5): 2 cun above the dorsal transverse crease of the wrist and between the radius and ulna.

4. Quchi (LI 11): midway on the line connecting the lateral end of transverse cubital crease and lateral epicondyle of the humerus.

5. Chize (LU 5): on the cubital crease and on the radial side of the tendon of m. biceps brachii.

6. Quze (PC 3): on the cubital crease and on the ulnar side of the tendon of m. biceps brachii.

7. Lieque (LU 7): superior to the styloid process of the radius, 1.5 cun above the transverse crease of the wrist.

8. Xuehai (SP 10): 2 cun above the mediosuperior border of the patella.

9. Zusanli (ST 36): 3 cun below Dubi (ST 35) and one finger-breadth from the anterior crease of the tibia.

10. Shangjuxu (ST 37): 3 cun below Zusanli (ST 36).

11. Xiajuxu (ST 39): 3 cun below Shangjuxu (ST 37).

12. Fenglong (ST 40): 8 cun superior to the external mallelous, and 2 finger-breadth from the anterior crest of the tibia.

13. Sanyinjiao (SP 6): 3 cun directly above the tip of the medial mallelous, and on the posterior border of the medial aspect of the tibia.

14. Gongsun (SP 4): in the anterior and inferior border of the base of the 1st metatarsal bone and at the junction of the red and white skin.

15. Neiting (ST 44): anterior to the second metatarsodigital

汉英对照
Chinese-English
Edition of
Acupuncture
Cosmetology

针灸美容

Part 1 The Basic Theory of Acupuncture Cosmetology

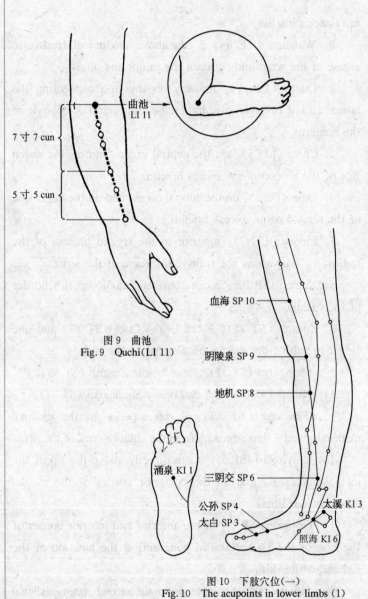

曲池
LI 11

7寸 7 cun

5寸 5 cun

图 9　曲池
Fig. 9　Quchi(LI 11)

血海 SP 10

阴陵泉 SP 9

地机 SP 8

涌泉 KI 1

三阴交 SP 6

公孙 SP 4
太白 SP 3

太溪 KI 3

照海 KI 6

图 10　下肢穴位（一）
Fig. 10　The acupoints in lower limbs（1）

joint and at the web margin between the 2nd and 3rd toes.

(See Fig. 7, Fig. 8, Fig. 9, Fig. 10 and Fig. 11)

汉英对照
Chinese-English
Edition of
Acupuncture
Cosmetology
针灸美容
Part 1 The Basic Theory of Acupuncture Cosmetology

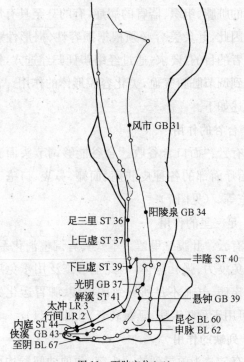

图 11　下肢穴位(二)
Fig. 11　The acupoints in lower limbs (2)

Section 2　The distal acupoints

The acupoints located below the elbows and knee joints of the 14 meridians, especially the 12 regular meridians can be used not only for local problems, but also for problems of zang-fu organs and tissues along the running course of the meridians, or even for the problems of the whole body. Therefore it's

第二节　具有循经远治作用的穴位

十四经穴,尤其是十二经脉在四肢肘、膝关节以下的腧穴,不仅能治疗局部病症,而且还可以治疗本经循行所及的远隔部位的脏腑、组织、器官的病症,有的甚至具有影响全身的作用。因此,针灸美容必须根据损容性、损形性病症的表现或求美者的目的、要求,通过经络辨证归经选穴,针灸这些腧穴而达到调节脏腑气血,美化容貌形体的作用。常用的这些穴位简述如下。

一、合谷的作用

古代有云:"面口合谷收。"合谷能够调节头面五官的气血,用于治疗面部的各种皮肤病、面瘫、鼻炎、口疮、蝴蝶斑、脱发、痤疮等。(见图 7)

二、足三里的作用

古代有云:"肚腹三里留。"本穴具有调整消化系统功能、增强机体免疫力、强壮身体,因此能够广泛用于免疫力低下的损容性疾病、气血不足所导致的消瘦、脾胃运化失调的肥胖等,还可用于预防疾病、延缓衰老。(见图 11)

三、列缺的作用

古代有云:"头项寻列缺。"头部、颈项的问题均可应用本穴进行调整。(见图 8)

四、委中的作用

古代有云:"腰背委中求。"腰部、背部的痤疮、疼痛、侧弯、椎体增生、突出等均可应用本穴。(见图 12)

important for acupuncture cosmetology to select these distal acupoints based on syndrome differentiation according to the beauty-impairing or figure-impairing manifestations or the patients' wishes to regulate zang-fu organs, qi and blood and achieve the goal of beauty. The common acupoints with above functions are as follows:

1. Action of Hegu (LI 4)

It's recorded in the ancient literature that "Hegu (LI 4) is always selected for face and mouth problems". The acupoint Hegu (LI 4) can regulate qi and blood of head and face and is always used for varieties of skin diseases, facial palsy, rhinitis, mouth ulcer, chloasma, loss of hair and acne. (See Fig. 7)

2. Action of Zusanli (ST 36)

It's recorded in the ancient literature that "Zusanli (ST 36) is always selected for abdominal problems". The acupoint Zusanli (ST 36) can regulate digestive function, enhance immunity and strengthen the body and is always used for beauty-impairing diseases due to immune deficiency, emaciation due to qi and blood deficiency and obesity due to spleen and stomach failing to transport and transform. In addition, this acupoint can also be used to prevent disease and delay the aging process. (See Fig. 11)

3. Action of Lieque (LU 7)

It's reported in the ancient literature that "Lieque (LU 7) is always selected for head and nape problems". The acupoint Lieque (LU 7) can be used for treatment of head, neck and nape problems. (See Fig. 8)

4. Action of Weizhong (BL 40)

It's recorded in the ancient literature that "Weizhong (BL 40) is always selected for lower back and back problems". The

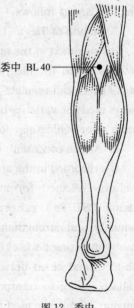

第三节 具有整体调整作用的穴位

身体的某些腧穴,对机体的不同状态,可起着双向的良性的整体调整作用,针灸美容重在整体调整,以调动内在积极因素,治本为主。常用的穴位简述如下。

一、足三里的调整作用

本穴具有良好的调整脾胃乃至整体功能的作用,既可治疗消瘦,又可治疗肥胖。(见图 11)

二、膈俞的调整作用

膈俞是血的会穴,能活血养血,祛风通络。可广泛用于雀斑等损容性病症的治疗。(见图 6)

三、血海的调整作用

妇女以血为本。本穴能够活血化瘀,用于治疗与瘀血有关的黄褐斑、皮肤色暗粗糙、皮肤瘙痒、毛发枯槁等。(见图 10)

四、三阴交的调整作用

本穴是足太阴、厥阴、少阴经

委中 BL 40

图 12 委中
Fig. 12 Weizhong (BL 40)

的会穴,可同时调整肝、脾、肾三脏及三经,有养血活血的作用,既可用于血虚导致的面色苍白、口唇色淡,又可用于血瘀导致的面色褐黑、口唇紫暗。能够广泛用于治疗先天不足、后天失养的各种损容性疾病;治疗与情志因素有关、与内分泌失调有关的各种损容性、损形性疾病。(见图 10)

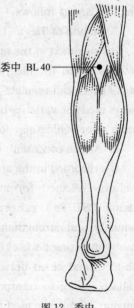

汉英对照

Chinese-English
Edition of
Acupuncture
Cosmetology

针灸美容

上篇 ◉ 针灸美容基础理论

acupoint Weizhong (BL 40) can be used for treatment of acne, pain, and skoliosis in lower back and back, hyperplasia of vertebrae and herniation of lumbar intervertebral disc. (See Fig. 12)

Section 3
The acupoints for whole-body regulation

Some acupoints can produce benign dual regulation on different state of organism. Acupuncture cosmetology aims to regulate the whole body to activate the internal positive factors and target the root cause. The common acupoints of this type are as follows:

1. Regulation of Zusanli (ST 36)

This acupoint has quite good function in regulating the spleen and stomach and even the body as a whole. It can be used for both emaciation and obesity. (See Fig. 11)

2. Regulation of Geshu (BL 17)

This acupoint is the influential acupoint of blood. It can be used to circulate and nourish blood, remove wind and clear meridians. This acupoint is extensively used for beauty-impairing diseases such as freckles, etc. (See Fig. 6)

3. Regulation of Xuehai (SP 10)

TCM theory holds that blood is extremely important for women. This acupoint can circulate blood to resolve stasis and is always used for blood stasis-related problems such as chloasma, rough skin in dark color, skin itching and dry hair. (See Fig. 10)

4. Regulation of Sanyinjiao (SP 6)

The acupoint Sanyinjiao (SP 6) is a crossing acupoint of spleen, liver and kidney meridians and therefore can be used to

汉英对照
Chinese-English
Edition of
Acupuncture
Cosmetology

针灸美容 Part 1 The Basic Theory of Acupuncture Cosmetology

汉英对照

Chinese-English
Edition of
Acupuncture
Cosmetology

针灸美容

上篇 ● 针灸美容基础理论

五、 大椎的调整作用

本穴是身体所有阳经的会穴。既有很好的泄热作用。常用于面部脓疱疮、痤疮、酒皶鼻等，又有极佳的强壮作用，用于肢体不温、面色晦暗、颈项不适等。（见图 6）

六、 命门的调整作用

命门位于第二腰椎棘突下，是身体的强壮穴。具有强身健体的作用。用于调整内分泌失调、素体免疫力功能低下导致的各种损容性疾病。（见图 6）

其他具有类似作用的有关元、气海等穴位。

七、 膻中的调整作用

膻中是周身气的会穴。具有理气宽胸降逆的作用。常用于情志因素导致的面部晦暗、蝴蝶斑、乳房胀痛、胸闷气促等。（见图 5）

八、 日月的调整作用

日月穴位于乳头直下第七肋间隙，是胆的募穴。善于疏理肝胆之气，可调节因情志所伤导致的各种损美性疾患。（见图 13）

regulate the three organs and three meridians. It can nourish and circulate blood and is used for pale complexion and lips due to blood deficiency as well as dark-brown complexion and purple lips due to blood stasis. This acupoint is always used for varieties of beauty-impairing diseases resulting from congenital deficiency and acquired malnutrition as well as conditions related to emotional fluctuation and endocrine disorder. (See Fig. 10)

5. Regulation of Dazhui (GV 14)

The acupoint Dazhui (GV 14) is a crossing acupoint of all yang meridians and can work well for clearing away heat. It's always used for facial pustules, acne and brandy nose. In addition, it can also be used for strong health protection and such conditions as cold limbs, a dark complexion and discomfort of neck and nape. (See Fig. 6)

6. Regulation of Mingmen (GV 4)

The acupoint Mingmen (GV 4) is located in the depression below the spinous process of L_2 and regarded as a health-protection acupoint of the body. It's always used for varieties of beauty-impairing diseases due to endocrine disorder and congenital immune deficiency. (See Fig. 6)

Acupoints with similar actions include Guanyuan (CV 4) and Qihai (CV 6).

7. Regulation of Danzhong (CV 17)

The acupoint Danzhong (CV 17) is the influential acupoint of qi and can regulate qi, soothe the chest and down-regulate adverse flow of qi. It's always used for a dark complexion, chloasma, distending pain of breasts, chest stuffiness and fast breath due to emotional factors. (See Fig. 5)

8. Regulation of Riyue (GB 24)

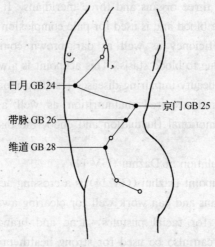

日月 GB 24

京门 GB 25

带脉 GB 26

维道 GB 28

图 13　日月、京门、带脉、维道
Fig. 13　Riyue（GB 24），Jingmen（GB 25），
Daimai（GB 26）and Weidao（GB 28）

九、 京门穴的调整作用

京门位于第十二肋端的下缘，是肾经的原穴。该穴不仅善于疏理肝胆之气，同时有良好的调节人体水液代谢作用。（见图 13）

十、 中脘穴的调整作用

本穴是人体脏腑之腑的会穴，也是胃经的募穴。可以调节腑气，健胃通肠消脂。用于肥胖、多食、腹胀、痤疮、面部皱纹、酒皶鼻、荨麻疹、便秘等。（见图 5）

十一、 带脉穴的调整作用

带脉，位于第十一肋端直下平肚脐水平线处。能调节内分泌。对于妇女因月经不调、带下病、盆腔炎等引起的面色晦暗、黄褐斑、痤疮或肥胖、腹部胀满等损容性病症。（见图13）

The acupoint Riyue (GB 24) is located directly below nipples and at the 7th intercostal space. It is the front-Mu acupoint of the gallbladder and can regulate qi of the liver or gallbladder. This acupoint is always used for beauty-impairing conditions due to emotional injury. (See Fig. 13)

9. Regulation of Jingmen (GB 25)

The acupoint Jingmen (GB 25) is located at the lower border of the free end of the 12th rib. It is the front-Mu acupoint of the kidney. This acupoint can not only regulate qi of the liver or gallbladder but also regulate water metabolism of the body. (See Fig. 13)

10. Regulation of Zhongwan (CV 12)

The acupoint Zhongwan (CV 12) is the influential acupoint of the fu-organs and the front-Mu acupoint of the stomach, and as a result it can regulate qi of fu-organs, benefit the stomach, clear intestine and remove fat. It's always used for obesity, polyphagia, abdominal distension, acne, facial wrinkles, brandy nose, urticaria and constipation. (See Fig. 5)

11. Regulation of Daimai (GB 26)

The acupoint Daimai (GB 26) is located directly below the free end of the 11th rib and at the level with the umbilicus and can regulate endocrine system. It's always used for a dark complexion, chloasma and acne due to irregular menstruation, leucorrhea and pelvic inflammation or such figure-impairing problems as obesity and abdominal distension. (See Fig. 13)

12. Regulation of Shenque (CV 8)

The acupoint Shenque (CV 8) is located at the center of the umbilicus and regarded as the root of Yuan-primordial qi. It can regulate the spleen and stomach, remove skin rashes and stop itching, and therefore it's always used for urticaria. In

十二、 神阙穴的调整作用

神阙穴,肚脐正中,是人体元气之根。具有调理脾胃、祛疹止痒的作用。用于荨麻疹。此外艾灸此穴又有很好的强身健体作用。围刺该穴周围腹部皮肤,可治疗肥胖。(见图5)

十三、 阳陵泉穴的调整作用

阳陵泉是筋的会穴,又是胆经的合穴、下合穴。具有强健周身筋骨、疏肝利胆、清泄湿热。用于肥胖、筋骨酸痛无力、面目黄肿、口舌疱疹等。(见图 11)

十四、 悬钟穴的调整作用

悬钟,位于外踝高点上 3 寸,是髓的会穴。用于斑秃、脱发、耳鸣、耳聋、健忘、面色萎黄、筋骨酸痛等。(见图 11)

十五、 章门穴的调整作用

章门,人体脏腑之脏的会穴,脾经的募穴。有调节脏气,健脾利湿。用于消化不良、肥胖、腹胀、便溏、面色萎黄、蝴蝶斑、黄褐斑等。(见图 5)

十六、 太冲穴的调整作用

太冲,位于足背第一、第二趾骨结合部之间凹陷中。是肝经的原穴。能很好地调整因情志导致的内分泌失调而出现的各种损容性疾患。(见图 11)

addition, moxibustion on this acupoint can strengthen the body resistance. Surrounding puncture on abdominal skin of this acupoint can work well for obesity. (See Fig. 5)

13. Regulation of Yanglingquan (GB 34)

The acupoint Yanglingquan (GB 34) is the influential acupoint of tendon and the He-sea acupoint or lower He-sea acupoint of the gallbladder meridian. It can strengthen tendons and bones, soothe the liver or gallbladder, and clear dampness-heat. This acupoint is always used for obesity, soreness, pain and weakness of tendons and bones, a sallow complexion with facial puffiness and mouth or tongue ulcer. (See Fig. 11)

14. Regulation of Xuanzhong (GB 39)

The acupoint Xuanzhong (GB 39), the influential acupoint of marrow, is located at 3 cun above the tip of the external mallelous and always used for alopecia areata, loss of hair, tinnitus, deafness, poor memory, a sallow complexion and soreness and pain of tendons and bones. (See Fig. 11)

15. Regulation of Zhangmen (LR 13)

The acupoint Zhangmen (LR 13) is the influential acupoint of zang-organs and the front-Mu acupoint of the spleen. It can regulate qi of zang-organs, strengthen the spleen and remove dampness. This acupoint is always used for dyspepsia, obesity, abdominal distension, loose stool, a sallow complexion, chloasma and freckles. (See Fig. 5)

16. Regulation of Taichong (LR 3)

The acupoint Taichong (LR 3), the Yuan-primary acupoint of the liver meridian, is located on the dorsum of the foot and in the depression distal to the junction of the 1st and 2nd metatarsal bones. This acupoint can regulate endocrine disorder due to emotional factors and the subsequent beauty-

十七、 太溪穴的调整作用

太溪位于足内踝高点与跟腱之间凹陷中，为肾经的原穴。具有滋阴泄热，生发防脱的功效。治疗脱发、斑秃、面色无华或黧黑、毛发枯焦早白等。（见图 10）

此外，身体的一些腧穴还具有相对的特异性，针对某些特殊症候具有特殊作用的穴位，如：大椎泄热，能够治疗血热导致的痤疮、酒皶鼻、面疖、脱发等。十二井穴（是十二经井穴的统称），主要用于泄热作用，一般用点刺放血。

impairing conditions. (See Fig. 11)

17. Regulation of Taixi (KI 3)

The acupoint Taixi (KI 3), the Yuan-primary acupoint of the kidney meridian, is located in the depression between the tip of medial mallelous and the tendo calcaneus. It can nourish yin, clear away heat, promote hair growth and prevent hair loss. This acupoint is always used for loss of hair, alopecia areata, a lusterless or dark complexion, and dry hair or premature gray hair. (See Fig. 10)

In addition, some acupoints have specific functions targeting on some special groups of symptoms and signs, for example, Dazhui (GV 14) can be used to clear away heat and treat acne, brandy nose, facial furuncles and loss of hair due to blood-heat; and the 12 Jing-well acupoints (the general term of Jing-well acupoints of the 12 regular meridians) can be used to clear away heat through blood-letting.

汉英对照

Chinese-English
Edition of
Acupuncture
Cosmetology

针灸美容

Part 1 The Basic Theory of Acupuncture Cosmetology

第五章　针灸美容的取穴配穴原则

在针灸美容治疗之前,首先要对求美者进行辨证,在此基础上方可以论治。而论治的关键,就是要进行合理的选穴。正确的取穴配穴和施治是提高疗效的根本。

第一节　局部取穴

局部取穴,就是选用病损所在部位局部和邻近穴位进行调理的一种方法。如酒皶鼻取素髎、迎香等。

第二节　循经取穴

当经脉分布所及的部位或相关脏腑、组织、器官发生病损时,可选用该经脉的穴位进行调理。如目赤肿痛,取合谷、太冲、睛明等等,因目为肝之窍,阳明经、太阳经均循经至此。

第三节　辨证取穴

根据中医的四诊八纲、脏腑辨证选取穴位。如斑秃,头发成片脱落,并伴头昏目眩、健忘失眠、舌淡苔白、神疲乏力等,属于血虚风盛,应选用风池、膈俞、脾俞、足三里、神门(见图 8)、三阴交、血海等以养血祛风。

Chapter 5
The principle on acupoint selection & combination of acupuncture cosmetology

Prior to the treatment of cosmetic acupuncture, syndrome differentiation is the first step for appropriate treatment followed by reasonable selection of acupoints. Correct selection and combination of acupoints as well as the subsequent treatment are essentials to the therapeutic effect.

Section 1　Selection of local acupoints

Selection of local acupoints refers to adopt acupoints at the affected area or adjacent acupoints to regulate the disorder, for example, to select Suliao (GV 25) and Yingxiang (LI 20) for brandy nose.

Section 2　Selection of distal acupoints

When certain areas along the running courses of meridians or corresponding zang-fu organs and tissues are involved with pathologic changes, distal acupoints of the involved meridians can be selected for regulation, for example, to select Hegu (LI 4), Taichong (LR 3) and Jingming (BL 1) for redness, swelling and pain of eyes, for the liver opens into the eyes and both Yangming and Taiyang meridians pass through the eye area.

Section 3
Selection of acupoints based on syndrome differentiation

Selection of acupoints can also be based on the four diagnostic methods, syndrome differentiation by eight

汉英对照

Chinese-English Edition of Acupuncture Cosmetology

针灸美容

Part 1　The Basic Theory of Acupuncture Cosmetology

第四节　经验取穴

选用对某些病损具有特效的穴位。如宋代窦材《扁鹊心书》载："人于无病，常灸关元、气海、命门、中脘……亦可保百年寿。"王执中《针灸资生经》云："旧传有人年老而颜如童子者，盖每岁以鼠粪灸脐中一壮故也。"因此，选用诸如关元、气海、中脘、足三里，具有延缓衰老、美容益颜、消除皱纹的作用。耳尖放血可以清热明目等。

由于针刺美容的最大特点在于全身调整，因此，必须局部与全身取穴相结合，方有较好疗效。局部取穴可以通过活络，改善循环，促进表皮细胞新陈代谢以消除斑点、斑疵等病损，并能增强肌肉弹性，而全身取穴则着重于平衡脏腑，调节各系统的功能以达到美容的目的。

principles and syndrome differentiation of zang-fu organs, for example, to select Fengchi (GB 20), Geshu (BL 17), Pishu (BL 20), Zusanli (ST 36), Shenmen (HT 7), Sanyinjiao (SP 6) and Xuehai (SP 10) for alopecia with associated symptoms including dizziness, blurred vision, poor memory, insomnia, a pale tongue with white coating and lassitude, for the TCM syndrome pattern of above condition is blood deficiency stirring wind and the above acupoints can nourish blood and remove wind.

Section 4
Selection of acupoints based on experience

Some acupoints have specific actions on certain problems. For example, the *Bian Que Xin Shu* by Dou Cai in the Song dynasty states that "even without any problems, frequent moxibustion on Guanyuan (CV 4), Qihai (CV 6), Mingmen (GV 4) and Zhongwan (CV 12) ... can work for longevity". The *Zhen Jiu Zi Sheng Jing* by Wang Zhi-zhong states that "moxibustion on umbilicus with mice feces every year makes those with old ages but young faces". Therefore acupoints including Guanyuan (CV 4), Qihai (CV 6), Zhongwan (CV 12) and Zusanli (ST 36) can be selected to delay aging, beautify the face and remove wrinkles. Blood letting on ear apex can clear away heat and brighten eyes.

The remarkable characteristic of acupuncture cosmetology is whole-body regulation, and as a result only with the combination of local acupoints and general acupoints, can a better effect achieved. The local acupoints can improve qi and blood circulation and promote metabolism of epidermal cells to remove spots and patches and enhance muscle elasticity. The

汉英对照

Chinese-English
Edition of
Acupuncture
Cosmetology

针灸美容

上篇 ● 针灸美容基础理论

一、 单穴与组穴

临床证实可选用单穴,亦可用几个穴位配为一组进行,若欲增强某一方面功能者,可用单穴,以突出其效用;欲调理整体功能者,可选用一组穴位,以增强效果。

二、 近穴与远穴

近穴,即近端取穴,是指选用病损病症局部或邻近部分的穴位,通过改善皮肤的局部状况达到美容目的的取穴方法。远穴,即远端取穴,是指选取远离病损局部,具有不仅能防治局部病症,而且能防治其所属经脉循行所涉及的距离较远部位的脏腑、组织、器官的病症,甚至有改善全身状况等作用的穴位的取穴方法。

general acupoints can balance zang-fu organs and regulate functions of each system to guarantee the cosmetic effect.

1. Single acupoint and group of acupoints

It's been proved by clinical practice that a single acupoint or a group of acupoints can both be selected, the former for enhancing certain aspect of function, and the latter for regulating the whole-body function.

2. Selection of local acupoints and distal acupoints

Selection of local acupoints, i. e. , selection of proximal acupoints, is an approach to select acupoints located at or adjacent to the affected area that can obtain beautification through improving the local skin conditions. Selection of distal acupoints, i. e. , selection of distant acupoints, is an approach to select acupoints located away from the affected area that can prevent and treat not only the local problems, but also the problems of distant zang-fu organs, tissues and organs along the running course of meridians, or even improve general condition of the body.

第六章　针灸美容的常用方法

　　针法是用不同的针具刺激腧穴或一定的部位,再施以适当手法,使求美者产生酸麻胀痛或冷热等感觉,以调整人体的功能,改善气血运行状况,达到美容及健身祛病,治疗损容性疾病的目的。灸法则是采用艾绒等各种药物烧灼、熏熨体表的一定部位或腧穴,通过药物的渗透及局部热效应,使肌体产生各种生理反应,通过经络的作用治疗损容性疾病,达到美化容貌、美化形体的目的。由于针法和灸法在治疗上常常结合应用,因此合称针灸。

　　随着社会发展和科学进步,在腧穴、经络的基础上,传统的针法灸法结合现代科学知识,形成了许多新的针法灸法,如：电针、水针、三棱针、皮肤针、皮内针、拔罐、穴位埋线、穴位注射、激光、电热针等；传统的经络学、腧穴学理论与西医学、生物学知识相结合,形成了在一些特定部位内取穴,并有着特定针灸方法的新的方法,如：耳针、头针、腕踝针等。针灸美容临床与普通针灸临床一样,既使用传统的针法、灸法,又使用现代的一些刺激方法,有时还要两者结合。各种方法都有其操作特点和适用范围,针灸美容临床除了治疗损容性疾病以外,还要注重保健、抗衰老、尽量减少痛苦、不破坏正常组织等问题,因此需要掌握多种治疗方法,才能在临床根据具体情况灵活施治,必要时综合治疗。

Chapter 6
The common methods of
acupuncture cosmetology

Acupuncture aims to regulate function of the human body and improve circulation of qi and blood by stimulating acupoints or certain areas with varieties of needles plus appropriate manipulations, resulting in soreness, numbness, distension, pain or cold and hot sensation to obtain cosmetic effect, strengthen the body resistance and treat beauty-impairing conditions. Moxibustion aims to produce varieties of physiological reactions and treat beauty-impairing conditions through penetration of medication and thermal effect of local area by applying moxa wool or other materials on certain areas or acupoints on the body surface. As the above two methods are always combined in clinical practice, they are always called acupuncture and moxibustion.

With social and scientific advances, modern scientific knowledge tends to be integrated into the traditional acupuncture and moxibustion therapies based on acupoints and meridians. As a result, many new acupuncture and moxibustion techniques appeared such as electric acupuncture, acupoint injection, three-edged needle, dermal needle, intradermal needle, cupping, catgut embedding, laser and electric heat needle. In addition, some new special methods such as ear acupuncture, scalp acupuncture and wrist-ankle acupuncture also appear resulting from the combination of traditional theory on meridians and acupoints with modern medicine and biology. Just like ordinary acupuncture clinic, cosmetic acupuncture includes traditional acupuncture and

汉英对照

Chinese-English
Edition of
Acupuncture
Cosmetology

针灸美容

Part 1 The Basic Theory of Acupuncture Cosmetology

汉英对照

Chinese-English
Edition of
Acupuncture
Cosmetology

针灸美容

上篇 ⊙ 针灸美容基础理论

第一节 针刺美容

一、 针刺前的准备

1. 选择针具：针刺美容多用不锈钢制成的毫针，由于针刺美容多选面部及耳部穴位，而头面部皮肤及肌肉浅薄，因此选用针具不宜过长，以针身长度 0.5～2 寸为宜。

2. 选择体位：针刺头面部穴位时卧位、坐位均可，对有条件的地方最好取比较舒适，能持久保持的卧位，也可预防晕针的发生。

另外，在针刺前应对初针者做好解释工作，使之对针刺常识有所了解，消除紧张情绪，使针刺治疗发挥更好的效果。

3. 针具与部位消毒：可煮沸消毒或高压消毒，也可将针具置于 75％乙醇内，浸泡 30 min，取出拭干后用。皮肤在选定穴位后，一般先用 1％的碘酒消毒，再用 75％的乙醇脱碘即可。操作者手指亦要消毒，以免感染。可先用肥皂水将手洗干净，待干后用 75％乙醇拭擦即可。

moxibustion as well as modern stimulating methods or sometimes the combination of the two. Different methods have different operation characteristics and indications, and varieties of therapies are necessary for cosmetic acupuncture in terms of correct choice or comprehensive therapy, for it targets not only on beauty-impairing diseases, but also on health protection, delay of aging process and reduce pain without damaging normal tissue.

Section 1 Cosmetic acupuncture

I. Preparation prior to needling

1. Selection of needles: filiform needles made from stainless steel are often adopted for acupuncture cosmetology, as most acupoints are located in face and auricles with shallow or thin muscles, the selected needles shall not be too long and they are usually 0.5 - 1.5 cun in length of the needle body.

2. Selection of posture: for head and facial acupoints, the patients can take lying or sitting positions and an appropriate comfortable position is easy to maintain and important to prevent needle faint.

In addition, the practitioner shall explain to the patients before the treatment and enable them to understand the common knowledge of acupuncture, ease their nervousness and guarantee a better effect.

3. Sterilization of needles and areas to treat: the needles can be sterilized in boiling water or in an autoclave or soaked in 75% alcohol for 30 minutes and then wiped clean after that. It is recommended that disposable needles be used. The areas to treat need to be sterilized with 1% iodine first and then removed the iodine with 75% alcohol. What's more, the fingers of the practitioner also need to be sterilized to prevent

汉英对照

Chinese-English
Edition of
Acupuncture
Cosmetology

针灸美容

上篇 ● 针灸美容基础理论

4. 针刺的角度与深度：头面部肌肉不甚丰富,故一般情况下适宜斜刺,将针身与皮肤呈45度角倾斜刺入,或沿皮刺,将针身与皮肤呈15度角左右沿皮刺入。

5. 针刺的用针要领：美容保健,施针宜和缓,刺激强度宜适中,不宜过力。一般来说,留针不宜过久,得气后即可出针,针刺深度也应因人而异,对年老体衰者,进针不宜过深;形体肥胖者则可适当深刺。

二、 针刺的注意事项

由于人的生理功能和生活条件因素所致,在针刺时,还应注意以下几个方面事项。

1. 过于饥饿、疲劳、精神过度紧张时,不宜立即进行针刺。

2. 孕妇慎刺。妊娠初期3个月内禁刺,以免引起流产。在月经期间,亦不宜针刺,尤其是腰腹部的穴位。

3. 若皮肤有感染、溃疡、瘢痕或肿瘤的部位,也不宜针刺。

4. 常有自发性出血或损伤后出血不止者,不宜针刺。

5. 某些部位要掌握针刺的深度,以免损伤内脏,而头面部的承泣穴、囟会穴、脑户穴、神庭穴、玉枕穴等,体穴的神阙、乳中、缺盆等为古籍记载中的禁针之穴。(见图1、图5)

infection: to wash clean with soapy water and then wipe clean with 75% alcohol.

4. Angle and depth of needling: due to thin muscles in the head and face, generally the needles are usually inserted obliquely to form an angle of 45° or subcutaneously to form approximately an angle of 15°.

5. Key principles of acupuncture: for acupuncture cosmetology, needling shall be gentle and moderate with appropriate stimulation. Generally it's not advisable to retain the needles for too long, and actually the needles can be removed as soon as the patients got needling sensation. The depth of needle varies from different people: not too deep for the aged with weak constitution; and relatively deeper for obese people.

II. Precautions

Due to human physiological functions as well as limitations of living conditions, the following aspects shall be considered:

1. It's not advisable to apply immediate acupuncture to those with hunger, fatigue or mental nervousness.

2. It's contraindicated to puncture pregnant women, especially those within 3 months to avoid miscarriage and it is not advisable to apple acupuncture to women during menstruation period, especially to the acupoints on the lumbar and abdominal regions.

3. It's not advisable to puncture those with skin infection, ulceration, scar and tumor.

4. It's not advisable to puncture those with frequent spontaneous hemorrhage or persistent hemorrhage after trauma.

5. Appropriate depth shall be controlled on some acupoints to avoid injury of internal organs. It's contraindicated to puncture such acupoints in the head and face as Chengqi (ST

6. 凡遇过饥、过饱、醉酒、大怒、大惊、劳累过度等情况，不宜针刺，孕妇产妇不宜针刺。

第二节　灸法美容

应用艾绒或某种药物在穴位或患处熏灼、贴敷、借灸火的热力，通过经络穴位的作用，达到治疗损容性疾病和美容益颜健体的目的。《医学入门》言："药之不及，针之不到，必须灸之。"因此，灸法也是针灸美容的主要手段。

常用的美容灸法有隔物灸、艾条灸、温灸器灸等。

一、灸法的操作

1. 隔物灸：是将某种药物置于艾炷与施灸部位的皮肤之间进行灸疗。是美容最常用的方法之一。根据间隔物的不同，常用的有隔姜灸、隔蒜灸、隔盐灸、隔附子饼灸、隔葱灸等，其中以隔姜灸最为常用。

2. 艾条灸：是将艾绒用纸包裹卷成圆柱形的艾卷，点燃一端进行施灸。常用的温和灸（在固定的高度，使施灸部位产生温和舒适的感觉）、雀啄灸（对准施灸部位，一起一落如同鸟雀啄食）、回旋灸（离施灸部位一定高度平行往复回旋熏灸）。

1), Xinhui (GV 22), Naohu (GV 17), Shenting (GV 24), Yuzhen (BL 9) and body acupoints including Shenque (CV 8), Ruzhong (ST 17) and Quepen (ST 12) in ancient literature. (See Fig. 1 and Fig. 5)

6. It's not advisable to puncture those with starvation, overeat, alcoholic intoxication, outrage, panic and fatigue as well as pregnant or puerperant women.

Section 2　Cosmetic moxibustion

Moxibustion is a therapy to fumigate or apply moxa-wool or a certain kind of drug to acupoints or affected areas to treat beauty-impairing conditions, beautify the appearance and strengthen the body resistance through heating of fire. The *Yi Xue Ru Men* (*Introduction to Medicine*) states that "when a disease that may not respond to medication or acupuncture, moxibustion is suggested". Therefore moxibustion is also a major means for acupuncture cosmetology.

The commonly-used cosmetic moxibustion methods include material-partitioned moxibustion, moxa-stick moxibustion and moxibustion through special instrument.

Ⅰ. Manipulations of moxibustion

1. Material-partitioned moxibustion: This is one of the most common methods for cosmetology: to place certain material between the moxa cone and skin during moxibustion. The most common materials include ginger, garlic, salt, Fuzi (*Radix Aconiti Lateralis*) cake and spring onion, especially ginger.

2. Moxa-stick moxibustion: to light one end of the paper-wrapped columniform moxa wool and apply moxibustion, this method includes mild-warm moxibustion (to bring mild warm

3. 温针灸：在留针的毫针针柄上插入 2 cm 左右的艾卷施灸。用于需要针加灸的损容性病症。

4. 温灸器灸：在特制的容器盛装艾绒进行施灸。目前市场上有各种各样的温灸器。常见的有温筒灸、温灸盒灸等。

二、 注意事项

1. 施灸时，应注意避免烫伤施灸处的皮肤或受术者的衣物等。

2. 对于阴虚发热、实热证，孕妇的腹部、腰骶部、合谷、三阴交、肩井（见图 6）、昆仑（见图 11）、至阴（见图 11）等部位不宜施灸。

3. 不同灸法的应用应根据求美者的具体病情、体质、症候、部位选用。

第三节　耳针美容

中医学认为，"耳者宗脉之所聚也"、"十二经脉、三百六十五络，其血气皆上于面而走空窍"。五脏六腑、皮肤九窍、四肢百骸等部位，通过经络与耳郭密切联系。因此，当人体某一脏腑或部位发生病变时，可能因经络的传导作用，会在耳郭的相应部位出现异常反应，表现为皮肤色泽、形态、压痛敏感及电特性改变等。

and comfortable sensation to the local area at a fixed height),
sparrow-pecking moxibustion (to lift the moxa stick up and
down toward the selected area like birds pecking) and rotation
moxibustion (to apply paralleled rotary moxibustion at a certain
height away from the selected area).

3. Moxibustion with warming needle: to wrap the needle
handle with a moxa roll about 2 cm for moxibustion, this
method is indicated for beauty-impairing conditions that require
both acupuncture and moxibustion.

4. Moxibustion with special instrument: to apply
moxibustion within special-made instrument containing moxa
wool, the commonly-used instrument now in the market
includes warm tubes and mild moxibustion boxes.

Ⅱ. Precautions

1. To avoid burning or scalding the patients' skin or clothes
during moxibustion.

2. It's not advisable to apply moxibustion to those with
fever due to yin deficiency, excessive heat syndrome and
abdomen or lumbosacral region as well as acupoints Hegu (LI
4), Sanyinjiao (SP 6), Jianjing (GB 21)(See Fig. 6), Kunlun
(BL 60)(See Fig. 11) and Zhiyin (BL 67)(See Fig. 11) of
pregnant women.

3. To select different moxibustion methods on the basis of
the customers' actual condition, constitution, symptoms and
different parts of the body.

Section 3   Cosmetic auricular acupuncture

TCM holds that "all meridians assemble in ears", and
"qi and blood of all 12 regular meridians and 365 collaterals
ascend to face and other facial orifices". Five-zang and six-fu

汉英对照
Chinese-English
Edition of
Acupuncture
Cosmetology
针灸美容
Part 1 The Basic Theory of Acupuncture Cosmetology

耳部的神经血管较丰富,特别是在耳甲腔的三角窝,刺激该处的神经有调整机体代谢平衡失调的作用。刺激迷走神经,可影响胰岛素值,抑制食欲以达到减肥的目的。刺激其他相应的部位可以达到祛斑、祛痤的目的;耳穴疗法结合背部放血、拔罐在美容方面具有更佳的疗效,美容从业人员掌握以上技能可以提高自己的临床水平及应对行业竞争的能力,也可以在美容机构建立自己的特色。

一、 耳穴的分布规律

耳穴分布总的规律如同一个在子宫中倒置的胎儿,头部朝下,臀部和下肢朝上,胸腹部、躯干在中间。

1. 与头面部相应的穴位在耳垂和对耳屏。

2. 与上肢相应的穴位在耳舟。

3. 与躯干和下肢相应的穴位在对耳轮和对耳轮上、下脚。

4. 与胸腔脏器相应的耳穴多分布在耳甲腔。

5. 与腹腔脏器相应的耳穴多分布在耳甲艇。

6. 与消化道相应的耳穴多分布在耳轮脚周围。

7. 消化道在耳轮脚周围环形排列。

8. 与耳鼻咽喉相应的耳穴多分布在耳屏四周。

(见图 14、图 15)

汉英对照

Chinese-English
Edition of
Acupuncture
Cosmetology

针灸美容

上篇 ◉ 针灸美容基础理论

organs, skin and nine orifices, and four limbs and all bones of the body closely relate to ears through meridians. Therefore, when disorders occur in internal organs or other parts of the body, abnormal reactions may appear at corresponding auricular areas through the conduction of meridians, manifesting as changes of skin color, shape, tenderness and electric property.

The auricular area is full of nerves and blood vessels, especially the triangle fossa in the cavity of concha. Stimulating the nerves in this area can regulate disordered organic metabolism; stimulating valgus nerve can affect insulin, inhibit appetite and lose weight; stimulating other corresponding areas can remove chloasma and acne; and the combined ear therapy with blood letting and cupping on the back can have much better effect. By mastering above techniques, the cosmeticians can improve their clinical level and professional competitiveness and also establish characteristic items among cosmetology institutions.

Ⅰ. Distribution law of the auricular acupoints

The general distribution law of auricular acupoints (like an inverted fetus in the uterus): head in the lower part, buttocks and lower limbs in the upper part, and chest and abdomen as well as torso in the middle.

1. Acupoints located on the lobule and antitragus are related to the head and face.

2. Acupoints located on the scapha are related to the upper limbs.

3. Acupoints located on antihelix and its two crura are related to torso and lower limbs.

4. Acupoints located on cavity of concha are related to

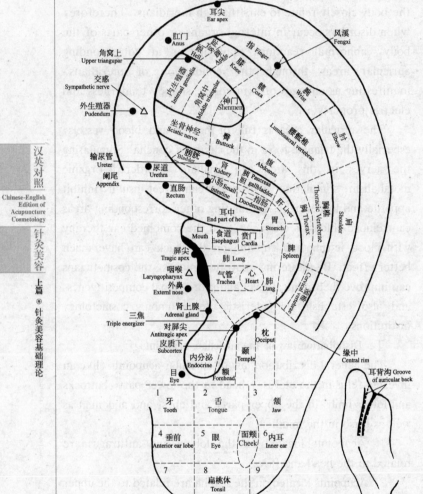

图 14　耳穴分布图(一)

Fig. 14　Distribution map of ear acupoints (1)

thorax organs.

5. Acupoints located on cymba of concha are related to abdominal organs.

6. Acupoints located around helix crus are related to alimentary tract.

7. The alimentary tract appeared ring alignment around helix crus.

8. Acupoints located around tragus are related to ears, nose and throat.

(See Fig. 14 and Fig. 15)

汉英对照

Chinese-English Edition of Acupuncture Cosmetology

针灸美容 Part 1 The Basic Theory of Acupuncture Cosmetology

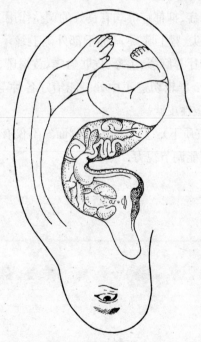

图 15　耳穴分布图（二）
Fig. 15　Distribution map of ear acupoints（2）

二、 常用的耳穴分布、定位与主治

1. 耳尖：耳郭向耳屏方向对折时，耳郭上面的尖端处。对于头面五官的各种损容性疾病，如麦粒肿、目赤肿痛、荨麻疹、湿疹、痤疮、皮肤瘙痒等均有效。

2. 荨麻疹点（风溪点）：位于耳舟上，指与腕两穴之间。对各种过敏导致的损容性疾患，如湿疹、荨麻疹、风疹、痤疮、过敏性皮肤病、过敏性鼻炎均有效。

3. 神门：三角窝内，对耳轮上、下脚交叉处。具有消炎止痛、抗过敏、止痛止痒、镇定等作用。对于各种痛证、炎症、过敏症、焦虑症、抑郁症等均有良好的调整作用。

4. 下屏尖（肾上腺）：耳屏下部外侧上缘。具有抗过敏、抗炎作用，治疗荨麻疹、湿疹、皮肤瘙痒、黄褐斑、蝴蝶斑等。

5. 脑干：屏轮切迹正中处。能治疗各种与脑部功能失调有关及过敏性皮肤病。

6. 脑（皮质下）：对耳屏的内侧面。不仅有消炎止痛、镇静的作用，还能调节视力。

Ⅱ. Distribution, location and indications of commonly-used ear acupoints

1. Ear apex: at the tip of auricle when folded towards tragus, this acupoint is indicated for beauty-impairing conditions of head, face and five sensory organs such as stye, redness, swelling and pain of eyes, urticaria, eczema, acne and skin itching.

2. Urticaria point (Fengxi point): on the scapha between finger and wrist, this acupoint is indicated for beauty-impairing conditions due to allergic reactions such as eczema, urticaria, rubella, acne, allergic skin diseases and allergic rhinitis.

3. Ear-Shenmen: at bifurcating point between superior and inferior antihelix crus in the triangle fossa, this acupoint can subdue inflammation and pain, relieve allergic reaction, stop itching and calm the mind and is therefore indicated for varieties of pain syndrome, inflammation, allergic reactions, anxiety and depression.

4. Infratragic apex (adrenal gland): at the upper border of lateral aspect of inferior part of tragus, this acupoint can relieve allergic reaction and subdue inflammation and is therefore indicated for urticaria, eczema, skin itching and chloasma.

5. Brain stem: at the midpoint of helix-tragic notch, this acupoint is indicated for disorders related to cerebral dysfunction and allergic skin diseases.

6. Brain (subcortex): at the medial aspect of antitragus, this acupoint can not only subdue inflammation, relieve pain

汉英对照
Chinese-English
Edition of
Acupuncture
Cosmetology

针灸美容 Part 1 The Basic Theory of Acupuncture Cosmetology

7. 平喘（又称对屏尖）：对耳屏的尖端。不仅有调节呼吸中枢的作用，还可以用于治疗鼻炎、哮喘、过敏性瘙痒、湿疹、荨麻疹等。

8. 耳中（又名膈）：耳轮角上。可用治各种皮肤病，如顽固性皮肤瘙痒、银屑病、湿疹、荨麻疹、黄褐斑、蝴蝶斑、脱发等。

9. 轮1～6：从耳轮结节下缘至耳垂中部的下缘分成5等份，共6点。自上而下依次分为轮1、轮2、轮3、轮4、轮5、轮6。用于各种面部炎症、热证，如痤疮、目赤肿痛、咽喉肿痛等。

10. 内分泌：屏间切迹的内侧面。具有调整机体内分泌作用。用于肥胖症、湿疹、荨麻疹、风疹、突眼等。

11. 面颊区：耳垂5、6区交界线的周围。可用于治疗所有面部损容性病症。如痤疮、黄褐斑、皱纹、面色萎黄无华、面瘫、面痛、面肌痉挛等。

（见图14）

三、 注意事项

1. 注意耳郭的消毒，避免感染。若耳郭有严重炎症时，禁止针刺。

2. 对于有严重器质性疾病或体质极度虚弱、精神高度紧张者，手法应轻缓柔和。

and calm the mind but also eyesight.

7. Pingchuan (antitragus): at the tip of antitragus, this acupoint can regulate respiratory center and is also indicated for rhinitis, asthma, allergic itching, eczema and urticaria.

8. Middle ear (diaphragm): on helix crus, this acupoint is indicated for varieties of skin diseases such as intractable skin itching, psoriasis, eczema, urticaria, chloasma and loss of hair.

9. Helix 1 - 6: region from lower border of auricular tubercle to midpoint of lower border of lobule is divided into five equal parts, and the points marking the division are respectively helix 1, 2, 3, 4, 5, and 6, and these acupoints are indicated for inflammation and heat symptoms in the face such as acne, redness, swelling and pain of eyes and sore throat.

10. Endocrine: at the medial aspect of intratragic notch, this acupoint can regulate endocrine and is therefore indicated for obesity, eczema, urticaria, rubella and exophthalmus.

11. Cheek: around the cross line of the 5th and 6th area of earlobe, this acupoint is indicated for beauty-impairing conditions such as acne, chloasma, wrinkles, sallow complexion, facial palsy, facial pain and facial spasm.

(See Fig. 14)

Ⅲ. Precautions

1. Strict antisepsis of auricle is necessary to avoid infection and it's prohibited for ear acupuncture in case of severe inflammation.

2. Gentle and mild manipulation shall be adopted for those

3. 有习惯性流产的孕妇、怀孕 3 个月以上的妇女,应禁用或慎用耳针,避免引起流产、早产。

第四节　拔罐美容

图 16　拔罐法
Fig. 16　Cupping

拔罐法是利用某种方法使罐内形成负压而吸附于施术的部位,使局部皮肤充血,而达到疏通经络、调和气血、排除局部病理产物的作用。(见图 16)

常用的罐具有玻璃罐、橡胶罐、竹罐、陶罐、金属罐等,以玻璃罐最为普及。

一、拔罐法的操作

拔罐的方法有火罐、针罐、刺血拔罐、抽气罐等。

1. 火罐法:应用火焰在罐内燃烧形成负压,将罐吸附在皮肤上。之后可留罐(吸附后停留于局部一定时间)、闪罐(吸附后迅速拔起,再反复操作数次,直至局部皮肤潮红、充血为度)、走罐(吸附后在上下或左右反复推移火罐,使皮肤红润、充血,再起罐)。

2. 针罐:适合于需要针刺又需要拔罐的病症。在留针之后再以针刺部位为中心拔罐。

with severe organic diseases, or extremely weak constitution and mental nervousness.

3. It's not advisable or prohibited to apply ear acupuncture to women with habitual miscarriage or after 3-month pregnancy to avoid miscarriage and premature labor.

Section 4　Cosmetic cupping

Cupping is a therapy in which a jar is attached to the skin surface to cause local congestion through the negative pressure created by introducing heat in the form of an ignited material, working to dredge meridians, harmonize qi and blood and remove local pathologic products. (See Fig. 15)

The common types of jars include glass, rubber, bamboo, pottery and metal ones and glass cups are the most common.

Ⅰ. **Manipulations of cupping**

The cupping methods include fire cupping, cupping after needling, and cupping following blood letting and vacuum cupping.

1. Fire cupping method: to attach the cup to the skin surface through the negative pressure created by fire burning, and after that the following procedures can be selected: retaining of cups (to retain the cups in local areas after attachment for some time); flash cupping (to remove the cups immediately after attachment repeat several times of cupping and removal until the local skin turned red or congested) and moving cupping (to move the cup either from upward to downward or from left to right several times until the local skin turned red and congested).

2. Cupping after needling: to apply cupping therapy centered on needling area during retaining of needles, and this

3. 刺血拔罐：在施术的部位先行梅花针叩打或三棱针等针具点刺出血，再行拔罐，以加强出血。是治疗痤疮、丹毒、皮癣等常用的方法。

二、 注意事项

1. 走罐操作前应在罐口和走罐的部位涂上适量的润滑剂，适合于皮肤肌肉丰厚的部位。针罐的选择应高于留针的针柄，以免拔罐后将针过度的插入皮肤之中造成损伤。

2. 留罐期间要注意观察罐内的皮肤充血或出血的状况，避免时间过长，过度充血或皮肤起泡等不良后果发生。一般以 5～15 min 为宜。

3. 对于皮肤有过敏、溃疡或孕妇的腹部、腰骶部禁用拔罐。

4. 用火罐应注意避免灼伤或烫伤皮肤。

第五节　三棱针美容

三棱针为不锈钢制造，身长约 6 cm，尖端三刃面，针尖锋利，针身圆润。根据需要选择大、中、小 3 型。主要是用来刺破受术者身上的某个穴位或表浅血络，放出一定量的血液，从而达到美容美体的目的。

method is indicated for those who need both needling and cupping.

3. Cupping following blood letting: to prick the selected area first with plum-blossom needle or three-edged needle for blood letting and then apply cupping to enhance bleeding, and this method is indicated for acne, erysipelas and psoriasis.

II. Precautions

1. It's advisable to apply some appropriate amount of lubricants to the mouth of cups and selected area and try to select the skin with thick muscles. For cupping after needling, the cups shall be higher than the needle handle to avoid pushing the needles and injuring the skin.

2. It's advisable to keep observing the skin congestion or bleeding during retaining of cups to avoid such consequences as over-congestion or blisters, and the time limit ranges from 5 to 15 minutes.

3. It's not advisable to apply cupping to those with skin allergy and ulcer and it's prohibited to apply cupping to abdomen and lumbosacral region of pregnant women.

4. Skin burn or scald shall be absolutely avoided.

Section 5
Cosmetic technique by three-edged needle

The three-edged needle is made from stainless steel and about 6 cm in length. The needle has a sharp tip with three edges and a round body. Three-edged needles in large, medium and small sizes can be used to prick a certain acupoint or superficial vessels for blood letting and obtain the goal of facial beauty or body shaping.

汉英对照

Chinese-English
Edition of
Acupuncture
Cosmetology

针灸美容

Part 1 The Basic Theory of Acupuncture Cosmetology

一、三棱针操作

临床常用的操作方法有缓刺、速刺、散刺、密刺4种。

1. 缓刺：对准被刺的部位缓缓刺入0.5～1分，再缓缓退出，血液自然流出至停止为止。常用于头面、四肢的部位放血。

2. 速刺：快速点刺所选部位1～2分，再迅速退出。常用于指趾末端的部位放血。

3. 散刺（围刺、豹文刺）：以所选部位为中心，对其周围点刺10～20针。常用于局部痈肿、痤疮、酒皶鼻等。

4. 密刺：用轻刺或梅花针叩打所选局部，使其微量出血。常用于治疗各种皮肤病，如顽癣、脱发、神经性皮炎等。

二、注意事项

1. 注意施术部位严格消毒，避免感染。

2. 严重贫血、低血压、严重静脉曲张、有出血倾向者，不适合采用本法。

第六节 皮肤针美容

皮肤针也是针刺美容最常用的一种方法。根据针的排列、多少，有梅花针（5枚针组成）、七星针（7枚针组成）、罗汉针（18枚针组成）、丛针（多枚针组成）。

I. Operations

Clinically there are three operative methods: slow pricking, fast pricking, scattered pricking and dense pricking.

1. Slow pricking: To prick the selected area 0.05 - 0.1 cun slowly and then withdraw slowly until blood comes out and stop naturally. It's always used for blood letting in head, face and four limbs.

2. Fast pricking: To prick the selected area 0.1 - 0.2 cun rapidly and then withdraw immediately. It's always used for blood letting in terminals of fingers or toes.

3. Scattered pricking (also called surrounding or leopard-spot pricking): To prick 10 - 20 times around the selected area. It's always used for local abscess, acne and brandy nose.

4. Dense pricking: To prick the selected area slightly or tap with plum-blossom needle until slight bleeding. It's always used for varieties of skin problems such as intractable tinea, loss of hair and neurodermatitis.

II. Precautions

1. Strict aseptic operation is applied to prevent infection.

2. This therapy shall in no case be applied for those with severe anemia, hypotension, severe varicose veins, and hemorrhagic tendency.

Section 6　Cosmetic technique by dermal needle

Dermal needle is also commonly used for acupuncture cosmetology. By the alignment and numbers of needle, dermal needles include plum-blossom needle (five needles), seven-star needle (seven needles), arhat needle (18 needles) and luster needles (numerous needle).

一、 皮肤针操作

施术者右手持针柄,以环指、小指将针柄末端固定在小鱼际肌处,以中指、拇指挟持针柄,示指按在针柄中段。均匀、有节奏地叩刺所选的部位。刺激强度分轻、中、重 3 种。频率以每分钟 80～100 次为宜。

1. 轻叩刺:叩刺局部皮肤潮红,有轻微疼痛感。

2. 中叩刺:介于轻、重叩刺之间。

3. 重叩刺:叩刺局部皮肤有较明显的痛感,但能忍受,局部皮肤明显发红,有轻微出血。

针刺美容最常用的是轻、中度叩刺。每日或隔日 1 次,14 日为 1 个疗程。两个疗程之间间隔 1 周。

二、 注意事项

1. 施术前详细检查针具,做好针具、施术部位的消毒。

2. 施术中注意观察受术者的反应。术后注意保持局部卫生,避免感染。

第七节　皮内针美容

皮内针是以特制的小型针具固定于腧穴的皮内或皮下,进行较长时间埋藏的一种方法,又称埋针法。适合于较长时间需要留针的病症。常用的皮内针有颗粒型、揿针型 2 种。

Ⅰ. Manipulations of dermal needle

To hold the handle of the needle with the right hand, more specifically, to use the ring finger and small finger to fix the end of needle handle to hypothenar, use the middle finger to pinch the needle hand and place the index finger to the middle part of the needle handle, and then tap the selected area evenly and rhythmically. The tapping intensity can be mild, moderate and heavy, and the tapping frequency is usually from 80 to 100 times per minute.

1. Mild tapping: until the local skin turned slightly red with slightly pain sensation.

2. Moderate tapping: in between the mild and heavy tapping.

3. Heavy tapping: until obvious redness of the local skin with slight bleeding and obvious but tolerable pain sensation.

The mild and moderate tapping is more common for cosmetic acupuncture. The tapping can be done once every day or every other day and 14 days make up one treatment course. There is an interval of one week between two treatment courses.

Ⅱ. Precautions

1. Detailed check-up of needles and strict sterilization of needles and selected areas are necessary prior to treatment.

2. It's advisable to observe the customers' reaction during tapping and keep local area clean after tapping to prevent infection.

Section 7
Cosmetic technique by intradermal needle

The intradermal needle therapy, also called needle

一、 操作方法

将皮内针浸泡在盛有 75% 的乙醇的平碟中，在穴位消毒后，用镊子夹住针柄，刺入真皮内（揿针型）或沿皮下刺入（颗粒型），然后用小方形胶布粘住固定。

二、 注意事项

1. 操作前应进行严格的局部消毒。埋针局部应保持干燥、卫生。暑热天埋针时间不能超过 2 日，以避免感染。

2. 皮内针应选用易于固定且不妨碍肢体活动的穴位。若有不适体征，应重埋或改用他穴再用。

第八节　火针美容

采用钨或钨合金、不锈钢制造，直径 0.5～1 mm，24～26 号，长约 2 寸的火针。对于体表痣的治疗，则采用三头火针。

火针主要用于痣、扁平疣、老年斑等损容性病症。

一、 火针操作

求美者取舒适位置，施术者先将部位常规消毒后，将火针在酒精灯上烧灼至针身通红（不锈钢针）或白而发亮（钨或钨合金针）后，迅速刺入所选部位，并立即退针。针刺的深度依治疗所需、个体体质和所选部位而定。肌肉丰厚的部位，2～5分，肌肉浅薄处，1～2分。

embedding therapy, is an approach to implant the specially-made short needles into the skin or subcutaneous region for long-term stimulation. This method is indicated for those conditions that require long-time needle retaining. The commonly-used intradermal needles include grain-like type and thumb tag type.

Ⅰ. **Manipulations**

To soak the intradermal needles into a plate containing 75% alcohol first; after sterilization of the acupoints, to pinch the needle handle with forceps and insert into dermis (thumb tag type) or subcutaneous region (grain-like type) and then to fix it with adhesive tape.

Ⅱ. **Precautions**

1. To make strict local sterilization prior to operation and keep local area dry and clean. In summer months, the embedding time shall be no more than 2 days to prevent infection.

2. To select acupoints easy to stabilize without affecting the movement of limbs and apply re-embedding or change acupoints in case of uncomfortable signs.

Section 8   Cosmetic technique by fire needle

Generally No. 24 - 26 fire needles 0.5 - 1 mm in diameter and 2 cun in length made from tungsten or tungalloy or stainless steel are adopted, and three-headed fire needles are always adopted for nevus on body surface.

Fire needles are mainly indicated for such beauty-impairing conditions as nevus, flat wart and senile plaque.

Ⅰ. **Manipulations**

To make routine sterilization of the selected area after the

汉英对照

Chinese-English
Edition of
Acupuncture
Cosmetology

针灸美容

Part 1 The Basic Theory of Acupuncture Cosmetology

二、 注意事项

1. 严格消毒,避免感染。

2. 掌握解剖,取穴准确,深浅适当,避开血管脏器,避免遗留瘢痕。

第九节 穴位注射美容

穴位注射是根据所患的损容性病症的需要,根据腧穴的治疗作用和药物的药理作用进行腧穴和药物的选择,将药物注射入穴位之中,通过二者的作用达到美容健体的目的。

躯干、四肢的穴位注射常用的针头为 2～5 ml 的普通注射器和针头,面部穴位则常用 1 ml 的皮试注射器和针头。

一、 穴位注射的操作

所选的穴位常规消毒后,将针头迅速刺入,然后缓慢上下提插,得气后回抽,如无回血,即可缓缓将药物推入。注射结束后退针,并用消毒干棉球压迫即可。

customer takes a comfortable position; next to burn the fire needle on alcohol lamp until redness of the needle body (stainless steel needle) or whiteness and shine (tungsten or tungalloy); and then insert into the selected area rapidly and remove immediately. The depth of needles shall be adjusted according to the therapeutic principle, individual constitution and location of the area, usually 0.2 – 0.5 cun for areas with thick muscle and 0.1 – 0.2 cun for areas with thin muscle.

Ⅱ. Precautions

1. Strict sterilization is necessary to prevent infection.

2. To be familiar with anatomy, make correct location of acupoints, puncture in appropriate depth and avoid blood vessels or internal organs to prevent left-over scars.

Section 9
Cosmetic technique by acupoint injection

Acupoint injection is a therapy for beautification and health protection by injecting medication into acupoints based on the therapeutic action of acupoints and pharmacological action of medications according to the need of beauty-impairing conditions.

The ordinary syringe and 2 – 5 ml needle is always adopted for acupoints in torso and limbs, and skin-test syringe and 1 ml needle for acupoints in face.

Ⅰ. Manipulations of acupoint injection

After routine sterilization of the selected acupoints, to insert the needle rapidly followed by slow lifting and thrusting and then draw back upon arrival of qi, and then if no blood flashback, to inject the medication slowly, and after that to remove the needle and press the area with dry cotton ball.

可每日或隔日 1 次，穴位可左右交替。7～10 日为 1 个疗程，隔 3～5 日再行第二个疗程。

二、 常用美容作用药物的选择

要获得良好的穴位注射美容效果，除了掌握正确的操作方法以外，选择适应损容性病症的药物极为关键。

1．具有清热解毒、消炎作用的药物：板蓝根注射液、银黄注射液等。

2．具有活血祛瘀、调经养颜的药物：复方当归注射液、丹参注射液等。

3．具有补益气血、强壮身体、美容益颜的药物：胎盘注射液、黄芪注射液、生脉注射液等。

4．具有消除色素沉着的注射液：维生素 C 注射液、丹参注射液、当归注射液等。

三、 注意事项

1．严格施行无菌操作，谨防感染。

2．注意药物的药理作用、剂量、配伍禁忌、副作用、过敏反应等。

3．避免将注射药物注入关节腔、脊髓腔和血管内。注意不可注射过深造成内脏损伤，如气胸、膀胱损伤等。

The acupoint injection can be done once every day or every other day. The acupoints can be selected left-rightly alternately. 7 - 10 days make up one treatment course and second treatment course starts after an interval of 3 - 5 days.

II. Selection of common medications for cosmetology

Besides correct manipulations, selection of appropriate medications is also extremely important for better cosmetic effect through by acupoint injection.

1. Medications that clear away heat, remove toxic substance, and subdue inflammation: Yuxingcao (cordate okuttuynia), Banlangen (Isatis root) injection and Yinhuang (honeysuckle flower and skullcap) injection.

2. Medications that circulate blood to resolve stasis, regulate menstruation, and beautify face: compound Danggui (angelica) injection and Danshen (Red sage root) injection.

3. Medications that supplements qi and blood, strengthen the body resistance, and beautify face: Taipan (placenta) injection, Huangqi (astragalus) injection and Shengmai (red ginseng, lilyturf root and fruit of Chinese magnoliavine) injection.

4. Medications that remove pigmentation: vitamin C injection, Danshen (red sage root) injection and Danggui (angelica) injection.

III. Precautions

1. Strict asepsis is necessary to prevent infection.

2. Be careful about the pharmacological actions, dose, incompatibility, side effects and allergic reaction of the medications for injection.

3. Medications shall not be injected into joint cavity, spinal cavity and blood vessels; and over-deep injection shall be

4. 注射结束后应注意让受术者稍事休息,并注意观察注射后的反应。

5. 体质明显虚弱、有晕针史、局部感染、有皮肤病者不宜使用本法。

第十节　穴位激光美容

激光疗法是通过激光的光、热、压力和电磁效应作用于经络、穴位,从而达到美容目的的一种疗法。这种疗法具有无痛、无菌、快速的美容治疗效果,是常用的针灸美容方法。

穴位激光美容医疗机有氦氖、二氧化碳、氩离子、氦镉激光医疗机。目前最广泛应用于临床的是氦-氖激光医疗机。随着激光疗法的普及,许多损容性病症可以用激光治疗,常见的有斑秃、湿疹、牛皮癣、荨麻疹、酒皶鼻、痤疮、丹毒、神经麻痹等。

一、　氦-氖激光医疗机的操作方法

选择好合适的体位,将激光机对准所选的部位。在照射前可将电流旋钮置于第二或第三档上,然后开启电源开关,当指示灯亮,氦-氖激光器发出红色的激光。治疗完毕关闭电源开关即可。

汉英对照
Chinese-English
Edition of
Acupuncture
Cosmetology

针灸美容

上篇 ◉ 针灸美容基础理论

avoided to prevent damaging internal organs, leading to such consequences as pneumothorax and injury of urinary bladder.

4. It's advisable to ask the patients to rest for a while after acupoint injection and observe their reactions.

5. It's not advisable to apply this therapy to those with weak constitution, history of needle faint, local infection and skin diseases.

Section 10
Cosmetic technique by laser therapy on acupoints

Laser therapy is a cosmetic approach to act on meridians and acupoints through the light, heat, pressure and electromagnetic effect of laser. This aseptic therapy works fast without pain and is therefore commonly used for cosmetic acupuncture.

There are four types of laser therapy instrument: Helium-Neon, carbon dioxide, argon ion and helium-cadmium laser instrument, but the first one is the most common one. As laser therapy becomes more and more popular, many beauty-impairing conditions can be treated with laser such as alopecia areata, eczema, psoriasis, urticaria, brandy nose, acne, erysipelas and neural paralysis.

I. Manipulations of H-N laser instrument

To ask the patients to take an appropriate posture and focus the laser instrument on the selected area; to place the knob of electric current to the 2nd or 3rd gear prior to radiation; then to switch on the electricity, and when the indication lamp turns bright, the H-N laser starts to give off red lights; and finally to switch off the electricity after radiation.

91

汉英对照

Chinese-English
Edition of
Acupuncture
Cosmetology

针灸美容

上篇 ⊙ 针灸美容基础理论

二、 注意事项

1. 激光机在使用前应详细检查有无漏电、混线现象，并检查地线是否接好，以防止触电或烧毁机器等事故发生。

2. 若启动后激光管不亮或出现闪辉现象，表明启动电压过低，应立即断电，并将电流调节旋钮沿顺时针方向转 1～2 档，停 1 min 再将电源开关打开。顺时针电流增大至 6 mA，以免损坏激光管。

3. 激光器使用时间最长不宜超过 4 h。开始宜从小剂量、短时间开始，在没有反作用、副作用后，方可逐渐增加照射时间。

4. 疗程应根据病情、个体的体质、敏感程度等情况而定。

5. 在治疗时，施术者与受术者均要戴激光防护眼镜，切不可对视激光束，以免损伤眼睛。

II . Precautions

1. Prior to application, detailed check up on electrical leakage, crossed wires and well-connected ground wire is necessary to prevent electric shock or burning out the machine.

2. Failure of laser tube to bright or flashing bright after switching on indicates that the trigger voltage is too low, so in case that happens, to turn off the power immediately, make 1 - 2 gear clockwise rotation of the electric current knob, and then to pause for one minute and re-switch on the electricity and increase the clockwise electric current to 6 mA to prevent damaging the laser tube.

3. The application of laser shall never exceed 4 hours, starting from small dose and short period. The radiation time can only be increased after no adverse reaction or side effects occur.

4. The treatment course depends upon the actual condition, individual constitution and degree of sensitivity.

5. It's advisable for practitioners and patients to wear laser-protective glasses and avoid directly looking at the laser beam to prevent damaging eyes.

汉英对照

Chinese-English
Edition of
Acupuncture
Cosmetology

针灸美容

中篇
针灸美容治疗

Part 2
The Treatment of Acupuncture Cosmetology

第七章 皮肤科病症的针灸美容

中医学认为任何表现于面部皮肤和其他部位皮肤的病变,都是由于体内某些脏腑的功能或结构发生了变化而影响了其功能。针灸美容就是基于这样的理论,根据皮肤病变的不同和病变部位的不同,分别选取不同的与之相适应的穴位进行刺激,来调节相应的脏腑,内调外治地改善皮肤。

第一节 黄褐斑

黄褐斑是一种以面生褐斑,形如蝴蝶为特征的皮肤病。主要分布于眼周、面颊、颧部及口周。也称"蝴蝶斑"、"黧黑斑"等。本病是由于色素代谢异常所引起的疾病。多见于女性青年,儿童和男性青年亦有之。尤以妊娠期女性(妊娠斑)为多。此病多因邪毒壅滞肌肤,经脉失畅;或饮食不洁,虫积内生,以致虫毒气滞,郁于颜面肌肤所致。

中医学认为,本病与肝、脾、肾三脏功能失调有关。由于情志不遂,肝气郁结,日久血随气停,瘀血阻络于面而发病;或饮食不节,劳累奔波,伤及脾土,土不制水,水气上泛,气血不能濡润而发病;或过度劳累,恣情纵欲,耗伤肾精,水不制

Chapter 7
The acupuncture cosmetology for dermatology conditions

TCM considers that any conditions manifesting on facial skin or other parts of the skin are associated with functional or structural changes of some internal organs. Just based on this knowledge, acupuncture cosmetology aims to regulate the corresponding zang-fu organs to treat skin problems by selecting different acupoints according to different skin conditions and pathologic areas.

Section 1   Chloasma

Chloasma, also known as " butterfly patches " or "melasma", is a skin problem characterized by brown and butterfly-shaped patches that usually occurs around one's eyes, cheek, zygomatic region and mouth. Chloasma is thought to be related to abnormal metabolism of pigment. Although it can also affect children and young men, it is particularly common in women, especially pregnant women (mask of pregnancy). TCM holds that this skin problem is caused by either retention of pathogenic toxic in skin leading to obstruction of meridians or qi stagnation and retention of parasitic infestation in facial skin due to unclean food.

According to TCM theory, chloasma is related to dysfunction of the liver, spleen and kidney. Emotional distress and chronic liver-qi stagnation may cause blood stasis, and then the stagnant blood may obstruct the meridian-qi flow in the face and result in skin discoloration; improper diet or fatigue may

汉英对照

Chinese-English Edition of Acupuncture Cosmetology

针灸美容

Part 2　The Treatment of Acupuncture Cosmetology

火,虚火上炎,火燥相结而发为斑。西医学认为,黄褐斑与许多因素有关,如遗传、妊娠、内分泌、日光照射、微生态失衡、代谢异常等。其中妊娠性黄褐斑,多见于口服避孕药的妇女或患有生殖器官疾病的女性。长期的紫外线照射可使黑色素细胞增殖。而有些患有某种慢性疾病,如慢性肝病、肿瘤、结核病等及内分泌疾病、营养不良,如缺乏维生素 A、维生素 C、维生素 E 及某些微量元素等均可见黄褐斑。

一、 针刺美容法

1. 耳针:

(1) 取穴:心、肺、交感、皮质下、内分泌、过敏点(风溪)。月经不调者加子宫、腹;重症失眠者加神经衰弱点、神门;慢性肝胆病者加肝炎区、胰胆、脾。

(2) 方法:每次取 4～5 个耳穴。常规消毒后。用皮内针(揿针)或王不留行籽帖压上穴,留针(籽)2～3 d,每日自行按压 4～5 次。

impair the spleen-earth, and then spleen failing to transport and transform normally and leading to up-floating of water-dampness and malnutrition of qi and blood, which may gradually result in skin discoloration; or over-exertion and indulgence may consume kidney-essence, and then kidney-water failing to control fire and leading to up-flame of deficient fire, and the mixture of fire and dryness may eventually result in skin discoloration. Modern medicine considers that chloasma is related to such factors as heredity, pregnancy, endocrine, and exposure to sunlight, micro-ecological imbalance and abnormal metabolism. The chloasma in pregnant women is usually found in women who took oral contraceptives or suffered from reproductive organ diseases. Long-term ultraviolet irradiation may cause proliferation of melanocytes. In addition, chloasma may also occur as a result of chronic conditions such as chronic liver diseases, tumor, tuberculosis or endocrine problems and malnutrition involving lack of vitamin A, vitamin C, vitamin E as well as some trace elements.

I. Cosmetic acupuncture

1. Auricular needle

1.1 Selection of ear acupoints: heart, lung, sympathetic nerve, subcortex, endocrine, and allergic point (Fengxi). In addition, Zigong (uterus) and abdomen are added for those with irregular menstruation; neurasthenia point and ear-Shenmen are added for those with severe insomnia; and hepatitis area, pancreas and spleen are added for those with chronic liver diseases.

1.2 Method: Each time 4 - 5 acupoints were selected. After routine sterilization, intradermal needles (thumb-tag needle) or cowherb seeds were pressed to stick to above

2. 拔罐：

(1) 取穴：身柱（见图 6）、大椎、膈俞、期门、章门、曲池、血海。

(2) 方法：每次 2～3 穴，拔罐。大椎、身柱可行刺络拔罐。

3. 针刺：

(1) 取穴：迎香（双）、四白、颧髎（见图 1）、太阳、下关、气海、肾俞（双）、肝俞（双）、丰隆、血海、阴陵泉、三阴交、太冲。

(2) 方法：常规消毒后，毫针针刺，行平补平泻法，得气后留针 15～30 min。毫针针刺气海、肾俞、肝俞，行平补平泻法，不留针，再加艾灸。每日或隔日治疗 1 次，7 次为 1 个疗程。必要时，休息 1～3 日，再行第二个疗程。

4. 艾灸：

(1) 取穴：患部、气海、关元、脾俞（双）、肾俞（双）、肝俞（双）。

acupoints. The intradermal needles or seeds remained for 2 - 3 days and 4 - 5 times of self-pressure each day.

2. Cupping

2.1   Selection of acupoints: Shenzhu (GV 12)(See Fig. 6), Dazhui (GV 14), Geshu (BL 17), Qimen (LR 14), Zhangmen (LR 13), Quchi (LI 11) and Xuehai (SP 10).

2.2   Method: Each time 2 - 3 acupoints were applied cupping. The acupoints Dazhui (GV 14) and Shenzhu (GV 12) can be applied cupping after blood-letting.

3. Body needle

3.1   Selection of acupoints: bilateral Yingxiang (LI 20), Sibai (ST 2), Quanliao (SI 18)(See Fig. 1), Taiyang (EX-HN 5), Xiaguan (ST 7), Qihai (CV 6), bilateral Shenshu (BL 23), bilateral Ganshu (BL 18), Fenglong (ST 40), Xuehai (SP 10), Yinlingquan (SP 9), Sanyinjiao (SP 6) and Taichong (LR 3).

3.2   Method: After routine sterilization, the above acupoints were punctured with filiform needles by even reinforcing-reducing manipulations and the needles remained for 15 - 30 minutes after arrival of qi. The acupoints Qihai (CV 6), Shenshu (BL 23) and Ganshu (BL 18) were punctured with filiform needles by even reinforcing-reducing manipulation and then removed immediately but applied moxibustion instead. The above treatment was done once every day or every other day, and 7 times make up one treatment course. If necessary, the second treatment course may start after an interval of 1 - 3 days.

4. Moxibustion

4.1   Selection of acupoints: the affected area, Qihai (CV 6), Guanyuan (CV 4), bilateral Pishu (BL 20), bilateral

汉英对照

Chinese-English
Edition of
Acupuncture
Cosmetology

针灸美容

中篇 ◎ 针灸美容治疗

（2）方法：艾炷灸患部中央 3～7 壮（无瘢痕灸）。艾条温灸气海、肾俞、肝俞 5～10 min。每日或隔日治疗 1 次，7 次为 1 个疗程。必要时，休息 1～3 d，再行第二个疗程。

5. 皮肤针：

（1）取穴：后颈部足太阳经、胸椎 7～10 两侧、小腿内侧肝脾肾经、带脉、期门、三阴交。

（2）方法：每次选用 1～2 个部位，轻度叩刺至皮肤潮红即可。

6. 穴位注射：

（1）取穴：足三里、曲池。

（2）方法：用当归或川芎注射液穴位注射，每个穴位1～2 ml。

二、 注意事项

在治疗期间应注意饮食、生活起居的调节。避免辛辣、温燥、寒凉食物。加强身体锻炼，避免过度操劳，保证充足睡眠。同时，注意防晒。避免使用过多美白、增白的方法。

Shenshu (BL 23) and bilateral Ganshu (BL 18).

4.2 Method: the center of the affected area was applied moxa-cone moxibustion (scarless moxibustion) for 3 - 7 zhuang (here means a unit of moxa-cone); the acupoints Qihai (CV 6), Shenshu (BL 23) and Ganshu (BL 18) were applied warm moxibustion with moxa stick for 5 - 10 minutes. The above treatment was done once every day or every other day, and 7 times make up one treatment course. If necessary, the second treatment course may start after an interval of 1 - 3 days.

5. Dermal needle

5.1 Selection of acupoints: the foot-Taiyang meridian on the nape area, bilateral area from T_{7-10}, the liver, spleen and kidney meridians in the medial aspect of the lower leg, the Daimai(GB 26), Qimen (LR 14) and Sanyinjiao (SP 6).

5.2 Method: Each time 1 - 2 acupoints were selected for mild tapping until the local skin turns red.

6. Acupoint injection

6.1 Selection of acupoints: Zusanli (ST 36) and Quchi (LI 11).

6.2 Method: Each acupoint was injected 1 - 2 ml of Danggui (root of Chinese angelica) or Chuanxiong (rhizome of chuanxiong) injection.

Ⅱ. Precautions

During treatment one needs to care about diet and regulate life styles; avoid hot-spicy, warm-dry and cold food; more physical exercises but avoid over-exertion; have adequate sleep; and avoid too much exposure to sunlight and overuse of cosmetic products for whitening.

第二节　痤疮

痤疮是一种以面生粟疹、脓疱,破后出白粉汁,多伴疼痛,消退后常可结疤为特征的皮肤病。属于中医学的"酒刺"、"痤"、"面疱"、"肺风粉刺"等。本病多见于青年男女,好发于颜面,偶见于胸背。

中医学认为,痤疮的病因多由于肺胃火热,熏蒸颜面;或过食肥甘厚味,脾胃积热,又感风毒之邪,凝滞肌肤而成。此外,女性冲任不调或气滞血瘀亦可导致。西医学认为,本病的发生与雄性激素分泌增加,皮脂腺分泌旺盛,毛囊口堵塞,痤疮棒状杆菌繁殖或体内微量元素缺乏等多种因素有关。

一、针刺美容法

1. 毫针:

(1)取穴:病灶局部、大椎、曲池、合谷、膈俞。肺胃积热,配太阳、列缺、内庭、鱼际、肺俞、胃俞;阴虚火旺,配内关、三阴交、太溪、太冲、行间(见图11)、神门;冲任不调,配中极(见图5)、气海、地机(见图10)、太冲、章门、期门;痰瘀凝结,配丰隆、肝俞、脾俞、血海、阴陵泉、太白(见图10)、太冲。

Section 2   Acne

Acne is a common skin disease characterized by whiteheads or pimples on the face followed by whitening liquid discharges, pain and scarring of the skin. It falls under the TCM category of "whelk", "furuncle", "facial pustules" or "lung-wind comedo". Acne usually affects adolescents and appears on the face and sometimes on chest and back.

TCM holds that acne can be caused by three possible reasons: the fire-heat of the lung and stomach fumigating the face; heat accumulation of the spleen and stomach due to overeat of sweet and fatty food plus pathogenic wind attacking the skin; and women with disorder of Chong (Thoroughfare Vessel) and Ren (Conception Vessel) meridians or blood stasis due to qi stagnation. Modern medicine considers that acne is related to such factors as excessive secretion of androgens, over-production of sebum, blockage of follicular pores, multiplying of Bacillus acnes or lack of trace elements.

I . Cosmetic acupuncture

1. Filiform needles

1.1   Selection of acupoints: the local focus, Dazhui (GV 14), Quchi (LI 11), Hegu (LI 4) and Geshu (BL 17). In addition, Taiyang (EX-HN 5), Lieque (LU 7), Neiting (ST 44), Yuji (LU 10), Feishu (BL 13) and Weishu (BL 21) are added for those with heat accumulation of the lung and stomach; Neiguan (PC 6), Sanyinjiao (SP 6), Taixi (KI 3), Taichong (LR 3), Xingjian (LR 2) and Shenmen (HT 7) are added for those with fire hyperactivity due to yin deficiency; Zhongji (CV 3)(See Fig. 5), Qihai (CV 6), Diji (SP 8)(See Fig. 10), Taichong (LR 3), Zhangmen (LR 13) and Qimen (LR 14) are added for women with disorder of Chong and Ren

汉英对照
Chinese-English
Edition of
Acupuncture
Cosmetology
针灸美容
Part 2 The Treatment of Acupuncture Cosmetology

（2）方法：每次取 3～4 个穴位，行泻法或平补平泻法。病灶局部以毫针围刺。隔日 1 次，10 次为 1 个疗程。

2. 耳针：

（1）取穴：面颊、肺、胃、大肠、脾、神门、内分泌。阴虚火旺，配肾、心、交感；冲任不调，配肝、子宫、卵巢、肾；痰瘀凝结，配皮质下、心、膈、肝。

（2）方法：应用毫针或皮内针、王不留行籽配穴。3～5 d 1 次，每日自行按压 3～4 次，使耳部充血、发胀。10 次为 1 个疗程。

3. 皮肤针：

（1）取穴：胸椎 5～12 两侧、项部足太阳膀胱经、合谷、曲池、大椎、肺俞、大肠俞（见图 6）。阴虚火旺，配腰骶部，三阴交；冲任不调，配腰骶部、带脉、归来（见图 5）。

meridians; and Fenglong (ST 40), Ganshu (BL 18), Pishu (BL 20), Xuehai (SP 10), Yinlingquan (SP 9), Taibai (SP 3)(See Fig. 10) and Taichong (LR 3) are added for those with mixture of phlegm-stasis.

1.2 Method: Each time 3 - 4 acupoints were selected for reducing or even reinforcing-reducing manipulation. The local focus was applied surrounding puncture with filiform needles. The above treatment was done once every other day and 10 times make up one treatment course.

2. Auricular needle

2.1 Selection of acupoints: cheek, lung, stomach, large intestine, spleen, ear-Shenmen and endocrine. In addition, kidney, heart and sympathetic nerve are added for those with fire hyperactivity due to yin deficiency; Liver, Zigong (uterus), ovary and kidney are added for those with disorder of Chong and Ren meridians; and subcortex, heart, diaphragm and liver are added for those with mixture of phlegm-stasis.

2.2 Method: Filiform needles or intradermal needles or cowherb seeds were pressed to stick on certain selected acupoints once every 3 - 5 days, 3 - 4 times of self-pressure each day until congestion and distension of the ear, and 10 times make up one treatment course.

3. Dermal needle

3.1 Selection of acupoints: bilateral area from T_{5-12}, the Bladder meridian of foot-Taiyang in the nape area, Hegu (LI 4), Dazhui (GV 14), Feishu (BL 13) and Dachangshu (BL 25). In addition, lumbosacral region and Sanyinjiao (SP 6) are added for those with fire hyperactivity due to yin deficiency; and lumbosacral region, Daimai (GB 26) and Guilai (ST 29) are added for women with disorder of Chong and Ren

（2）方法：中等叩刺，局部稍微出血，大椎穴、肺俞再加拔罐，留罐 5 min，3 d 1 次，10 次为 1 个疗程。

4. 穴位注射：

（1）取穴：合谷（双）、足三里（双）、三阴交（双）。

（2）方法：每次取 1～2 个穴位，复发丹参注射液或自血注射，每穴 1 ml。每周 2 次，7 次为 1 个疗程。

二、注意事项

1. 保持心情舒畅，劳逸结合，避免郁怒。避免受冷、热刺激，避免游泳等水上运动。少食膏粱厚味、辛辣之品，多吃新鲜蔬菜及水果，保持大便通畅。

2. 保护皮肤清洁，预防感染，停用接触性致病物质，禁用皮质类固醇、溴、碘类药物，防止诱发痤疮或病情迁延、恶化。

第三节　雀斑

雀斑是一种以鼻、面部出现褐色斑点，边缘清晰，不融成片为特征的损容性皮肤病。多见于青春发育期的女性。

中医学认为，本病的发生与禀赋不足、肾水不能荣华于面、郁火结滞血分，复受风邪侵袭而成。西医学认为，本病与遗传、日光照射等有关。

汉英对照
Chinese-English
Edition of
Acupuncture
Cosmetology

针灸美容

中篇 ◉ 针灸美容治疗

meridians.

3.2 Method: Moderate tapping was applied to the selected acupoints until slight bleeding of the local area; cupping was combined to the acupoints Dazhui (GV 14) and Feishu (BL 13) for 5 minutes after tapping. The above treatment was done once every 3 days and 10 times make up one treatment course.

4. Acupoint injection

4.1 Selection of acupoints: bilateral Hegu (LI 4), bilateral Zusanli (ST 36) and bilateral Sanyinjiao (SP 6).

4.2 Method: Each time 1 - 2 acupoints were injected 1 ml of compound Danshen (red sage root) injection or auto-blood injection.

Ⅱ. Precautions

1. Keep a peaceful mind, balance work and rest and avoid depressed anger; avoid cold or hot stimulation as well as water-related sports like swimming; reduce greasy and spicy food but take more fresh vegetables and fruits and keep a smooth bowel movement.

2. Keep skin clean and prevent infection, stop using contact pathogenic substance, corticosteroid and bromine or iodine-contained medications to prevent triggering, delaying or worsening acne.

Section 3　Freckle

Freckle is a discosmetic skin disease that usually occurs to girls in puberty characterized by brown spots on the nose and face with clear borderlines and absence of merging into patches.

TCM holds that freckle is caused by kidney-water failing to

汉英对照

Chinese-English
Edition of
Acupuncture
Cosmetology

针灸美容

Part 2　The Treatment of Acupuncture Cosmetology

一、 针灸美容法

1. 毫针：

（1）取穴：病灶局部，合谷、太冲；肾水亏损，配太溪、照海（见图 10）、肾俞、命门；火郁血热，配行间、内庭、血海、膈俞、三阴交。

（2）方法：每次取 4～5 穴，按常规针刺，行平补平泻手法。病灶局部用短针平刺、围刺法。隔日 1 次，10～15 次为 1 个疗程。

2. 火针：

（1）取穴：病灶局部。

（2）方法：取"三头火针"烧至温热。在局部常规消毒后，迅速掮灼局部，至雀斑完全消失为宜。根据雀斑面积多少，分批分次进行。治疗间隔 3～5 d。

3. 耳针：

（1）取穴：相应部位、面颊区、肾、肝、内分泌、神门、皮质下。

（2）方法：每次选 3～4 穴，皮内针或王不留行籽埋穴 3～5 d，每穴每日按压 4～5 次。5 次为 1 个疗程。

nourish the face due to congenital deficiency, retention of stagnant fire in the blood-stage and an attack of exogenous pathogenic wind. Modern medicine considers that freckle is related to heredity and sunlight and so on.

I. Cosmetic acupuncture

1. Filiform needles

1.1 Selection of acupoints: the local focus, Hegu (LI 4) and Taichong (LR 3). In addition, Taixi (KI 3), Zhaohai (KI 6)(See Fig. 10), Shenshu (BL 23) and Mingmen (GV 4) are added for those with kidney-water insufficiency; and Xingjian (LR 2), Neiting (ST 44), Xuehai (SP 10), Geshu (BL 17) and Sanyinjiao (SP 6) are added for those with stagnant fire and blood heat.

1.2 Method: Each time 4 - 5 acupoints were selected for routine puncture with even reinforcing-reducing manipulation. The local focus was applied subcutaneous surrounding puncture by short needles. The above treatment was done once every other day and 10 - 15 times make up one treatment course.

2. Fire needle

2.1 Selection of acupoints: the local focus.

2.2 Method: After routine sterilization of the local area, the heated "three-headed fire needle" was applied to scratch the focus immediately until the freckles totally disappeared. The treatment may contain several times according to the areas of freckles. There should be 3 - 5 days of interval between treatment courses.

3. Auricular needle

3.1 Selection of acupoints: the corresponding areas, cheek, kidney, liver, endocrine, ear-Shenmen and subcortex.

3.2 Method: Each time 3 - 4 acupoints were selected.

汉英对照

Chinese-English
Edition of
Acupuncture
Cosmetology

针灸美容

Part 2 The Treatment of Acupuncture Cosmetology

汉英对照

Chinese-English
Edition of
Acupuncture
Cosmetology

针灸美容

中篇 ● 针灸美容治疗

4. 三棱针：

（1）取穴：大椎、耳尖。

（2）方法：每次取 1 个部位，三棱针点刺放血。适用于火郁血热者。

5. 艾灸：

（1）取穴：大椎、曲池、三阴交。

（2）方法：以艾条温灸上穴至局部温热感、皮肤红晕为度。每穴 15～20 min，每日或隔日 1 次，10 次为 1 个疗程。为巩固疗效，可继续每周或隔周 1 次。

二、 注意事项

1. 火针治疗后在皮肤结痂期（5～7 d 可自行脱落）应注意避免沾水或手抓，避免感染。

2. 注意避免暴晒太阳，应尽量少晒或使用遮光保护用品。

3. 注意多吃水果、蔬菜、硬果类食物，补充足够的维生素。

第四节　扁平疣

扁平疣，俗称扁瘊。多见于青年男女，尤其是青春期前后的少女，所以又称青春扁平疣。是发于身体各处扁平如芝麻、绿豆或黄豆大小、颜色近似肤色的良性赘生物。

The intradermal needles (thumb-tag needle) or cowherb seeds were pressed to stick to above acupoints for 3 - 5 days, 4 - 5 times of self-pressure each day, and 5 times make up one treatment course.

4. Three-edged needle

4.1 Selection of acupoints: Dazhui (GV 14) and ear apex.

4.2 Method: One acupoint was selected each time for blood-letting with three-edged needle. This method is indicated for those with stagnant fire and blood heat.

5. Moxibustion

5.1 Selection of acupoints: Dazhui (GV 14), Quchi (LI 11) and Sanyinjiao (SP 6).

5.2 Method: Moxa stick was applied to the above acupoints until the local skin turned red with warm sensation, 15 - 20 minutes for each acupoint. The moxibustion was done once every day or every other day, and 10 times make up one treatment course. In addition, the moxibustion once every week or every other week can consolidate the therapeutic effect.

Ⅱ. Precautions

1. Avoid wetting water or hand scratching during the skin scab-forming period (5 - 7 days) after fire needle therapy to prevent infection.

2. Avoid over-exposure to sunlight and reduce using shading-protection products.

3. Take more fruits, vegetables and hard nuts to supplement adequate vitamin.

Section 4 Flat wart

The flat wart, also called verruca plana or juvenile wart as

汉英对照
Chinese-English
Edition of
Atupuncture
Cosmetology

针灸美容 Part 2 The Treatment of Acupuncture Cosmetology

　　中医学认为,本病多由于外感风热或肝气郁结、气滞血瘀,发于肌肤而致。《灵枢·经脉》有"虚则生肬"之说。西医学认为,本病属于一种病毒性皮肤病,免疫功能缺陷或低下的人易感发病。

　　一、针灸美容法

　　1. 毫针:

　　(1) 取穴:合谷、曲池、列缺、血海。肝经郁热,配太冲或行间、外关;脾虚气血不和,配足三里、三阴交。

　　(2) 方法:毫针针刺,行平补平泻。10～15 次为 1 个疗程。

　　2. 皮肤针:

　　(1) 取穴:病灶局部、颈椎、胸椎 3～10 的夹脊、合谷、风池、血海、太渊(见图 8)、太阳、曲池。

　　(2) 方法:中等强度叩刺。疣体及其基地部重叩刺,其周围皮肤轻叩刺。每周 2～3 次。

it frequently occurs to adolescents, especially girls in puberty refers to sesame-shaped, mung bean or yellow bean-sized and skin color-liked benign neoplasm that can appear anywhere on the body.

TCM holds that flat wart is caused by either external contraction of wind-heat or liver-qi stagnation and subsequent blood stasis. The *Ling Shu* • *Jing Mai* (Chapter on meridians from *the Miraculous Pivot*) states that "deficiency causes warts". Modern medicine considers that flat wart is a viral skin disease related to functional defect or hypofunction of immune system.

I. Cosmetic acupuncture

1. Filiform needle

1.1　Selection of acupoints: Hegu (LI 4), Quchi (LI 11), Lieque (LU 7), and Xuehai (SP 10). In addition, Taichong (LR 3) or Xingjian (LR 2) and Waiguan (TE 5) are added for those with stagnant heat in the liver meridian; and Zusanli (ST 36) and Sanyinjiao (SP 6) are added for those with disharmony between qi and blood due to spleen deficiency.

1.2　Method: The above acupoints were punctured with filiform needles by even reinforcing-reducing manipulation, and 10 - 15 times make up one treatment course.

2. Dermal needle

2.1　Selection of acupoints: the local focus, cervical vertebra, Jiaji (EX-B 2) acupoints from T_{3-10}, Hegu (LI 4), Fengchi (GB 20), Xuehai (SP 10), Taiyuan (LU 10)(See Fig. 8), Taiyang (EX-HN 5) and Quchi (LI 11).

2.2　Method: The above acupoints were applied moderate tapping; the warts and their base were applied severe tapping and their surrounding skin was applied mild tapping. The

汉英对照

Chinese-English
Edition of
Acupuncture
Cosmetology

针灸美容

中篇 ● 针灸美容治疗

3. 耳针：

（1）取穴：病灶相应区耳穴、肝、胆、肺、脾、皮质下、交感。

（2）方法：揿针或王不留行籽埋穴。每周1次，5次为1个疗程。

4. 穴位注射：

（1）取穴：病灶局部、颧髎、颊车、攒竹、合谷。肝经郁热，配曲池、血海、外关、太冲；脾虚气血不和，配足三里、三阴交。

（2）方法：每次取3个穴位，常规操作，每穴注射药物0.5～1 ml，每周2～3次。肝经郁热，药用板蓝根注射液或10%川芎注射液；脾虚气血失和，药用维生素 B_{12} 加2%利多卡因注射液。

5. 火针疗法：

（1）取穴：母疣（疣体较大的）。

（2）方法：火针烧刺疣根部四周，再在疣中心加刺1针。5～7 d 母疣自行脱落，其他疣群也可逐渐消失。

tapping was done 2 - 3 times every week.

3. Auricular needle

3. 1   Selection of acupoints: the corresponding ear acupoints of the local focus, liver, gallbladder, lung, spleen, subcortex and sympathetic nerve.

3. 2   Method: Thumb-tag needles or cowherb seeds were pressed to stick on the ear acupoints, once every week and 5 times make up one treatment course.

4. Acupoint injection

4. 1   Selection of acupoints: the local focus, Quanliao (SI 18), Jiache (ST 6), Cuanzhu (BL 2) and Hegu (LI 4). In addition, Quchi (LI 11), Xuehai (SP 10), Waiguan (TE 5) and Taichong (LR 3) are added for those with stagnant heat in the liver meridian; and Zusanli (ST 36) and Sanyinjiao (SP 6) are added for those with disharmony between qi and blood due to spleen deficiency.

4. 2   Method: Each time 3 acupoints were injected 0. 5 - 1 ml of medication after routine sterilization, 2 - 3 times each week. The medicinal Banlangen (Isatis root) injection or 10% Chuanxiong (rhizome of chuanxiong) injection was applied to those with stagnant heat in the liver meridian; and medicinal vitamin B_{12} plus 2% lidocaine injection was applied to those with disharmony between qi and blood due to spleen deficiency.

5. Fire needle

5. 1   Selection of acupoints: the mother-wart (the bigger ones).

5. 2   Method: The heated needle was applied to burn or puncture around the root area of the warts and another needle was applied to puncture the center of the warts. The mother-warts may fall off spontaneously within 5 - 7 days and other

汉英对照

Chinese-English
Edition of
Acupuncture
Cosmetology

针灸美容

中篇 ◉ 针灸美容治疗

6. 三棱针：

(1) 取穴：病灶局部。

(2) 方法：术者左手捏紧疣的基底部，使之苍白，用消毒好的小号三棱针从疣顶部垂直刺入基底部，快速出针，起针后渗出少量血为宜。一般10 d左右表面干燥或成块状，半月后可完全脱落痊愈。

7. 艾灸疗法：

(1) 取穴：手大骨空、小骨空(拇指指间关节背侧及小指第二指间关节背侧)。

(2) 方法：针尖向上刺入，得气后接电针。取锯齿波，每隔5 min逐渐加大刺激量，通电25 min。

二、 注意事项

1. 注意生活起居，避免与患者接触而传染；避免局部搔抓或热水洗烫而加重病情，甚至导致局部恶化。

2. 多食瓜果类食物，如丝瓜、苦瓜、枇杷、绿豆等，或薏苡仁、土茯苓、赤小豆等。

第五节　神经性皮炎

神经性皮炎，又称慢性单纯性苔藓。是一种以皮肤阵发性瘙痒和皮肤苔藓样变(皮肤增厚、皮沟加深、多角形丘疹)为特征的慢性炎症性皮肤病。多生于颈项，又称"摄领疮"。

warts may gradually disappear.

6. Three-edged needle

6.1 Selection of acupoints: the local focus.

6.2 Method: The acupuncturist pinches the basal part of the warts tightly to make it turn pale, and then inserts perpendicularly from top to the basal part with sterilized small-sized three-edged needle and after that withdraw the needle rapidly. The effect would be better if there were a small amount of bleeding after removal of the needle. It usually takes about 10 days to make the skin surface dry or lumpy and about 15 days for complete falling off.

7. Moxibustion

7.1 Selection of acupoints: the dorsal aspect of interphalangeal joint of the thumb and the dorsal aspect of the second interphalangeal joint of the little finger.

7.2 Method: The acupoint was punctured with needle tip upward and then connected the needle with electric stimulator for 25 minutes, using sawtooth wave and gradually increasing stimulation every 5 minutes.

Ⅱ. Precautions

1. Keep regular life style, avoid contacting with people suffering from flat warts, avoid local scratching or washing with hot water that may worsen the condition or make the local area deteriorate.

2. Take more melons or fruits such as towel gourd, bitter gourd, loquat, and green bean or Yiyiren (*Semen Coicis*), Tufuling (*Rhizoma Smilacis Glabrae*) and red beans.

Section 5　Neurodermatitis

Neurodermatitis, also known as chronic lichen simplex, is a

　　中医学认为，本病多由于风、湿、热之邪蕴于肌肤或日久血虚生风化燥所致，与情绪波动密切相关。西医学认为，本病与大脑皮质兴奋、抑制失调有关。内分泌异常、胃肠功能失调、自体中毒等因素有关，局部的刺激、摩擦、搔抓、日晒、出汗、饮酒等物理、机械刺激可诱发或加重本病的发作。

一、针灸美容法

1. 毫针：

（1）取穴：病灶局部、大椎、风池、曲池、膈俞、合谷、太冲、血海、风市（见图 11）。肝郁化火，配行间、支沟、侠溪（见图 11）；湿热蕴结，配阴陵泉、三阴交、太白；血虚生风，配足三里、太渊、肝俞、肾俞、脾俞、太溪。

（2）方法：病灶局部采用毫针围刺，针尖均朝向病灶中心。其他腧穴每次选用 3～5 个，毫针平补平泻，留针 30 min。每日或隔日 1 次。

chronic inflammatory skin disease characterized by paroxysmal skin itching and lichenification (thickening skin, deepening skin grooves and polygon papules). As cervical area is the most common site of an outbreak, neurodermatitis is also called "cervical neurodermatitis".

TCM holds that neurodermatitis is closely related to the following three factors: accumulation of wind, dampness and heat in skin; chronic blood deficiency stirring wind and leading to dryness; and emotional stress or tension. Modern medicine considers that it is related to excited cerebral cortex and inhibition disorder, for example, endocrine disorder, functional disorder of gastrointestine, and autotoxicosis. Such physical or mechanical irritation as local irritation, friction, scratching, sun exposure, sweats, and alcohol drinking may trigger or worsen the attacks of neurodermatitis.

Ⅰ. Cosmetic acupuncture

1. Filiform needle

1.1   Selection of acupoints: the local focus, Dazhui (GV 14), Fengchi (GB 20), Quchi (LI 11), Geshu (BL 17), Hegu (LI 4), Taichong (LR 3), Xuehai (SP 10), and Fengshi (GB 31)(See Fig. 11). In addition, Xingjian (LR 2), Zhigou (TE 6), and Xiaxi (GB 43)(See Fig. 11) are added for those with liver-qi stagnation transforming into fire; Yinlingquan (SP 9), Sanyinjiao (SP 6) and Taibai (SP 3) are added for those with accumulation of dampness-heat; and Zusanli (ST 36), Taiyuan (LU 9), Ganshu (BL 18), Shenshu (BL 23), Pishu (BL 20) and Taixi (KI 3) are added for those with blood deficiency stirring wind.

1.2   Method: the local focus was applied surrounding puncture by filiform needles, all needle tips were toward the

汉英对照

Chinese-English
Edition of
Acupuncture
Cosmetology

针灸美容

中篇 ● 针灸美容治疗

2. 皮肤针：

（1）取穴：病灶局部、夹脊穴。

（2）方法：病灶周围常规消毒，皮肤针围绕病灶根部周围皮肤重叩，稍许出血，再选用比病灶区稍大的火罐拔罐，出血适量即可。每周1～2次。夹脊穴轻叩刺，隔日1次。

3. 三棱针：

（1）取穴：耳后静脉。

（2）方法：常规消毒后，以三棱针刺破耳后静脉，放血2～5滴。

4. 穴位注射：

（1）取穴：曲池、血海、合谷、太冲。体虚，配足三里。

（2）方法：每次2～3穴，用丹参注射液或当归注射液或自血进行注射，隔日1次，7次为1个疗程。

5. 耳针：

（1）取穴：病灶相应区、风溪、肺、脾、肝、心、内分泌、肾上腺、皮质下。

（2）方法：每次除病灶外，再取3～5穴，毫针针刺，隔日1次，留针30～60 min，15次为1个疗程。或揿针、王不留行籽埋穴，10次为1个疗程。

center of focus. Each time 3 - 5 acupoints among the above were punctured with even reinforcing-reducing manipulation. The needles retained for 30 minutes, and the treatment was done once every day or every other day.

2. Dermal needle

2.1 Selection of acupoints: the local focus and Jiaji (EX-B 2) acupoints.

2.2 Method: The root area of the focus was applied severe tapping after routine sterilization until slight bleeding, and then cupping (slightly larger size than the focus) was applied with appropriate amount of bleeding. The treatment was done 1 - 2 times a week. The Jiaji (EX-B 2) acupoints were applied mild tapping once every other day.

3. Three-edged needle

3.1 Selection of acupoints: the posterior auricular vein.

3.2 Method: the auricular vein was done pricked by three-edged needle after routine sterilization and then squeezed 2 - 5 drops of blood.

4. Acupoint injection

4.1 Selection of acupoints: Quchi (LI 11), Xuehai (SP 10), Hegu (LI 4), and Taichong (LR 3). In addition, Zusanli (ST 36) is added for those with weak constitution.

4.2 Method: Each time 2 - 3 acupoints were injected Danshen (*Radix Salviae Miltiorrhizae*) or Danggui (*Radix Angelicae Sinensis*) injection or auto-blood injection. The injection was done once every other day and 7 times make up one treatment course.

5. Auricular needle

5.1 Selection of acupoints: the corresponding area of the focus, Fengxi, lung, spleen, liver, heart, endocrine, adrenal

6. 艾灸：

（1）取穴：病灶局部。

（2）方法：以大蒜汁涂抹病灶局部，再以绿豆大小的艾炷（每炷间隔0.5寸）施直接灸，灸后覆盖消毒敷料。每10 d 1次。

二、 注意事项

1. 注意情绪调节。饮食应清淡，避免辛辣、海鲜食物，戒烟酒等。

2. 局部病灶处应避免搔抓或热水洗烫，或用刺激性的药物外涂，以免加重病情。

第六节　荨麻疹

荨麻疹，也称"瘾疹"、"风瘙瘾疹"等。是一种以皮肤出现鲜红色或苍白色风团，时隐时现，瘙痒不堪，消退后不留痕迹为特点的过敏性疾病。

中医学认为，本病的发生与禀赋不足，风邪外袭，或妇女冲任失调，营卫不和，过食鱼虾荤腥之物而致化风生燥，阻于肌肤而致。西医学认为，本病是过敏导致皮肤黏膜血管扩展、通透性增强而产生的一种瘙痒性、局限性、暂时性的表皮或黏膜的水肿反应。龋齿、反复发作的扁桃体炎症、肠道寄生虫等可诱发本病。

gland, and subcortex.

5. 2   Method: Another 3 – 5 acupoints were selected in addition to the local focus were applied filiform puncture once every other day, 30 – 60 min each time and 15 minutes make up one treatment course; the ear acupoints can also be applied with thumb-tag needles or cowherb seeds and 10 times make up one treatment course.

6. Moxibustion

6. 1   Selection of points: the local focus.

6. 2   Method: The local focus was squashed with garlic juice first and then applied direct moxibustion with green bean-sized moxa cone (0. 5 cun in between moxa cones) and after that covered with aseptic dressing. The moxibustion was done once every 10 days.

Ⅱ. Precautions

1. Keep a peaceful mind, take bland food and avoid spicy food and seafood and stay away from cigarettes or alcohol.

2. Avoid scratching or washing the local focus with hot water, and avoid using external usage of irritation medications to prevent worsening the condition.

Section 6   Urticaria

Urticaria, also called "hidden rashes" or "wind-related hidden rashes" in Chinese medicine, is an allergic skin disease characterized by hit-and-miss and itching bumpy weals in bright red or pale color but no left-over marks after disappearance.

TCM holds that urticaria is related to the following factors: congenital weak constitution plus an attack of exogenous wind; disharmony between ying-nutrient and wei-defense due to disorder of Chong and Ren meridians for women; or overeating of seafood

汉英对照
Chinese-English
Edition of
Acupuncture
Cosmetology

针灸美容

Part 2 The Treatment of Acupuncture Cosmetology

一、针灸美容法

1. 毫针：

（1）取穴：风池、血海、曲池、膈俞。偏于风寒，配风门、肺俞；偏于风热，配大椎、内庭；冲任不调，配气海、关元、地机、三阴交；有过敏病史，配中脘、足三里、三阴交、丰隆；痒甚，配神门。

（2）方法：毫针针刺，行平补平泻。关元、气海、肺俞、足三里行补法。每日 1 次，10～15 次为 1 个疗程。

2. 三棱针：

（1）取穴：大椎、耳背静脉。

（2）方法：常规消毒后，用三棱针点刺大椎或挑刺耳背静脉出血，大椎再拔罐，出血量可至 5 ml。用于风热型荨麻疹。

including fish or shrimp leading to wind-dryness that obstructs the skin. Modern medicine considers that urticaria is an itchy, local, and temporary edema of epidermis or skin mucosa produced by allergy-related vasodilation of skin mucosa and increased permeability. Dental caries, recurrent tonsillitis and parasitic infection may trigger this condition.

I. Cosmetic acupuncture

1. Filiform needle

1.1 Selection of acupoints: Fengchi (GB 20), Xuehai (SP 10), Quchi (LI 11), and Geshu (BL 17). In addition, Fengmen (BL 12) and Feishu (BL 13) are added for wind-cold; Dazhui (GV 14) and Neiting (ST 44) are added for wind-heat; Qihai (CV 6), Guanyuan (CV 4), Diji (SP 8) and Sanyinjiao (SP 6) are added for disorder of Chong and Ren meridians; Zhongwan (CV 12), Zusanli (ST 36), Sanyinjiao (SP 6), and Fenglong (ST 40) are added for allergic history; and Shenmen (HT 7) is added for severe itching.

1.2 Method: Except for reinforcing manipulation on Guanyuan (CV 4), Qihai (CV 6), Feishu (BL 13) and Zusanli (ST 36), all the other acupoints were punctured with even reinforcing-reducing manipulation. The treatment was done once every day and 10 - 15 times make up one treatment course.

2. Three-edged needle

2.1 Selection of acupoints: Dazhui (GV 14) and posterior auricular vein.

2.2 Method: The acupoint Dazhui (GV 14) and posterior auricular vein were pricked with three-edged needle for bleeding (5 ml) after routine sterilization and followed by cupping on Dazhui (GV 14). This therapy is indicated for wind-heat urticaria.

汉英对照

Chinese-English
Edition of
Acupuncture
Cosmetology

针灸美容

中篇 ● 针灸美容治疗

3. 灸法：

（1）取穴：神阙、膈俞、血海、足三里、关元。

（2）方法：用艾条点燃，隔姜悬灸上穴，以局部皮肤潮红为度。每日 1 次，15～20 次为 1 个疗程。适用于冲任不调，或有过敏性病史的荨麻疹。

4. 耳针：

（1）取穴：病灶相应区耳穴、肺、脾、肝、神门、肾上腺、皮质下、交感。

（2）方法：每次取 3～5 穴，毫针针刺，每日或隔日 1 次，或揿针、王不留行籽埋穴。5 d 1 次，7 次为 1 个疗程。

5. 穴位注射：

（1）取穴：曲池、足三里、三阴交。

（2）方法：常规消毒后，取适量自血，注射上穴，每穴 1 ml，每周 1 次。

二、 注意事项

1. 忌食诱发过敏的海鲜荤腥食物。有条件时可查过敏原，避免再次接触。

2. 加强营养和必要的锻炼，增强自身体质，预防外邪侵袭。

3. Moxibustion

3.1 Selection of acupoints: Shenque (CV 8), Geshu (BL 17), Xuehai (SP 10), Zusanli (ST 36) and Guanyuan (CV 4).

3.2 Method: The above acupoints were applied ginger-partitioned moxibustion until the local skin turned slight red. The treatment was done once every day and 15 - 20 times make up one treatment course. This therapy is indicated for those with disorder of Chong and Ren meridians or an allergic history.

4. Auricular needle

4.1 Selection of acupoints: the corresponding ear acupoints of the local focus, lung, spleen, liver, ear-Shenmen, adrenal gland, subcortex and sympathetic nerve.

4.2 Method: Each time 3 - 5 acupoints were selected for either filiform needling or sticking of thumb-tag needle or cowherb seeds. The filiform needling was done once every day or every other day and the thumb-tag needle or cowherb seeds were changed once every 5 days, and 7 times make up one treatment course.

5. Acupoint injection

5.1 Selection of acupoints: Quchi (LI 11), Zusanli (ST 36) and Sanyinjiao (SP 6).

5.2 Method: Appropriate amount of auto-blood was injected into the above acupoints after routine sterilization, 1 ml for each acupoint and the injection was done once every week.

Ⅱ. Precautions

1. Avoid seafood that may trigger allergic reaction and avoid re-contacting sensitinogens if they can be detected.

2. Take well-balanced diet and physical exercises and prevent attack by exogenous pathogenic factors.

第七节　斑秃

斑秃,俗称"鬼舐头"、"油风"等。是一种以无自觉症状而头发突然成片脱落、头皮正常为特点的皮肤病。可发生于任何年龄,但以青壮年为多。

中医学认为,本病的发生与情志抑郁、过度劳累、睡眠不足而致心脾两虚、肝肾不足,精血无以随气上荣毛发皮肤,复感风邪而致。西医学认为,本病可由多种原因导致,有先天性或遗传性因素,也有后天性因素,后者与精神创伤、过度紧张等引起高级中枢功能失调,皮质下自主神经、内分泌系统或自身免疫紊乱、B 族维生素缺乏,头皮毛囊、皮脂腺萎缩而致。

一、　针灸美容法

1. 毫针:

(1) 取穴:病灶局部、太溪、血海、曲池、合谷。心烦易怒,配太冲、行间、肝俞;瘙痒甚,配大椎、风池。

(2) 方法:毫针针刺,病灶局部围刺,血海、太溪施补法,曲池、合谷施平补平泻法。留针 30 min,每 5 min 行针 1 次。

2. 皮肤针:

Section 7   Alopecia areata

Alopecia areata, also known as "hair-cutting by ghosts" or "oily wind" in folklore, is a skin disease characterized by sudden patchy loss of hair but still with normal scalp. It can occur at any age but mostly adolescents or young people.

TCM holds that this condition is related to the following factors: deficiency of both the heart and spleen or deficiency of both the liver and kidney due to emotional depression, fatigue and poor sleep, leading to the failure of essence-blood in nourishing the hair and skin, and external contraction of wind can be another predisposing factor. Modern medicine considers that this condition can be caused by hereditary or genetic or postnatal factors such as psychic trauma or stress-related functional disorder of central nerve, derangement of subcortex autonomic nerve, endocrine system or autoimmune system, lack of vitamin B group and atrophy of scalp hairy follicle and sebaceous gland.

I . Cosmetic acupuncture

1. Filiform needle

1.1   Selection of acupoints: the local focus, Taixi (KI 3), Xuehai (SP 10), Quchi (LI 11) and Hegu (LI 4). In addition, Taichong (LR 3), Xingjian (LR 2) and Ganshu (BL 18) are added for those with restlessness and irritability; and Dazhui (GV 14) and Fengchi (GB 20) are added for those with severe itching.

1.2   Method: The local focus was applied surrounding puncture. Except for reinforcing manipulation on Xuehai (SP 10) and Taixi (KI 3), all the other acupoints were punctured with even reinforcing-reducing manipulation. The needles retained for 30 minutes and were manipulated once every

汉英对照
Chinese-English
Edition of
Acupuncture
Cosmetology

针灸美容

Part 2 The Treatment of Acupuncture Cosmetology

（1）取穴：病灶局部，脊柱两侧的条索状、结节状阳性物，颈、腰、骶部，太渊、内关等穴。

（2）方法：皮肤针叩刺病灶区域，从脱发区边缘开始呈螺旋状向中心均匀密刺，直至皮肤潮红或少量渗血，再涂以适量的生姜汁。其他区域或穴位一般叩刺，隔日 1 次。

3. 耳针：

（1）取穴：病灶相应区耳穴、肺、肾、交感、内分泌、神门、肾上腺。

（2）方法：以毫针针刺，得气留针 30 min，每 5 min 捻针 1 次，隔日 1 次。或以揿针、王不留行籽埋穴，5 d 1 次，7 次为 1 个疗程。

4. 穴位注射：

（1）取穴：心俞、肺俞、膈俞、脾俞、风池、大椎、曲池、血海。

（2）方法：每次取穴 2～3 个，以维生素 B$_{12}$ 注射液，或维生素 B$_1$、维生素 B$_6$ 注射液，每次 1 支注射，每日 1 次，10 次为 1 个疗程。间隔 3～5 d 再行第二个疗程。

5 minutes.

2. Dermal needle

2.1 Selection of acupoints: the local focus, bilateral cordlike spots of the spine, nodule-like positive reaction points, neck, lower back, lumbosacral regions, Taiyuan (LU 9) and Neiguan (PC 6) and so on.

2.2 Method: The above acupoints were punctured with filiform needles. The needles retained for 30 minutes after arrival of qi and were manipulated once every 5 minutes. The treatment was done once every other day. The thumb-tag needle or cowherb seeds can also be stuck to the above acupoints and changed once every 5 days, and 7 times make up one treatment course.

3. Auricular needle

3.1 Selection of acupoints: the corresponding ear acupoints of the local focus, lung, kidney, sympathetic nerve, endocrine, ear-Shenmen and adrenal gland.

3.2 Method: The acupoints were selected for either filiform needling or sticking of thumb-tag needle or cowherb seeds. The filiform needling was retained for 30 minutes after qi arrival, twisted per 5 minutes and done once every other day and the thumb-tag needle or cowherb seeds were changed once every 5 days, and 7 times make up one treatment course.

4. Acupoint injection

4.1 Selection of acupoints: Xinshu (BL 15), Feishu (BL 13), Geshu (BL 17), Pishu (BL 20), Fengchi (GB 20), Dazhui (GV 14), Quchi (LI 11) and Xuehai (SP 10).

4.2 Method: Each time 2 - 3 points were selected for injection 1 tube of Vitamin B_{12}, or Vitamin B_1 or B_6. The injection was done once every day and 10 times make up one

二、 注意事项

1. 调节情绪,保持心情愉悦。

2. 调整饮食起居,营养均衡,劳逸结合。

3. 保持头发卫生,避免过频洗发或使用过强碱性洗发用品。

第八节 黑痣

黑痣,又称"色素痣",俗称"黑子"、"黑子痣",是一种肤起黑褐色斑点略隆起于皮面的痣。可发于身体各处,男女可见,出生后或青春期、中年后始发,可随年龄增长而生长,不会自然消失。

中医学认为,本病主要由于先天禀赋不足,肾中浊气,或因孙络之血,滞于卫分,阳气束结,坚而不散;或由风邪搏于血气,变化而成。西医学认为,本病是由痣细胞构成的含有黑色素的先天性良性新生物,与遗传有关。

一、 针灸美容法

火针:

(1) 取穴:痣区。

(2) 方法:常规消毒后,以 26 号 1.5~2 寸短针用酒精灯将针尖烧红约 2 cm 后,迅速刺入痣的中心,一刺即出,针刺深度,一般与皮肤相平的痣宜浅刺,进针不可深过皮下;高出皮肤的痣可较深,均以不刺着正常皮肤为度。如为凸出大痣可以左手持镊子挟起痣的根部,右手持针将针尖与针身前端烧红,快速沿镊子底部如拉锯式去之,去后用消毒纱布包扎,以防感染。

treatment course. There should be an interval of 3 - 5 days between two treatment courses.

II. Precautions

1. Keep a peaceful mind and be happy.

2. Keep a regular life style; take well-balanced diet and balance work and rest.

3. Keep hair clean and avoid frequent hair washing or using alkaline shampoo.

Section 8   Black nevus

Black nevus, also called "pigmentation mole" or commonly known as "black moles", refers to black-brown spots slightly elevated on the skin surface. It can occur at anywhere of the body on both men and women after birth, during puberty or after middle ages. It may grow as ages but cannot disappear spontaneously.

TCM holds that this condition is related to the following factors: the turbid-qi retention in kidney due to congenital weak constitution or blood stasis of tiny collaterals obstructing the wei-defensive stage, leading to knotting of yang-qi and failing to disperse the hard masses; or exogenous pathogenic wind attacks the blood-qi. Modern medicine considers that this condition is a congenital benign overgrowth of skin pigment forming cells called melanocytes and related to heredity.

I. Cosmetic acupuncture

Fire needle

1. Selection of acupoints: the local focus.

2. Method: After routine sterilization and the needle tip was burnt red about 2 cm, a No. 26 short needle 1. 5 - 2 cun in length was inserted into the center of nevus rapidly and then removed immediately. As far as the needle depth, shallow puncture was

汉英对照
Chinese-English
Edition of
Acupuncture
Cosmetology
针灸美容
Part 2 The Treatment of Acupuncture Cosmetology

二、注意事项

1. 有些黑痣，如发现迅速增长，颜色显著加深，周围发红，出现多个卫星状小黑痣或经常出血，或附近淋巴结肿大者，可能为恶性病变的黑色素瘤，应及早去正规医院求诊，及时做手术切除，不可采用火针疗法。

2. 注意避免刺激黑痣，以防染毒成脓，或诱发恶变。

第九节　白癜风

白癜风，又称"白驳"、"斑白"等，是一种以皮肤白斑，斑内毛发变白，缠绵难愈为特征的皮肤病。青年多见，一般不危及健康。

中医学认为，本病多由于肝郁气滞或肝肾不足或脾失健运，血不荣肤，又外感六淫，肺气不宣，气血失和，毛窍闭塞而致。西医学认为，本病的病因尚不清楚，可能与自身免疫、家族史、黑色素的代谢异常、神经内分泌功能紊乱有关。

adopted for the nevus that leveled with the skin and the needle was not allowed to insert deeper than subcutaneous region, and relatively deep puncture was adopted for the nevus that elevated the skin. However, for both cases, the needles were not allowed to touch the normal skin. In case of the big nevus, the acupuncturist can pinch the root of nevus with forceps by using the left hand, hold the heated needle (needle tip and the front part of the needle body) with the right hand, and then removed it like dragsaw along the bottom of the forceps as fast as possible, and finally bind up with sterile gauze to prevent infection.

II. Precautions

1. Some black nevus, if grows fast in remarkably deeper color with redness around, multiple satellite-like small moles or frequent bleeding or adjacent enlargement of lymph nodes, may be malignant melanoma that require operations in a regular hospital as early as possible.

2. Avoid stimulating the black nevus to prevent purulence or inducing canceration.

Section 9　Vitiligo

Vitiligo, also called "white patches" or "gray-white patches" in Chinese, is an intractable skin disease characterized by white patches on the skin and the hair that grows on areas affected by vitiligo sometimes turns white. It usually occurs to young people and is not harmful to the general health.

TCM holds that vitiligo is caused by the following factors: the blood failing to nourish the skin due to liver-qi stagnation, or deficiency of the liver and kidney or spleen failing to transport and transform; and blockage of follicular pores due to lung-qi failing to disperse and disharmony between qi and blood

汉英对照

Chinese-English
Edition of
Acupuncture
Cosmetology

针灸美容

中篇 ◉ 针灸美容治疗

一、针灸美容法

1. 毫针:

(1) 取穴:病灶局部、风池、天枢、外关、合谷、太冲。风邪外袭,配肺俞、大椎、风门;寒凝肌肤,配关元、命门;肝郁气滞,配阳陵泉、膻中、期门;肝肾不足,配肝俞、肾俞、太溪、三阴交;久病瘀血阻滞,配膈俞、血海、三阴交。

(2) 方法:毫针病灶局部围刺,其他腧穴行平补平泻法,关元、命门、肾俞、肝俞、太溪、肺俞行补法,留针 30 min,间隔 5 min 行针 1 次,每日或隔日 1 次,10～15 次为 1 个疗程。

2. 艾灸:

(1) 取穴:病灶局部、关元、命门、气海、足三里、肝俞、肾俞、脾俞、肺俞。

resulting from external contraction of six exogenous factors. Modern medicine considers that the cause of vitiligo is unknown but possibly related to autoimmune system, family history, abnormal metabolism of melanin, and functional disorder of neuroendocrine.

I. Cosmetic acupuncture

1. Filiform needle

1.1　Selection of acupoints: the local focus, Fengchi (GB 20), Tianshu (ST 25), Waiguan (TE 5), Hegu (LI 4), and Taichong (LR 3). In addition, Feishu (BL 13), Dazhui (GV 14) and Fengmen (BL 12) are added for pathogenic wind attacking the body; Guanyuan (CV 4) and Mingmen (GV 4) are added for cold retention in the skin; Yanglingquan (GB 34), Danzhong (CV 17) and Qimen (LR 14) are added for liver-qi stagnation; Ganshu (BL 18), Shenshu (BL 23), Taixi (KI 3) and Sanyinjiao (SP 6) are added for deficiency of the liver and kidney; and Geshu (BL 17), Xuehai (SP 10) and Sanyinjiao (SP 6) are added for blood stasis due to chronic disease.

1.2　Method: the local focus was applied surrounding puncture; except for reinforcing manipulation for Guanyuan (CV 4), Mingmen (GV 4), Shenshu (BL 23), Ganshu (BL 18), Taixi (KI 3) and Feishu (BL 13), all the other acupoints were punctured with even reinforcing-reducing manipulation. The needles retained for 30 minutes and were manipulated once every 5 minutes. The treatment was done once every day or every other day, and 10 - 15 times make up one treatment course.

2. Moxibustion

2.1　Selection of acupoints: the local focus, Guanyuan (CV 4), Mingmen (GV 4), Qihai (CV 6), Zusanli (ST 36), Ganshu (BL 18), Shenshu (BL 23), Pishu (BL 20) and Feishu (BL 13).

汉英对照
Chinese-English
Edition of
Acupuncture
Cosmetology

针灸美容　Part 2 The Treatment of Acupuncture Cosmetology

（2）方法：每次除病灶局部外，可任选 2～3 个穴交替。以艾条温灸至局部肤色深红为度。每日 1 次，15～30 次为 1 个疗程。

3. 耳针：

（1）取穴：病灶相应区耳穴、肺、脾、肝、枕、内分泌、交感、肾上腺。

（2）方法：每次选用 3～5 个穴，毫针针刺，隔日 1 次，或撤针、王不留行籽埋穴，每日按压穴位 4～5 次，每穴 10 下，5～7 d 更换 1 次，10～15 次为 1 个疗程。

4. 皮肤针：

（1）取穴：病灶局部。

（2）方法：常规消毒后，皮肤针中等力度叩刺病灶及其周围，至皮肤充血或有轻微出血为度，每日 1 次，10～15 次为 1 个疗程。

5. 三棱针：

（1）取穴：病灶局部。

（2）方法：常规消毒后，以三棱针点刺病灶使之轻微出血，再拔火罐于上，留罐 3～5 min，每周 1 次。

6. 穴位注射：

（1）取穴：病灶局部。

（2）方法：常规消毒后，取自血适量，注入病灶皮肤浅层，至局部青紫色为度。每周 2 次，10 次为 1 个疗程。

2.2　Method: Each time 2 - 3 acupoints were selected in addition to the local focus were applied moxibustion with moxa stick until the local skin turned deep red. The moxibustion was done once every day and 15 - 30 times make up one treatment course.

3. Auricular needle

3.1 Selection of acupoints: the corresponding ear acupoints of the local focus, lung, spleen, liver, Occipit, endocrine, sympathetic nerve and adrenal gland.

3.2　Method: Each time 3 - 5 acupoints were selected for either filiform needling or sticking by thumb-tag needles or cowherb seeds. The acupoints were pressed 4 - 5 times per day, 10 times for each acupoint. The thumb-tag needles or cowherb seeds were changed once every 5 - 7 days and 10 - 15 times make up one treatment course.

4. Dermal needle

4.1　Selection of acupoints: the local focus.

4.2　Method: the focus and its surrounding area were applied moderate tapping with dermal needle until local congestion or slight bleeding. The treatment was done once a day and 10 - 15 times make up one treatment course.

5. Three-edged needle

5.1　Selection of acupoints: the local focus.

5.2　Method: the local focus was pricked for bleeding with three-edged needle after routine sterilization and followed by 3 - 5 minutes of cupping. The treatment was done once every week.

6. Acupoint injection

6.1　Selection of acupoints; the local focus.

6.2　Method: Appropriate amount of auto-blood was injected into the superficial layer of the skin on the local focus after routine sterilization until the local skin turned bluish-

7. 火针：

(1) 取穴：病灶局部。

(2) 方法：常规操作，以火针多点刺入病灶局部皮肤浅层(约1 mm)，每周1次。

二、 注意事项

1. 调摄情志，保持乐观，避免忧思恼怒。

2. 调节生活起居。避免接触使皮肤脱色的化学物质，避免外伤。注意衣着宽大，适度日晒，但避免严重晒斑。

3. 忌食辛辣、油腻，避免过食海鲜、维生素 C 等。多食核桃、花生、黑芝麻、芹菜、豆类、胡萝卜、苹果、葡萄干等。

第十节　银屑病

银屑病，又称"牛皮癣"、"松皮癣"。是一种以皮肤起红疹，上覆银屑，搔之而起，反复发作难愈，冬重夏轻为特征的皮肤病。多见于青壮年。好发于四肢伸侧、头皮、躯干等处，对称分布。

purple. The treatment was done twice every week and 10 times make up one treatment course.

7. Fire needle

7.1　Selection of acupoints: the local focus.

7.2　Method: By following the routine procedure, the superficial layer of the skin on the local focus was punctured by heated needle from different directions (about 1 mm). The treatment was done once every week.

II. Precautions

1. Keep a peaceful mind and an optimistic attitude and avoid anger or too much worry.

2. Keep a regular life style; avoid contacting chemical substances that may discolor the skin; avoid trauma; Have comfortable clothes and moderate sun exposure but prevent severe sunburn.

3. Avoid spicy or greasy food; avoid too much seafood or vitamin C; take more walnuts, peanuts, black sesames, celeries, beans, carrots, apples and raisins.

Section 10　Psoriasis

Psoriasis, also called " scaly tetter " or " dermatitis vegetans", is a common skin disease characterized by recurrent and intractable red rashes on the skin that are covered with silvery flakes, come off easily and appears severe in winter but mild in summer. It usually occurs to adolescents and appears symmetrically in extensor aspects of the four limbs, scalp and body trunk.

TCM holds that psoriasis is caused by the following factors: internal injury of seven emotions and chronic qi-stagnation transforming into fire; six exogenous pathogenic factors

汉英对照

Chinese-English
Edition of
Acupuncture
Cosmetology

针灸美容

中篇 ● 针灸美容治疗

中医学认为,本病多为情志内伤,郁久化火;或六淫外袭,阻塞经络,瘀于肌腠;或过食荤腥,胃肠积热,外透肌肤;或冲任失调,肝肾阴虚,肌肤失养所致。西医学认为,本病的发生与遗传、感染、代谢的障碍、免疫功能障碍、内分泌障碍等有关,但具体病因尚不完全明确。

一、 针刺美容法

1. 毫针:

(1)取穴:曲池、血海、合谷、三阴交、膈俞。血热风燥,配大椎、外关;血虚风燥,配足三里、膈俞。

(2)方法:毫针针刺,足三里行补法,余穴行平补平泻法,留针 20~30 min,每日或隔日 1 次,10 次为 1 个疗程。

2. 电针:

(1)取穴:曲池、合谷、血海、三阴交、足三里。

(2)方法:取 2 个或 4 个穴,加电针,断续波强刺激通电 20~30 min,隔日 1 次,10 次为 1 个疗程。

obstructing meridians and retention of stasis in muscular striae; heat accumulation in the stomach and intestine due to overeat of greasy food affecting the skin; or disorder of Chong and Ren meridians and yin deficiency of the liver and kidney leading to malnutrition of the body skin. Modern medicine considers that this condition is related to heredity, infection, metabolic disorder, dysfunction of immune system and endocrine disorder, but the specific etiology is still unclear.

I. Cosmetic acupuncture

1. Filiform needle

1.1　Selection of acupoints: Quchi (LI 11), Xuehai (SP 10), Hegu (LI 4), Sanyinjiao (SP 6) and Geshu (BL 17). In addition, Dazhui (GV 14) and Waiguan (TE 5) are added for those with blood heat and wind-dryness; and Zusanli (ST 36) and Geshu (BL 17) are added for those with blood deficiency and wind-dryness.

1.2　Method: Except for Zusanli (ST 36) that was punctured with reinforcing manipulation, all the other acupoints were punctured with even reinforcing-reducing manipulation. The filiform needles retained for 20 - 30 minutes. The treatment was done once every day or every other day and 10 times make up one treatment course.

2. Electric acupuncture

2.1　Selection of acupoints: Quchi (LI 11), Hegu (LI 4), Xuehai (SP 10), Sanyinjiao (SP 6) and Zusanli (ST 36).

2.2　Method: Electric stimulator was connected to 2 or 4 of the above acupoints for 20 - 30 minutes with discontinuous wave and strong intensity. The treatment was done once every other day and 10 times make up one treatment course.

汉英对照

Chinese-English
Edition of
Acupuncture
Cosmetology

针灸美容

中篇 ◉ 针灸美容治疗

3. 三棱针：

（1）取穴：大椎、陶道、肝俞、脾俞。

（2）方法：常规消毒后，三棱针点刺出血，再拔罐。留罐3～5 min。隔日1次。10～15次为1个疗程。

4. 灸法：

（1）取穴：病灶局部。

（2）方法：自制灸条（白芷、苍术各150 g、硫黄60 g,各研细末，加艾绒150 g制成药条）点燃，温灸病灶局部 15～30 min。每日1次,7～10次为1个疗程。

二、 注意事项

1. 忌食辛辣、酒酪、肥甘等辛热动风之品。

2. 注意加强自身锻炼、增强体质,避免感冒。

3. 保持居处干燥,避免潮湿。避免用热水烫洗病灶局部或用过强刺激性的外用药。

4. 和顺情志,避免恼怒忧思。

3. Three-edged needle

3.1 Selection of acupoints: Dazhui (GV 14), Taodao (GV 13), Ganshu (BL 17) and Pishu (BL 20).

3.2 Method: The acupoints were pricked for bleeding with three-edged needle after routine sterilization and followed by 3 - 5 minutes of cupping. The treatment was done once every other day and 10 - 15 times make up one treatment course.

4. Moxibustion

4.1 Selection of acupoints: the local focus.

4.2 Method: The local focus was applied with self-made moxa stick (herbal stick made from the fine powder of 150 g of Baizhi/*Radix Angelicae Dahuricae* and Cangzhu/*Rhizoma Atractylodis* as well as 60 g of Liuhuang/Sulphur) for 15 - 30 minutes. The treatment was done once every day and 7 - 10 times make up one treatment course.

Ⅱ. **Precautions**

1. Avoid spicy, alcohol and cheese and sweet and fatty food that may trigger wind.

2. Take more physical exercises to prevent common cold.

3. Keep residence dry and stay away from humidity; and avoid washing the local focus with hot water or using external lotions with excessive irritation.

4. Keep a peaceful mind and avoid anger or too much worry.

汉英对照

Chinese-English
Edition of
Acupuncture
Cosmetology

针灸美容

Part 2 The Treatment of Acupuncture Cosmetology

第八章　五官科病症的针灸美容

第一节　麦粒肿

麦粒肿,又称"偷针眼"、"土疳"等,是一种表现为眼睑皮肤红肿、疼痛为特征的五官科疾病。可数处同时发作或反复发作。

中医学认为,本病多因外感风热,或过食辛辣炙煿之品,脾胃积热上攻于目,加上卫生习惯不良或屈光不正、睡眠不足而罹患。西医学认为,本病是以睑缘的皮脂或睑板腺感染细菌所引起的眼睑急性化脓性炎症。

一、　针灸美容法

1. 三棱针:

(1) 取穴:耳尖、太阳。

(2) 方法:在常规消毒后,取耳尖或太阳穴三棱针点刺放血3～5滴,每周2次。对于麦粒肿早期常1次可愈。

2. 毫针:

(1) 取穴:丝竹空、太阳、合谷、天井(见图17)、行间。脾胃湿热,配内庭、丰隆;阴虚内热,配三阴交、太冲、太溪。

(2) 方法:毫针针刺,行泻法。每日或隔日1次。

Chapter 8
The acupuncture cosmetology
for ENT conditions

Section 1 Stye

Stye, also called "Tou Zhen Yan" or "Tu Gan" in TCM terms (meaning hordeolum), is an ENT disease manifesting red, swelling and painful eyelids. It may appear in different parts simultaneously or repeatedly.

TCM holds that stye is related to the following factors: external contraction of wind-heat, overeating of spicy food and accumulated heat in the spleen and stomach ascending and attacking eyes, plus bad hygienic habit or refractive errors and inadequate sleep. Modern medicine considers that stye is an acute suppurative inflammation resulting from bacterial infection of the oil glands of the eyelid or meibomian gland.

Ⅰ. Cosmetic acupuncture

1. Three-edged needle

1.1 Selection of acupoints: ear apex and Taiyang (EX-HN 5).

1.2 Method: the ear apex or Taiyang (EX-HN 5) was pricked with three-edged needle after routine sterilization for blood-letting of 3 - 5 drops. The treatment was done twice every week and usually the early-stage stye can be cured by once.

2. Filiform needle

2.1 Selection of acupoints: Sizhukong (TE 23), Taiyang (EX-HN 5), Hegu (LI 4), Tianjing (TE 10)(See Fig. 17), and Xingjian (LR 2). In addition, Neiting (ST 44) and Fenglong

汉英对照
Chinese-English
Edition of
Acupuncture
Cosmetology

针灸美容 Part 2 The Treatment of Acupuncture Cosmetology

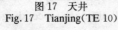

天井 TE 10

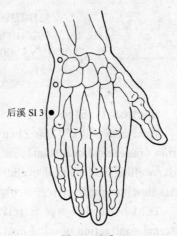

后溪 SI 3

图 17 天井
Fig. 17 Tianjing(TE 10)

图 18 后溪
Fig. 18 Houxi(SI 3)

3. 皮肤针：

（1）取穴：大椎、身柱、风池、肩胛内侧区阳性反应点。

（2）方法：中等力度叩刺，出少量的血液，大椎、反应点可加拔火罐。

4. 艾灸：

（1）取穴：后溪（见图18）、患侧眼部。

（2）方法：以麦粒大小艾炷施灸于健侧后溪穴，每次2壮，以局部皮肤充血红晕为度。患侧眼部以半圆形核桃壳做隔物灸，核桃壳可先在开水冲泡的菊花液中浸泡10～20 min，取出后放入眼镜框中让患者戴上，核桃半球面朝外，再用艾条施灸。二者均可每日1次。

5. 耳针：

（1）取穴：眼区。重症，可配神门、肝、脾、肺。

（2）方法：先在眼区找到敏感点，在常规消毒后，毫针针

(ST 40) are added for dampness-heat in the spleen and stomach; and Sanyinjiao (SP 6), Taichong (LR 3) and Taixi (KI 3) are added for internal heat due to yin deficiency.

2.2　Method: The above acupoints were punctured with filiform needles by reducing manipulations once every day or every other day.

3. Dermal needle

3.1　Selection of acupoints: Dazhui (GV 14), Shenzhu (GV 12), Fengchi (GB 20) and positive reaction points in medial aspect area of shoulder blade.

3.2　Method: The above acupoints were applied moderate tapping until slight bleeding; and Dazhui (GV 14) and reaction points were combined cupping.

4. Moxibustion

4.1　Selection of acupoints: Houxi (SI 3) (See Fig.18) and the affected-side eye area.

4.2　Method: The kernel-sized moxa cone was applied to the healthy-side Houxi (SI 3) for 2 zhuang until the local skin turned red. The walnut hull-partitioned moxibustion was applied to the affected-side eye area; the semicycle-shaped walnut hull was soaked in the boiled water with chrysanthemum for 10 - 20 minutes and then put into spectacles for the patients to wear, the semicycle of the walnut facing outward, followed by moxibustion with moxa stick. The above treatments can both be done once every day.

5. Auricular needle

5.1　Selection of acupoints: eye area, and ear-Shenmen, liver, spleen and lung are added for severe symptoms.

5.2　Method: The sensitive points around the eye area was found first and then punctured with filiform needles after

汉英对照

Chinese-English
Edition of
Acupuncture
Cosmetology

针灸美容

Part 2 The Treatment of Acupuncture Cosmetology

刺,留针 30 min,重症可配其他穴位。每日 1 次。

二、 注意事项

1. 注意局部卫生,避免以手擦、搓眼部,防止病毒扩散。

2. 忌食辛辣、海鲜、炙煿食物,多饮水,进食瓜果、蔬菜,保持大便通畅。

3. 适当锻炼,增强身体抗病能力。

第二节 突眼症

突眼症,多由于甲状腺功能亢进引起,是以眼球突出、眼球酸胀、眼睑肿胀、目赤畏光为主要表现的病症。

中医学认为,本病的发生主要与情志、体质因素有关,导致肝郁气滞、阴虚火旺、痰火交阻而致。西医学认为,本病的发生可由甲状腺功能亢进,内分泌失衡,或眶蜂窝织炎导致。

一、 针灸美容法

1. 毫针:

(1) 取穴:上明(眼球与眉毛之间的眼睑上)、阳白、养老(见图 19)、风池、合谷、太冲、照海。肝火上亢,配行间、内庭;阴虚火旺,配太冲、太溪、三阴交、肝俞、肾俞。

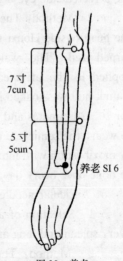

图 19　养老
Fig.19　Yanglao(SI 6)

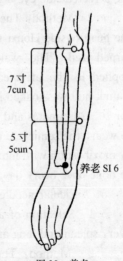图中标注:7寸 7cun;5寸 5cun;养老 SI 6

汉英对照
Chinese-English
Edition of
Acupuncture
Cosmetology
针灸美容
中篇 ◉ 针灸美容治疗

routine sterilization. The needles retained for 30 minutes. Other acupoints can be added for severe symptoms. The treatment was done once every day.

II. Precautions

1. Keep local area clean and avoid rubbing or twisting eye area with hands to prevent virus spreading.

2. Avoid spicy and fried food as well as seafood; drink more water; take more fruits and vegetables to keep normal bowel movement.

3. Take appropriate exercises to build up the body resistance.

Section 2 Exophthalmus

Exophthalmus is a condition mainly characterized by protrusion, soreness and distension of eyeballs, swelling of eyelids and red eyes with photophobia. It mostly results from hyperthyroidism.

TCM holds that exophthalmus is mainly related to emotional and constitutional factors, leading to liver-qi stagnation, hyperactivity of fire due to yin deficiency and mixture of phlegm and fire. Western medicine considers that it may result from hyperthyroidism, endocrine disorder or orbital cellulites.

I. Cosmetic acupuncture

1. Filiform needle

1.1   Selection of acupoints: Shangming (Extra point, location; the eyelid between eyeball and eyebrow), Yangbai (GB 14), Yanglao (SI 6)(See Fig. 19), Fengchi (GB 20), Hegu (LI 4) and Zhaohai (KI 6). In addition, Xingjian (LR 2) and Neiting (ST 44) are added for hyperactivity of liver-

（2）方法：患者平卧，施针者以手指固定眼球，选用 1 寸细毫针，缓慢从上明穴刺入 0.5 寸，避开血管、眼球，避免大幅度提插捻转，其他穴位常规针刺，平补平泻。留针 30 min。

2. 艾灸：

（1）取穴：臂臑（见图 20）、臑俞（见图 21）。

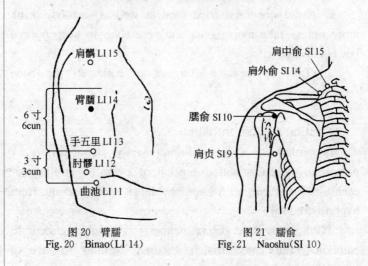

图 20　臂臑
Fig. 20　Binao(LI 14)

图 21　臑俞
Fig. 21　Naoshu(SI 10)

（2）方法：以麦粒大小艾炷直接灸两穴，15～18 壮，以局部皮肤充血红晕为度。隔日 1 次，10 次为 1 个疗程。

3. 激光疗法：

（1）取穴：扶突（见图 1）、耳门或睛明。

（2）方法：氦氖激光照射扶突 5～7 min，耳门或睛明，双侧交替照射，每次 3～5 min，每日 1 次，10 次为 1 个疗程。

二、 注意事项

1. 注意情绪的调摄，避免不良精神刺激，怡情养志。

2. 起居有时，劳逸结合，增强体质，提高抗病能力。

fire; and Taichong (LR 3), Taixi (KI 3), Sanyinjiao (SP 6), Ganshu (BL 17) and Shenshu (BL 23) are added for hyperactivity of fire due to yin deficiency.

1. 2   Method: After telling the patients to take lying position, the acupuncturist needs to immobilize the eyeball with his finger and then puncture Shangming (Extra) 0. 5 cun in depth slowly with 1-cun thin filiform needle. Attention: to avoid blood vessels and eyeball and large-amplitude lifting, thrusting and twisting are prohibited. The other acupoints were punctured with routine procedure by even reinforcing-reducing manipulations. The needle retained for 30 minutes.

2. Moxibustion

2.1   Selection of acupoints: Binao (LI 14) (See Fig. 20) and Naoshu (SI 10) (See Fig. 21).

2. 2   Method: The above two acupoints were applied direct moxibustion with kernel-sized moxa cone for 15 – 18 zhuang until the local skin turned red. The treatment was done once every other day and 10 times make up one treatment course.

3. Laser therapy

3.1   Selection of acupoints: Futu (LI 18), Ermen (TE 21) or Jingming (BL 1).

3. 2   Method: Futu (LI 18) was applied helium-neon laser radiation for 5 – 7 minutes. Bilateral Ermen (TE 21) or Jingming (BL 1) were applied laser radiation alternately for 3 – 5 minutes each time. The treatment was done once every day and 10 times make up one treatment course.

Ⅱ. Precautions

1. Keep a peaceful mind and avoid mental irritation.

2. Keep a regular life style, balance work and rest and do

3. 适当配服含碘剂,进食含碘食物,如紫菜、海带等。

第三节 眼睑瞤动

眼睑瞤动,又称"目瞤"、"眼皮跳"。是一种眼睑皮肤不由自主地抽搐瞤动的眼病。

中医学认为,本病的发生多与劳倦太过、久视,心脾两虚或肝肾阴虚,血虚风动而致。西医学认为,本病有间歇性与持续性两种。前者多由于精神疲劳或神经紧张而导致的某一肌束发生跳动性痉挛。后者,可由前者不能缓解,持续加重而来;也可因为局部炎症,或不明原因导致眼轮匝肌抽搐痉挛而致。

一、针灸美容法

1. 毫针:

(1) 取穴:丝竹空、瞳子髎、养老、光明(见图11)、风池、太冲、照海。

(2) 方法:毫针常规针刺,行平补平泻。每日1次,10次为1个疗程。

2. 耳针:

(1) 取穴:眼区、肝、肾上腺、脾、神门、皮质下。

(2) 方法:以揿针或王不留行埋针、埋籽,留针或留籽3～5 d,每日每穴按压4次。实证,可配耳尖放血。

physical exercises to build up body resistance.

3. Take iodine-contained preparation or food such as laver and kelp.

Section 3   Twitching of eyelids

Twitching of eyelids, also called "spasm of eyelids" or "flickering of eyelids", is an eye problem characterized by involuntary spasm or twitching of the eyelids.

TCM holds that this condition is related to fatigue, long-term eye using, deficiency of both the heart and spleen or yin deficiency of the liver and kidney and subsequent blood deficiency stirring wind. Modern medicine considers that this condition can be intermittent or persistent; the former is caused by jerking spasm of a muscle girdle due to mental fatigue or nervous tension, while the latter can be the result of failure of relief or further progression of the former. Local inflammation or convulsive spasm of orbicularis muscle caused by unknown reasons may also result in this condition.

Ⅰ. Cosmetic acupuncture

1. Filiform needle

1.1 Selection of acupoints: Sizhukong (TE 23), Tongziliao (GB 1), Yanglao (SI 6), Guangming (GB 37), Fengchi (GB 20), Taichong (LR 3) and Zhaohai (KI 6).

1.2 Method: the acupoints were punctured with even reinforcing-reducing manipulation, once every day and 10 times make up one treatment course.

2. Auricular needle

2.1 Selection of acupoints: eye area, liver, adrenal gland, spleen, ear-Shenmen, and subcortex.

2.2 Method: The thumb-tag needle or cowherb seeds

汉英对照
Chinese-English
Edition of
Acupuncture
Cosmetology

针灸美容

Part 2 The Treatment of Acupuncture Cosmetology

3. 皮肤针：

（1）取穴：眼眶周围、太阳。

（2）方法：以轻强度叩刺，以局部皮肤微红为度，每日 1 次，5 次为 1 个疗程。

4. 艾灸：

（1）取穴：眼眶周围、光明、足三里、养老。心脾两虚，配心俞、脾俞；肝肾阴虚，配肝俞、肾俞。

（2）方法：每次选用 4～5 穴，以艾条施灸，以皮肤温热潮红为度，每日 1 次，7 次为 1 个疗程。多用于虚证。

二、 注意事项

1. 调摄情志，饮食有节，起居有常，劳逸有度。

2. 加强身体锻炼，提高身体抗病能力。

3. 注意卫生，保护眼睛，对于长期用眼者，应多进食护眼食物，如枸杞子、菊花等。

were applied to above acupoints and changed once every 3 – 5 days. Each acupoint was pressed 4 times every day. For excessive syndrome, blood letting therapy on ear apex can be combined.

3. Dermal needle

3.1　Selection of acupoints: area around eye sockets and Taiyang (EX-HN 5).

3.2　Method: the selected area and acupoint were applied mild tapping until the local skin turned slight red, once every day and 5 times make up one treatment course.

4. Moxibustion

4.1　Selection of acupoints: area around eye sockets, Guangming (GB 37), Zusanli (ST 36) and Yanglao (SI 6). In addition, Xinshu (BL 15) and Pishu (BL 20) are added for deficiency of both the heart and spleen; and Ganshu (BL 18) and Shenshu (BL 23) are added for yin deficiency of the liver and kidney.

4.2　Method: Each time 4 – 5 acupoints were selected for moxibustion by moxa stick until the local skin turned slight red, once every day and 7 times make up one treatment course. This therapy is mostly indicated for deficient syndrome.

Ⅱ. Precautions

1. Keep a peaceful mind, proper diet, and regular life stye and balance work and rest.

2. Do appropriate physical exercises to build up the body resistance.

3. Keep local area clean and take care of eyes and take more eye-protecting foods such as wolfberry fruit and chrysanthemum flowers.

汉英对照

Chinese-English
Edition of
Acupuncture
Cosmetology

针灸美容

中篇 ◉ 针灸美容治疗

第四节 红眼病

红眼病,又称"火眼"、"天行赤眼",是以眼睑红肿、目赤肿痛、流泪痒感,甚至流脓等为主要症状的病症。多发于春、夏季。具有传染性、流行性。

中医学认为,本病的发生多由于多食膏粱厚味,或嗜饮无度,素体湿热隐伏,又外感风热,内外热毒暴发于上。西医学认为,本病的发生多由于细菌或病毒感染而致显著的结膜充血、水肿、黏液性或脓性分泌物为特征的急性结膜炎症。有急性传染性结膜炎、流行性角膜结膜炎、流行性出血性结膜炎3种。

一、 针灸美容法

1. 毫针:

(1) 取穴:丝竹空、太阳、曲池、委中、风池、合谷、太冲。

(2) 方法:常规毫针针刺,行平补平泻法,留针 30 min,间隔 5 min 行针 1 次,每日 1 次。

2. 三棱针:

(1) 取穴:耳尖、耳背静脉、太阳。

(2) 方法:每次取 1 穴,用三棱针点刺出血 3～5 滴,每日 1 次。

3. 皮肤针:

Section 4 Conjunctivitis

Conjunctivitis, also called "fire eyes" or "pink eyes", is an eye problem characterized by red and swelling eyelids, red, swelling and painful eyes, lacrimation and itching and sometimes even suppuration. It occurs more in spring and summer. It can be contagious and epidemic.

TCM holds that this condition is related to the following factors: overeat of greasy food, too much alcohol drinking, constitutional dampness-heat, plus external contraction of wind-heat. Modern medicine considers that this condition is an acute inflammation of conjunctiva due to bacterial or viral infection and characterized by conjunctiva congestion, edema, and sticky or purulent discharges. There are three types of conjunctivitis: acute contagious conjunctivitis, epidemic kerato-conjunctivitis and epidemic hemorrhagic conjunctivitis.

I. Cosmetic acupuncture

1. Filiform needle

1.1 Selection of acupoints: Sizhukong (TE 23), Taiyang (EX-HN 5), Quchi (LI 11), Weizhong (BL 40), Fengchi (GB 20), Hegu (LI 4) and Taichong (LR 3).

1.2 Method: the acupoints were punctured with even reinforcing-reducing manipulation, and manipulated once every 5 minutes. The needles retained for 30 minutes. The treatment was done once every day.

2. Three-edged needle

2.1 Selection of acupoints: ear apex, posterior auricular vein, and Taiyang (EX-HN 5).

2.2 Method: Each time one acupoint was pricked for bleeding of 3 – 5 drops, once every day.

3. Dermal needle

（1）取穴：眼眶周围、颈部、风池、太阳。

（2）方法：眼眶周围，轻度叩刺，以皮肤微红为度；其他穴位采用重叩刺，以皮肤微出血为度，隔日1次。

4. 挑治疗法：

（1）取穴：肩胛内侧区阳性反应点。

（2）方法：在常规消毒后，用粗针挑断皮下纤维或挤出少许血液，消毒后再加纱布覆盖。

5. 耳针：

（1）取穴：眼、目1、目2、肝。

（2）方法：毫针中等刺激，以耳部胀热为度。留针30 min，每日1次。

二、 注意事项

1. 注意个人卫生，避免交叉传染。

2. 注意劳逸结合，忌食辛辣炙煿之品，保持大便通畅。

第五节　酒皶鼻

酒皶鼻，俗称"红鼻子"、"赤鼻"，是一种以鼻部发红、上起丘疹、脓疱，状若酒糟为特征的慢性皮肤病。多见于中年以后的男女或嗜酒之人。

中医学认为，本病多为喜食辛辣、肥甘嗜酒，肺胃积热，上熏于鼻，复受风寒，血瘀凝滞而成。西医学认为，本病多由毛囊虫寄生于鼻而发。

3.1　Selection of acupoints: area around eye sockets, neck area, Fengchi (GB 20) and Taiyang (EX-HN 5).

3.2　Method: Except for mild tapping on area around eye sockets, the other acupoints were applied heavy tapping until slight bleeding of the local skin. The treatment was done once every other day.

4. Pricking therapy

4.1　Selection of acupoints: the positive reaction points in the medial aspect area of the shoulder girdle.

4.2　Method: After routine sterilization, the subcutaneous fiber was pricked with a thick needle or squeezed for some blood drops and then covered with sterile gauze.

5. Auricular needle

5.1　Selection of acupoints: eye, eye 1, eye 2 and liver.

5.2　Method: The acupoints were punctured with filiform needle by moderate stimulation until the auricle turned distension and hot. The needles retained for 30 minutes. The treatment was done once every day.

Ⅱ. Precautions

1. Keep local area clean and avoid cross infection.

2. Balance work and rest, avoid spicy and fried food and keep normal bowel movement.

Section 5　Brandy nose

Brandy nose, also called "red nose", is a chronic skin disease characterized by redness over nose with schlempe-shaped papulae and pustules. It occurs to both men and women after middle age or heavy drinkers.

TCM holds that this condition is related to the following factors: preference for spicy, sweet, and greasy food as well as

汉英对照

Chinese-English
Edition of
Acupuncture
Cosmetology

针灸美容

中篇

◉ 针灸美容治疗

一、 针灸美容法

1. 毫针：

（1）取穴：印堂、素髎、迎香、合谷。热盛，配曲池、外关、内庭。

（2）方法：毫针常规针刺，平补平泻，留针 20～30 min，隔日 1 次。

2. 三棱针：

（1）取穴：鼻部局部瘀血络脉显露处或鼻翼旁半月形中点。

（2）方法：每次选一处。在常规消毒后，取小三棱针放血，出血 3～5 滴，每 3 日 1 次。

3. 耳针：

（1）取穴：鼻部相应区耳穴、肺、胃、大肠、内分泌、肾上腺、神门。

（2）方法：每次取 3～5 穴，取短小毫针针刺，隔日 1 次，7 次为 1 个疗程。或揿针、王不留行籽埋穴。

4. 穴位注射：

（1）取穴：迎香。

（2）方法：在常规消毒后，取 0.25%～0.5%普鲁卡因注射液，注射两侧迎香各 0.5 ml，每周 2 次，10 次为 1 个疗程。

二、 注意事项

1. 注意调节情绪。避免过度冷热水刺激及不洁之物接触，避免感染。

alcohol may cause accumulated heat in the lung and stomach, which in turn may flare up to fumigate noses; plus external contraction of wind-cold and the subsequent blood stasis. Modern medicine considers that this condition is caused by mites in hair follicles.

I. Cosmetic acupuncture

1. Filiform needle

1.1   Selection of acupoints: Yintang (EX-HN 3), Suliao (GV 25), Yingxiang (LI 20) and Hegu (LI 4). In addition, Quchi (LI 11), Waiguan (TE 5) and Neiting (ST 44) are added for extreme heat.

1.2   Method: the acupoints were punctured with even reinforcing-reducing manipulation, once every day and 20 – 30 minutes each time.

2. Three-edged needle

2.1   Selection of acupoints: the local area with exposed blood stasis or half-moon midpoint of the nasal wing.

2.2   Method: Each time one spot was pricked with three-edged needle for bleeding of 3 – 5 drop, once every 3 days.

3. Auricular needle

3.1   Selection of acupoints: the corresponding ear acupoints of the nose, lung, stomach, large intestine, endocrine, adrenal gland and ear-Shenmen.

3.2   Method: Each time 3 – 5 acupoints were punctured with small and short filiform needle once every other day, and 7 times make up one treatment course. The thumb-tag needle or cowherb seeds can also be adopted.

4. Acupoint injection

4.1   Selection of acupoint: Yingxiang (LI 20).

4.2   Method: The bilateral Yingxiang (LI 20) were injected 0.5 ml liquid containing 0.25% – 0.5% Procaine, twice

汉英对照

Chinese-English Edition of Acupuncture Cosmetology

针灸美容

Part 2 The Treatment of Acupuncture Cosmetology

2. 饮食以清淡为好,忌食辛辣、酒等各种刺激性食物、饮料,少食肥甘,少饮浓茶等,保持大便通畅。

3. 尽早调治与本病有关的疾病,如月经不调、习惯性便秘、螨虫寄生等。

第六节　口舌疮

口舌疮,也称"口疳"、"口舌生疮",是一种口腔黏膜反复溃烂、疼痛,影响进食为主要表现的症候。多见于成年女性。

中医学认为,本病多由思虑过度、情志抑郁、过食辛辣肥甘,湿热熏蒸或素体禀赋、病后劳伤,阴虚火旺,上炎口舌而致。西医学认为,本病的发生与病毒感染、内分泌紊乱、维生素缺乏、消化功能紊乱有关。

一、针灸美容法

1. 三棱针:

(1) 取穴:金津、玉液(见图 22);四缝(见图 23);后溪。

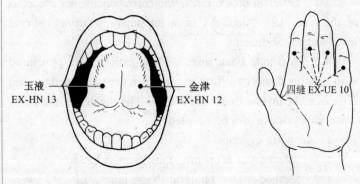

图 22　金津、玉液
Fig. 22　Jinjin(EX-HN 12) and Yuye(EX-HN 13)　Fig. 23　Sifeng(EX-UE 10)

every week and 10 times make up one treatment course.

Ⅱ. Precautions

1. Keep a peaceful mind and avoid irritation of cold or hot water as well as unclear substances to prevent infection.

2. Take bland food, avoid pungent foods including spicy food and alcohol and reduce sweet, fatty food and strong tea to keep normal bowel movement.

3. Regulate or get treatment of such relevant problems as irregular menstruation, habitual constipation and mites.

Section 6   Mouth or tongue ulcer

Mouth or tongue ulcer, also called "canker sores" or "mouth ulceration", is a group of symptoms characterized by recurrent ulceration and pain of oral cavity mucosa that affects food intake. It mainly occurs to adult women.

TCM holds that this condition is related to the following factors: mental stress, emotional depression, overeats of spicy, fatty and sweet food, fumigation of dampness-heat or congenital constitution of dampness-heat, chronic disease-related overstrain, and hyperactivity of fire due to yin deficiency. Modern medicine considers that this condition is related to viral infection, endocrine disorder, vitamin deficiencies and disturbance of digestive function.

Ⅰ. Cosmetic acupuncture

1. Three-edged needle

1.1   Selection of acupoints: Jinjin (EX-HN 12), Yuye (EX-HN 13)(See Fig. 22), Sifeng (EX-UE 10)(See Fig. 23) and Houxi (SI 3).

1.2   Method: The sublingual Jinjin (EX-HN 12) and Yuye (EX-HN 13) were pricked with three-edged needle for bleeding,

汉英对照
Chinese-English Edition of Acupuncture Cosmetology
针灸美容
Part 2 The Treatment of Acupuncture Cosmetology

（2）方法：以三棱针点刺舌下两静脉上的金津、玉液穴出血，以口吸吐出 2～3 口；或用三棱针刺入四缝穴皮下，挤出少许淋巴液或血液；或点刺后溪出血 3～5 滴。每周 2 次。

2. 毫针：

（1）取穴：地仓、照海、通里（见图 8）、廉泉（见图 1）。

（2）方法：毫针针刺，行平补平泻法，每日 1 次，每次 30 min，7～10 次为 1 个疗程。

3. 耳针：

（1）取穴：心、口、脾、胃、三焦。

（2）方法：用揿针或王不留行籽埋穴，3～5 d 更换 1 次，10 次为 1 个疗程。

4. 穴位敷贴疗法：

（1）取穴：涌泉。

（2）方法：以吴茱萸研细末，取适量配以陈醋调成糊状，敷贴双侧涌泉，再以纱布固定，24 h 后取下，5 次为 1 个疗程。

二、注意事项

1. 忌食辛辣炙煿饮食，少烟酒。

2. 多进食瓜果蔬菜，保持大便通畅。

3. 加强锻炼，增强体质，调节情志，起居有常。

4. 保持口腔卫生，早晚盥洗，饭后漱口。

2 - 3 times of spitting out; or Sifeng (EX-UE 10) was punctured subcutaneously with three-edged needle to squeeze some lymph fluid or blood; or Houxi (SI 3) was pricked for bleeding of 3 - 5 drops. The treatment was done twice every week.

2. Filiform needle

2.1 Selection of acupoints: Dicang (ST 4), Zhaohai (KI 6), Tongli (HT 5)(See Fig. 8) and Lianquan (CV 23)(See Fig. 1).

2.2 Method: the acupoints were punctured with even reinforcing-reducing manipulation, once every day, 30 minutes each time and 7 - 10 times make up one treatment course.

3. Auricular needle

3.1 Selection of acupoints: heart, mouth, spleen, stomach and Sanjiao.

3.2 Method: The thumb-tag needles or cowherb seeds were applied and changed once every 3 - 5 days, and 10 times make up one treatment course.

4. Acupoint injection

4.1 Selection of acupoint: Yongquan (KI 1).

4.2 Method: The bilateral Yongquan (KI 1) was applied with paste made from fine powder of Wuzhuyu (*Fructus Evodiae*) and mellow vinegar and then fixed with sterile gauze and removed after 24 hours. Five times make up one treatment course.

Ⅱ. Precautions

1. Avoid spicy and fried food and reduce alcohol drinking.

2. Take more fruits and vegetables to keep normal bowel movement.

3. Do physical exercises to build up the body resistance and keep a peaceful mind and regular life style.

4. Keep oral cavity clean: brush teeth twice a day and rinse out mouth after meals.

汉英对照

Chinese-English
Edition of
Acupuncture
Cosmetology

针灸美容

中篇 ◉ 针灸美容治疗

第九章　其他损美性病症的针灸美容

第一节　肥胖症

肥胖症,是指由于体内脂肪积聚过多,体重超过标准体重的 20% 以上者。所谓标准体重,国际上通常采用 Broca 计算法:标准体重(kg) = [身高(cm) − 100]×0.9(身高在 150 cm 以上者)。肥胖可发生于任何年龄,常见于 40 岁以上的成人。但近年来小儿超体重的人数日趋增加,已引起各方面的重视。

中医学认为,本病的发生与过食辛辣肥甘厚腻、劳逸失调、久坐久卧导致湿痰停滞、流溢肌肤,滞久化热,胃纳亢盛而致。西医学认为,肥胖有单纯性与继发性两种。前者多与家族肥胖、营养过剩有关;后者多因内分泌紊乱或与脑血管、心血管、高血压、动脉硬化、糖尿病等密切相关。小儿肥胖还受大脑发育的影响。

一、针灸美容法

1. 毫针:

(1) 取穴:神阙、关元、水分(见图 5)、四满(见图 5)、天枢、中脘、带脉、维道(见图 13)、丰隆、足三里、阳陵泉、阴陵泉、支沟、内关、三阴交。

Chapter 9
The acupuncture cosmetology for other beauty-impairing conditions

Section 1 Obesity

Obesity refers to a condition that the body weight exceeds 20% of the standard body weight due to an excess of body fat. The standard body weight is calculated by internationally recognized Broca's method: the standard body weight (kg) = [height (cm) − 100] × 0.9 (the height > 150 cm). Obesity can occur at age, but usually to adults above 40 years old. However, the numbers of obese children are also on the rise in recent years.

TCM holds that this condition is related to retention of dampness-phlegm manifesting on skin or chronic stagnation transforming into heat and leading to excessive appetite; either condition may result from overeats of spicy, fatty and sweet food, imbalance of work and rest and long-term sitting or lying position. Modern medicine considers that obesity has two types: simple obesity and secondary obesity, the former is related to family history and over-nutrition, while the latter is closely related to endocrine disorder or cardiocerebral vascular diseases, hypertension, arteriosclerosis and diabetes. The cerebrum development may also play a role in children's obesity.

I. Cosmetic acupuncture

1. Filiform needle

1.1 Selection of acupoints: Shenque (CV 8), Guanyuan (CV 4), Shuifen (CV 9)(See Fig. 5), Siman (KI 14)(See Fig.

（2）方法：每次取 5～8 个穴位，毫针围刺神阙穴四周皮肤，其他腧穴采用毫针针刺，行平补平泻法，留针 30 min，每 5 min 行针 1 次。腹部穴位也可采用透穴法，针刺朝向神阙穴。每日或隔日 1 次，10～15 次为 1 个疗程。

2. 皮肤针：

（1）取穴：足太阳膀胱经在背后的两条侧线（旁开后正中线 1.5 寸、3 寸）、天枢下至维道、足三里下至解溪（见图 11）。

（2）方法：以重度刺激叩刺所选部位，至皮肤潮红、微出血为度，隔日 1 次，10 次为 1 个疗程。

3. 耳针：

（1）取穴：口、食道、脾、胃、肝、三焦、大肠、饥点、丰隆、复溜、内分泌、肾上腺。

（2）方法：取 5 个穴位，毫针针刺，每日 1 次；或王不留行籽埋穴，3～5 日 1 换，10 次为 1 个疗程。

5), Tianshu (ST 25), Zhongwan (CV 12), Daimai (GB 26), Weidao (GB 28)(See Fig. 13), Fenglong (ST 40), Zusanli (ST 36), Yanglingquan (GB 34), Zhigou (SJ 6), Neiguan (PC 6) and Sanyinjiao (SP 6).

1.2 Method: Each time 5 - 8 acupoints were selected. The area around Shenque (CV 8) was applied with surrounding puncture. The other acupoints were punctured with even reinforcing-reducing manipulation and manipulated once every 5 minutes. The needles retained for 30 minutes. The acupoints on abdomen can also be punctured toward Shenque (CV 8). The treatment was done once every day or every other day and 10 - 15 times make up one treatment course.

2. Dermal needle

2.1 Selection of acupoints: the two bilateral lines of bladder meridian of foot-Taiyang (1.5 cun and 3 cun lateral to the spine), area from Tianshu (ST 25) to Weidao (GB 28) and from Zusanli (ST 36) to Jiexi (ST 41) (See Fig. 11).

2.2 Method: The selected areas were applied heavy tapping until the local skin turned slight red or bleeding. The treatment was done once every other day and 10 times make up one treatment course.

3. Auricular needle

3.1 Selection of acupoints: mouth, esophagus, spleen, stomach, liver, Sanjiao, large intestine, hunger points, Fenglong (ST 40), Fuliu (KI 7), endocrine and adrenal gland.

3.2 Method: Each time 5 acupoints were either punctured with filiform needle once every day or applied cowherb seeds once every 3 - 5 days, and 10 times make up one treatment course.

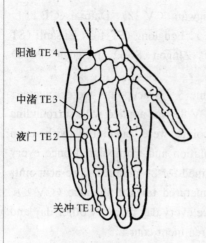

阳池 TE 4

中渚 TE3

液门 TE 2

关冲 TE 1

图 24　阳池
Fig. 24　Yangchi（TE 4）

4．艾灸疗法：

（1）取穴：阳池（见图24）、三焦俞（见图 6）为主穴；配以地机、命门、三阴交、大椎。

（2）方法：每次各取主、配穴 1 个，以生姜隔物灸，每次 5～6 壮，每日 1 次，30 次为 1 个疗程。

5．拔罐：

（1）取穴：肥胖区域、膈俞、肝俞、期门、章门、中脘、血海、三阴交。

（2）方法：膈俞、肝俞可以用刺络拔罐；肥胖区域可用走罐；其他采用火罐，留罐 10～15 min。

二、　注意事项

1．节制饮食，少食肥甘厚味，戒吃零食，尤其是在晚餐后。

2．调整生活起居，劳逸结合，增强体育锻炼。

3．积极治疗导致肥胖的原发病症。

第二节　黑变病

黑变病，又称"面黑"、"黧黑斑"、"面尘"等名。是一种以面部发生黑褐斑片、色如尘垢为特征的皮肤病。多见于中年以上妇女，好发于面颈部，亦可累及四肢等处。

4. Moxibustion

4.1　Selection of acupoints: Major acupoints: Yangchi (TE 4)(See Fig. 24) and Sanjiaoshu (BL 22)(See Fig. 6); adjunct acupoints: Diji (SP 8), Mingmen (GV 4), Sanyinjiao (SP 6) and Dazhui (GV 14).

4.2　Method: Each time one major acupoint and one adjunct acupoint were selected for 5 – 6 zhuang of ginger-partitioned moxibustion, once every day and 30 times make up one treatment course.

5. Cupping

5.1　Selection of acupoints: local obese area, Geshu (BL 17), Ganshu (BL 18), Qimen (LR 14), Zhangmen (LR 13), Zhongwan (CV 12), Xuehai (SP 10) and Sanyinjiao (SP 6).

5.2　Method: Geshu (BL 17) and Ganshu (BL 18) were applied cupping following blood-letting; the local obese area was applied moving cupping; and other acupoints were applied routine cupping for 10 – 15 minutes.

Ⅱ. Precautions

1. Reduce food intake, especially sweet and fatty food and avoid snacks, particularly after supper.

2. Regulate life style, balance work and rest and do physical exercises.

3. Get active treatment on primary diseases that led to obesity.

Section 2　Melanosis

Melanosis, also called "black complexion", or "black facial patches" or "dusty complexion", is a skin disease characterized by black-brown facial patches in dusty complexion. It frequently affects women above middle age and appears in the

中医学认为，本病多由于饮食不节、劳倦过度，气血不足或情志不畅，气滞血瘀或房室过度，阴阳虚损，肌肤失养导致。西医学认为，本病是一种光感性不明原因的皮炎，可能与维生素缺乏、化妆品刺激等有关。

一、针灸美容法

1. 毫针：

(1) 取穴：肝俞、脾俞、肾俞、太冲(或行间)、合谷、血海、曲池、足三里、太溪、三阴交。

(2) 方法：每次取 5 个穴位，毫针针刺，背俞穴、足三里、太溪，采用补法，其他用平补平泻法，留针 30 min，每隔 5 min 行针 1 次，10～15 次为 1 个疗程。

2. 耳针：

(1) 取穴：神门、交感、肾上腺、内分泌、子宫、肺、大肠。

(2) 方法：每次取 3～5 个穴位，毫针针刺，强刺激，留针 3～4 h，间断行针。每日或隔日 1 次。或以揿针埋穴，3～5 d 1 换，10 次为 1 个疗程。

face, neck or four limbs.

TCM holds that this condition is related to malnutrition of skin due to factors including improper diet, overexertion, deficiency of qi and blood, emotional depression, blood stasis due to qi stagnation, over-indulgence or deficiency of both yin and yang. Modern medicine considers that this condition is a type of dermatitis with unknown reasons resulting from vitamin deficiencies or cosmetics irritation.

I. Cosmetic acupuncture

1. Filiform needle

1.1　Selection of acupoints: Ganshu (BL 18), Pishu (BL 20), Shenshu (BL 23), Taichong (LR 3) [or Xingjian (LR 2)], Hegu (LI 4), Xuehai (SP 10), Quchi (LI 11), Zusanli (ST 36), Taixi (KI 3) and Sanyinjiao (SP 6).

1.2　Method: Each time 5 acupoints were selected for filiform needling. Except for reinforcing manipulations on back-Shu acupoints, Zusanli (ST 36) and Taixi (KI 3), the other acupoints were punctured with even reinforcing-reducing manipulations and manipulated once every 5 minutes. The needles retained for 30 minutes. And 10 - 15 times make up one treatment course.

2. Auricular needle

2.1　Selection of acupoints: ear-Shenmen, sympathetic nerve, adrenal gland, endocrine, Zigong (uterus), lung and large intestine.

2.2　Method: Each time 3 - 5 acupoints were selected for filiform needling with strong stimulation. The needles retained for 3 - 4 hours and were intermittently manipulated. The treatment was done once every day or every other day. The selected acupoints can also be applied embedding of thumb-tag

汉英对照
Chinese-English
Edition of
Acupuncture
Cosmetology

针灸美容 Part 2 The Treatment of Acupuncture Cosmetology

3. 穴位注射：

（1）取穴：三阴交、足三里、肝俞、脾俞、肾俞。

（2）方法：每次取 2 组穴位，以当归或丹参或川芎或黄芪注射液 1 支，按常规操作法，分别注射。隔日 1 次，10 次为 1 个疗程。

二、 注意事项

1. 怡情养志，调摄情绪。

2. 起居有常，劳逸结合。

3. 积极治疗原发病症。

第三节　皱纹

皱纹，即皮肤皱纹，分假性和真性两种，前者是指皮肤水分减少所产生的小皱纹，皮下脂肪减少所产生的暂时性皱纹；后者是指由假性皱纹进一步发展导致面部弹性纤维退化萎缩所产生的皱纹。可见假性是真性的前期阶段。多见于面部，尤其是额部、眼部鱼尾纹。针灸治疗应把握在假性皱纹阶段，通过穴位刺激，促使皮肤功能活化，增加和保持皮肤水分与脂肪。

中医学认为，本病与饮食不调、劳倦过度、脾胃虚弱或恣情纵欲、年老体衰，精血亏耗，肌肤失养有关。西医学认为，本病的发生是由于维持皮肤正常张力的弹性纤维减少，皮脂腺分泌减弱，皮下脂肪减少，使皮肤与其深部组织之间过于松弛而折叠形成。

一、 针灸美容法

1. 毫针：

汉英对照
Chinese-English
Edition of
Acupuncture
Cosmetology
针灸美容
中篇 ● 针灸美容治疗

needles once every 3 - 5 days, and 10 times make up one treatment course.

3. Acupoint injection

3.1   Selection of acupoints: Sanyinjiao (SP 6), Zusanli (ST 36), Ganshu (BL 18), Pishu (BL 20) and Shenshu (BL 23).

3.2   Method: Each time two pairs of acupoints were selected for 1-tube injection of Danggui (*Radix Ligustici Angelicae*) or Huangqi (*Radix Astragali*) injection respectively by routine procedure. The injection was done once every other day and 10 times make up one treatment course.

Ⅱ. **Precautions**

1. Keep a peaceful mind.

2. Keep a regular life style and balance work and rest.

3. Get active treatment of primary diseases.

Section 3　Wrinkles

Wrinkles, i.e., the skin wrinkles, has two types: pseudo ones (fine surface lines) and true ones (deep furrows), the former refers to small wrinkles due to reduction of water content or temporary wrinkles due to reduction of subcutaneous fat; while the latter refers to wrinkles due to degeneration or atrophy of facial elastic fiber as a result of further progression of the former. Regarded as the early-stage of the true wrinkles, the pseudo wrinkles mostly appear in the face, especially forehead and ocular regions as crow's feet or fishtail lines. Acupuncture intervention shall be applied for pseudo wrinkles to activate the skin function, increase and maintain the water content as well as fat of the skin through stimulating acupoints.

TCM holds that wrinkles are related to essence-blood

汉英对照
Chinese-English
Edition of
Acupuncture
Cosmetology

针灸美容 Part 2 The Treatment of Acupuncture Cosmetology

（1）取穴：额纹：皱纹局部、四白、印堂、头维、头临泣（见图 25）、上星、足三里；鱼尾纹：皱纹局部、丝竹空、瞳子髎、太阳、足三里；笑纹：皱纹局部、迎香、颧髎、颊车、夹承浆（见图 26）、合谷；颈纹：皱纹局部、扶突、天牖（见图 27）、翳风（见图 27）、风池、三阴交。

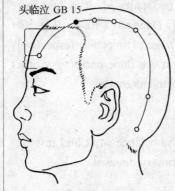

图 25　头临泣
Fig. 25　Toulinqi (GB 15)

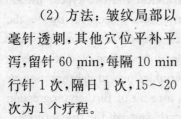

（2）方法：皱纹局部以毫针透刺，其他穴位平补平泻，留针 60 min，每隔 10 min 行针 1 次，隔日 1 次，15～20 次为 1 个疗程。

2. 灸法：

（1）取穴：皱纹局部、翳风、阳白、四白、百会、足三里、神阙。

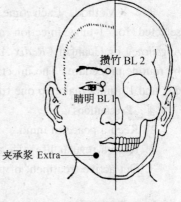

攒竹 BL 2

睛明 BL 1

夹承浆 Extra

图 26　夹承浆
Fig. 26　Jiachengjiang (Extra)

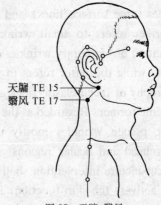

天牖 TE 15
翳风 TE 17

图 27　天牖、翳风
Fig. 27　Tianyou (TE 15) and
Yifeng (TE 17)

exhaustion and malnutrition of skin due to factors including improper diet, overexertion, deficiency of the spleen and stomach, or over-indulgence and aging process. Modern medicine considers that wrinkles, or folding of skin are caused by excessive loose between skin and its deeper tissues resulting from reduction of elastic fiber in maintaining normal tension of skin, decrease of sebaceous gland secretion as well as reduction of subcutaneous fat.

I. Cosmetic acupuncture

1. Filiform needle

1.1 Selection of acupoints: For wrinkles in forehead: local area, Sibai (ST 2), Yintang (EX-HN 3), Touwei (ST 8), Toulinqi (GB 15) (See Fig. 25), Shangxing (GV 23), and Zusanli (ST 36); For Crow's feet: local area, Sizhukong (TE 23), Tongziliao (GB 1), Taiyang (EX-HN 5), and Zusanli (ST 36); For laughter lines: local area, Yingxiang (LI 20), Quanliao (SI 18), Jiache (ST 6), Jiachengjiang (Extra) and Hegu (LI 4); and for neck lines: local area, Futu (LI 18), Tianyou (TE 16) (See Fig. 27), Yifeng (TE 17) (See Fig. 27), Fengchi (GB 20) and Sanyinjiao (SP 6).

1.2 Method: Except for puncturing from one side toward the other side, the other acupoints were punctured with even reinforcing-reducing manipulation. The needles retained for 1 hour and were manipulated once every 10 minutes. The treatment was done once every other day and 15 – 20 times make up one treatment course.

2. Moxibustion

2.1 Selection of acupoints: local area, Yifeng (TE 17), Yangbai (GB 14), Baihui (GV 20), Zusanli (ST 36) and Shenque (CV 8).

汉英对照

Chinese-English
Edition of
Acupuncture
Cosmetology

针灸美容 Part 2 The Treatment of Acupuncture Cosmetology

（2）方法：神阙以隔姜或隔盐灸，每次 3 壮，其他诸穴用艾条温和灸，每穴 10 min，以局部皮肤潮红为度，隔日 1 次，30 次为 1 个疗程。

3. 耳针：

（1）取穴：皱纹相应区耳穴、心、脾、肾、肝、内分泌、神门、皮质下、肾上腺。

（2）方法：每次选 5～8 个穴位，以毫针针刺，留针 30 min，每 10 min 行针 1 次，隔日 1 次，20～30 次为 1 个疗程。或以揿针、王不留行籽埋穴，每日按压 4 次，每穴 10 下，3～5 日 1 换，15～20 次为 1 个疗程。

4. 激光疗法：

（1）取穴：皱纹局部。

（2）方法：以氦氖激光治疗仪在距离皱纹局部 10 cm 处照射，每次 10～15 min，隔日 1 次，15～20 次为 1 个疗程。

二、 注意事项

1. 调摄情志，均衡营养，起居有常，劳逸结合。

2. 注意皮肤的清洁卫生，但不要过多清洗，每日早晚以温、冷水交替按摩面部。避免暴晒。

2.2 Method: Except for 3 zhuang of ginger- or salt-partitioned moxibustion on Shenque (CV 8), the other acupoints were applied moderate moxibustion by moxa stick, 10 minutes for each acupoint until the local skin turned slightly red. The treatment was done once every other day and 30 times make up one treatment course.

3. Auricular needle

3.1 Selection of acupoints: the corresponding ear acupoints of the wrinkle areas, heart, spleen, kidney, liver, endocrine, ear-Shenmen, subcortex and adrenal gland.

3.2 Method: Each time 5 - 8 acupoints were selected for filiform needling. The needles retained for 30 minutes and were manipulated once every 10 minutes. The treatment was done once every other day, and 20 - 30 times make up one treatment course. The selected acupoints can also be applied embedding thumb-tag needles or cowherb seeds, 4 times of self-pressure every day, 10 times for each acupoint, changed once every 3 - 5 days and 5 - 20 times make up one treatment course.

4. Laser therapy

4.1 Selection of acupoint: local area.

4.2 Method: He-Ne laser therapeutic instrument was applied for radiation at 10 cm away from the local wrinkles, 10 -15 minutes each time, once every other day and 15 - 20 times make up one treatment course.

Ⅱ. Precautions

1. Keep a peaceful mind, well-balanced diet, regular life style and balanced work and rest.

2. Keep local skin clean but avoid too much washing; massage face with alternate warm and cold water; and avoid sun exposure.

第四节　消瘦

消瘦,是指体重低于标准体重的 20% 以上。可发生于任何年龄。

中医学认为,本病的发生多由于先天不足、素体虚弱或饮食偏嗜,或情志抑郁,恣情纵欲等气血亏虚、肌肤失养而致。西医学认为,本病的发生多与遗传因素、精神因素、自身消化吸收功能、饮食习惯、内分泌疾病以及慢性消耗性疾病等因素有关。

一、针灸美容法

1. 毫针

(1) 取穴:肝俞、脾俞、肾俞、中脘、章门、足三里、天枢、气海、关元、太冲、太溪、神门。

(2) 方法:毫针针刺,行补法。留针 20~30 min。隔日 1 次,15~20 次为 1 个疗程。

2. 灸法:

(1) 取穴:神阙、肝俞、脾俞、肾俞、百会、中脘、章门、足三里、天枢、气海、关元、大椎。

(2) 方法:神阙、气海、中脘、关元、大椎可用隔姜灸,其他穴位可用艾条温灸,以局部皮肤潮红为度。

Section 4　Emaciation

Emaciation refers to the condition that the body weight is less than 20% of the standard body weight and can occur to all age groups.

TCM holds that this condition is caused by deficiency of qi and blood and malnutrition of skin due to such factors as congenital weak constitution, partiality of food, or emotional depression or over-indulgence. Modern medicine considers that the condition is related to such aspects as hereditary factor, mental factor, auto-digestive and absorptive function, dietary habit, endocrine disease and chronic consumptive disease.

Ⅰ. **Cosmetic acupuncture**

1. Filiform needle

1.1　Selection of acupoints: Ganshu (BL 18), Pishu (BL 20), Shenshu (BL 23), Zhongwan (CV 12), Zusanli (ST 36), Tianshu (ST 25), Qihai (CV 6), Guanyuan (CV 4), Taichong (LR 3), Taixi (KI 3) and Shenmen (HT 7).

1.2　Method: The acupoints were punctured with reinforcing manipulation. The needles retained for 20 – 30 minutes each time, once every other day and 15 – 20 times make up one treatment course.

2. Moxibustion

2.1　Selection of acupoints: Shenque (CV 8), Ganshu (BL 18), Pishu (BL 20), Shenshu (BL 23), Baihui (GV 20), Zhongwan (CV 12), Zhangmen (LR 13), Zusanli (ST 36), Tianshu (ST 25), Qihai (CV 6), Guanyuan (CV 4) and Dazhui (GV 14).

2.2　Method: Except for ginger-partitioned moxibustion on acupoints Shenque (CV 8), Qihai (CV 6), Zhongwan (CV 12), Guanyuan (CV 4) and Dazhui (GV 14), the other

汉英对照
Chinese-English
Edition of
Acupuncture
Cosmetology

针灸美容 Part 2 The Treatment of Acupuncture Cosmetology

3. 耳针：

(1) 取穴：脾、肝、肾、胃、大肠、神门、皮质下、内分泌、肾上腺。

(2) 方法：每次选用 5 个穴位,以王不留行籽埋穴,每日按压 4～5 次,每穴 10 下,3～5 d 1 换,10 次为 1 个疗程。

4. 穴位注射：

(1) 取穴：足三里、关元、气海、三阴交、脾俞、肾俞、肝俞。

(2) 方法：每次取 2～3 穴,以黄芪注射液或当归注射液 1 支注射。每周 1～2 次,10 次为 1 个疗程。

二、 注意事项

1. 怡情乐志,保持心情愉悦。

2. 适当加强饮食,多进食硬果类、菇类等含蛋白、脂类丰富的食物。

3. 增强体质锻炼,起居有常,劳逸结合。

4. 积极治疗原发病,调整机体的平衡。

第五节　眼袋

眼袋,是指眼睑下垂、局部隆起如袋状为主要特征的症状。多发生在下眼睑。有先天性与后天性两种。前者属于遗传,后者多由于眼睑皮肤长期受到不良刺激,如不正确按摩,爱流眼泪,长画眼线,导致眼睑皮肤松弛并萎缩而致。多见于中老年人。

acupoints were applied moxa-stick moderate moxibustion until the local skin turned slightly red.

3. Auricular needle

3.1 Selection of acupoints: spleen, liver, kidney, stomach, large intestine, ear-Shenmen, subcortex, endocrine and adrenal gland.

3.2 Method: Each time 5 acupoints were selected for embedding cowherb seeds, 4 - 5 times of self-pressure every day, and 10 times for each acupoint. The seeds were changed once every 3 - 5 days and 10 times make up one treatment course.

4. Acupoint injection

4.1 Selection of acupoints: Zusanli (ST 36), Guanyuan (CV 4), Qihai (CV 6), Sanyinjiao (SP 6), Pishu (BL 20), Shenshu (BL 23) and Ganshu (BL 18).

4.2 Method: Each time 2 - 3 acupoints were injected 1 tube of Huangqi (*Radix Astragali*) or Danggui (*Radix Ligustici Angelicae*) injection 1 - 2 times per week, and 10 times make up one treatment course.

Ⅱ. Precautions

1. Keep a peaceful and joyful mind.

2. Take well-balanced diet, especially more food rich in protein and lipoid such as hard nuts and mushrooms.

3. Do physical exercises; keep a regular life style and balance work and rest.

4. Get active treatment of primary diseases and regulate the body balance.

Section 5　Baggy eyelids

Baggy eyelids commonly occur to the lower eyelids in

中医学认为,本病多由于脾肾虚损,气血不足,无以上养或水湿内停,阻滞脉络而致。西医学认为,本病是由于眼睑皮肤松弛或眼轮匝肌过于肥厚、眶隔内脂肪球堆积而致。

一、 针灸美容法

1. 毫针:

(1) 取穴:眼袋局部、四白、瞳子髎、太阳、睛明、照海、申脉(见图 11)。

(2) 方法:以毫针针刺局部,行平补平泻法。隔日 1 次,10～15 次为 1 个疗程。

2. 电针:

(1) 取穴:眼袋局部、四白。

(2) 方法:毫针针刺后,接电针仪,以疏密波,见眼袋局部肌肉明显收缩,以求美者可接受为度,通电 20～30 min。每日或隔日 1 次,10 次为 1 个疗程。

汉英对照

Chinese-English
Edition of
Acupuncture
Cosmetology

针灸美容

中篇 ◉ 针灸美容治疗

middle or aged people and are mainly characterized by droopy eyelids and local bulging or enlarging like bags. They can be congenital or acquired; the former is due to heredity, while the latter is caused by loosened or atrophic skin of eyelid skin resulting from long-term pessimal stimulation such as incorrect massage, frequent lacrimation and make-up of drawing eye lines.

TCM holds that this condition is caused by either deficiency of qi and blood failing to nourish eyes or water-dampness retention obstructing meridians due to deficiency of the spleen and stomach. Modern medicine considers that this condition can be caused by loosened skin of eyelids or over-thickening of orbicularis muscle and deposit of oil globule inside orbital septum.

I. Cosmetic acupuncture

1. Filiform needle

1.1　Selection of acupoints: local area, Sibai (ST 2), Tongziliao (GB 1), Taiyang (EX-HN 5), Jingming (BL 1), Zhaohai (KI 6) and Shenmai (BL 62)(See Fig. 11).

1.2　Method: the local areas were punctured with even reinforcing-reducing manipulation, once every other day and 10 -15 times make up one treatment course.

2. Electric acupuncture

2.1　Selection of acupoints: local area and Sibai (ST 2).

2.2　Method: The electric stimulator was connected to the filiform needles for 20 - 30 minutes with intermittent wave; the intensity is up the patients' tolerance with obvious contracture of the local baggy muscle. The treatment was done once every day or every other day and 10 times make up one treatment course.

汉英对照

Chinese-English Edition of Acupuncture Cosmetology

针灸美容

Part 2 The Treatment of Acupuncture Cosmetology

汉英对照

Chinese-English
Edition of
Acupuncture
Cosmetology

针灸美容

中篇 ◎ 针灸美容治疗

3. 灸法：

（1）取穴：眼袋局部、足三里。

（2）方法：以艾条温和灸，每穴 10～15 min，以局部红晕为度。10 次为 1 个疗程。

4. 穴位敷贴：

（1）取穴：眼袋局部。

（2）方法：以黑豆研细末，茶水调成糊状，夜敷局部，次晨取下。每日 1 次，10 次为 1 个疗程。

5. 激光疗法：

（1）取穴：眼袋局部。

（2）方法：求美者双眼紧闭，用低功率氦氖激光，照射局部，每次 10～15 min，每日或隔日 1 次，10 次为 1 个疗程。

二、 注意事项

1. 注意情志调摄，劳逸结合，注意睡眠质量。

2. 增加营养并使营养均衡，可多进食瓜果蔬菜等维生素含量丰富的食物。

3. 可用稍强的指力，自行按摩局部，以局部皮肤发热出现红晕为度。

3. Moxibustion

3.1 Selection of acupoints: local area and Zusanli (ST 36).

3.2 Method: the selected places were applied with moxa-stick moderation moxibustion, 10 – 15 minutes for each acupoint until the local skin turned red, and 10 times make up one treatment course.

4. Acupoint application

4.1 Selection of acupoints: local area.

4.2 Method: The local area was applied the paste made from fine powder of black bean with tea water at night and removed the next morning. The treatment was done once every day and 10 times make up one treatment course.

5. Laser therapy

5.1 Selection of acupoints: local area.

5.2 Method: The low-frequency He-Ne laser instrument was applied to radiate the local area after the patient's eyes were closed, 10 – 15 minutes each time, once every day or every other day and 10 times make up one treatment course.

Ⅱ. Precautions

1. Keep a peaceful mind, balance work and rest and take care of the sleep quality.

2. Take well-balanced diet, especially more food rich in vitamins such as fruits and vegetables.

3. Apply self-massage on local area with slightly stronger finger power until the local skin turned red and warm.

下篇
针灸美容典型验案

Part 3
The Typical Case Reports of Acupuncture Cosmetology

汉英对照

Chinese-English
Edition of
Acupuncture
Cosmetology

针灸美容 下篇 ● 针灸美容典型验案

第十章 皮肤科病症的典型验案

第一节 黄褐斑

一、验案1

崔某,女,39岁,会计。2000年1月8日初诊。

主诉:10年前无明显诱因,面颊及唇周出现淡褐色斑,并逐渐加重,尤以近4年明显。伴有失眠、偏头痛,重时头痛如针刺,月经先期,色暗有块,大便秘结3～7 d一行。曾自做面部按摩、面膜美容等,口服中成药治疗,疗效不明显。刻诊:面色灰黄,布满黄褐色斑,额部、眼周、双侧面颊及唇周颜色呈深褐色;失眠,健忘,疲乏无力,右侧头部刺痛,胁肋胀痛,心烦易怒。此次月经提前1周来潮,色暗有血块,大便秘结,舌质暗红、少苔,脉沉细涩。诊断:黄褐斑。证属肝气郁结,气滞血瘀。治以疏肝理气,活血化瘀。采用飞腾八法即时开穴后溪,配以申脉,配大椎穴,以三棱针点刺3针后拔火罐,出血约1 ml,血色呈紫色。治疗3次后黄褐斑均变浅,面色由灰黄渐见红色。治疗1个疗程后,患者大部分色斑消退,尤以额部、眼周围消退明显,但口周色斑仍较明显,5个疗程后患者面色皮肤红润光泽,黄褐斑完全消退而告痊愈,伴随偏头痛、失眠症状明显改善,心烦易怒症状消失,月经如时来潮,色红无血块。

Chapter 10
The typical case reports of dermatology conditions

Section 1   Chloasma

Case 1

Cui, female, 39 years old, an accountant, came for the first visit on Jan. 8, 2000.

Chief complaints: The patient got light tan patches in cheeks and around lips 10 years ago without obvious inducing factors, and the patches gradually worsened, especially in the recent 4 years. Accompanying symptoms include: insomnia, migraine with stabling pain sensation in severe attacks, a preceded period containing blood clots in dark color, and constipation (one bowel movement every 3 - 7 days). Previous treatment: self-facial massage, cosmetic facial-mask and oral administration of patterned Chinese herbal products. Present symptoms and signs: gray-sallow complexion with yellow brown patches, deep brown patches in forehead, around eye sockets, bilateral cheeks and around lips, insomnia, poor memory, fatigue, right-sided stabling migraine, hypochondriac distension and pain, restlessness and irritability, period occurred 1 week earlier containing blood clots in dark color, constipation, a deep-red tongue with scanty coating and a deep, thready and hesitant pulse. Diagnosis: chloasma. TCM pattern: liver-qi stagnation and blood stasis. Therapeutic principle: to regulate liver-qi and circulate blood to resolve stasis. The eight methods of intelligent turtle were adopted to select the following three acupoints: Houxi (SI 3), Shenmai (BL 62) and Dazhui (GV

　　按语：飞腾八法治疗黄褐斑，是根据不调时辰人体经脉气血周流的变化，按时取一组八脉交会穴治疗，以协调全身阴阳、调理脏腑经络、益气养血、调节冲任、活血化瘀、疏通经络，使气血得以上荣于面，达到治疗目的。黄褐斑的主要病机为瘀血阻滞，气血不能上荣，刺血拔罐来使脉络通畅，气血上承，色斑消退。治疗期间，患者久病阴虚，可内服六味地黄丸调养，并尽量避免夏日强烈日光照射。

　　二、　验案2

　　张某，女，42岁。

14). The three acupoints were pricked with three-edged needle for about 1 ml of blood in purple color. After 3 times of treatment, the patient's yellow brown patches all turned light and her facial complexion turned from gray-sallow to red. After one treatment course, most of her pigmentation spots disappeared, especially those in forehead and around eye sockets, but those around lips still remained. After 5 treatment courses, the patient's skin turned red and lustrous and her chloasma completely disappeared. In addition, her migraine and insomnia were obviously improved, her restlessness and irritability disappeared, and her period came on time in red color but without blood clots.

Remarks: The eight methods of intelligent turtle for chloasma are based on the ancient theories of selecting a pair of eight confluent acupoints according to qi and blood circulation cycles of human meridians in terms of the day and hour to coordinate yin-yang, regulate zang-fu organs and meridians, supplement qi, nourish blood, regulate Chong and Ren meridians, circulate blood to resolve stasis, dredge meridians and ascend qi and blood to nourish the face. The major pathogenesis of chloasma lies in stagnant blood obstructing qi and blood from ascending to nourish the face. Cupping following blood-letting can clear meridians and ascend qi and blood to remove pigmentation spots. During the treatment, the patients may also take Liu Wei Di Huang Wan (a patterned Chinese herbal product) for yin deficiency and try to avoid intense sun exposure in summer months.

Case 2

Zhang, female, 42 years old.

Chief complaints: more than one year of facial

汉英对照
Chinese-English
Edition of
Acupuncture
Cosmetology

针灸美容

下篇◎针灸美容典型验案

主诉：面部色素沉着年余。患者1年前出现面部色素沉着，并逐渐加深。伴神疲、失眠、月经量少色淡，舌淡苔白，脉细。诊断：黄褐斑。证属气血虚弱，不能上荣于面部，皮肤失于濡润而致色素沉着。治以调理气血，补益脏腑，祛斑美容。针刺局部斑块、合谷（双）、三阴交（双）、足三里（双）、脾俞（双）、肾俞（双）、肝俞（双），补虚泻实，得气后留针30 min，每日1次，10次为1个疗程。贴压耳穴：面颊、肺、肝、脾、肾、内分泌、神门、卵巢、内生殖器、子宫，两耳交替贴压。经第一个疗程治疗后，斑色变浅，兼症好转，5个疗程后，黄褐斑消失，随访1年，未见复发。

按语：针刺局部色斑可疏调经气，活血化瘀，改善局部营养，增强细胞再生，清除堆积废物，促进色斑消退。体穴多取多气多血的手足阳明经，加上背俞穴，能调整肝、脾、肾的功能。"十二经脉三百六十五络，其气皆上于面而走空窍，其别气走于耳而为之听"。通过刺激与黄褐斑有关的耳穴，达到疏通经络、调和气血、活血化瘀、滋补肝肾的目的，最终获得祛斑美容的效果。

pigmentation. One year ago, the patient got facial pigmentation that gradually worsened. Accompanying symptoms and signs include: fatigue, insomnia, scanty menstruation in light color, a pale tongue with white coating, and a thready pulse. Diagnosis: chloasma. TCM syndrome pattern: deficiency of qi and blood failing to nourish the face and malnutrition or lack of moistening of the face. Therapeutic principle: to regulate qi and blood, tonify zang-fu organs and remove colored patches. Method: the local area, bilateral Hegu (LI 4), bilateral Sanyinjiao (SP 6), bilateral Zusanli (ST 36), bilateral Pishu (BL 20), bilateral Shenshu (BL 23) and bilateral Ganshu (BL 18) were punctured with reinforcing manipulation for deficient syndrome or reducing manipulation for excessive syndrome. The needles retained for 30 minutes, once every day and 10 times make up one treatment course. Auricular acupoints: cheek, lung, liver, spleen, kidney, endocrine, ear-Shenmen, ovary, inner genitalia, and Zigong (uterus). The two ears were applied seeds alternately. After the first visit course, the patient's pigmentation color turned light and her accompanying symptoms got improved. After 5 treatment courses, her chloasma disappeared. The one-year follow-up didn't found any relapse.

Remarks: Needling the colored spots can regulate meridian-qi, circulate blood to resolve stasis, improve local nutrition, enhance cell regeneration, and clear the deposit of wastes as well as pigmentation spots. Acupoints of Yang-ming meridians of both hand and foot that are full of qi and blood plus back-Shu acupoints can regulate the functions of the liver, spleen and kidney. Based on the theory that "qi of 12 regulate meridians and 365 collaterals ascends to face and qi of their divergent

汉英对照
Chinese-English
Edition of
Acupuncture
Cosmetology

针灸美容 Part 3 The Typical Case Reports of Acupuncture Cosmetology

三、 验案 3

蔡某,女,27 岁,学生。2004 年 4 月 7 日初诊。

主诉：面部色素沉着 3 年余,近半年逐渐加深,曾用多种外用药,症状反复。伴体倦神疲、记忆力下降、纳呆便溏、月经量少色淡,舌淡苔白,脉沉细。诊断：黄褐斑。查体：面部双侧见色素沉着,面积 2~4 cm^2,颜色淡深相间。取皮损局部消毒,采用美容针在皮损局部多针围刺,以将病处包围为宜。再取曲池、外关、合谷、血海、足三里、三阴交、关元、气海、列缺针刺,关元、气海行补法加灸,余穴平补平泻,两者均留针 30 min,隔日 1 次,10 次为 1 个疗程。治疗 1 个疗程后皮损区缩小,颜色变淡,治疗 3 个疗程,黄褐斑基本消失,巩固治疗 1 个疗程,随访 1 年,未见复发。

meridians reaches the ears", stimulating auricular acupoints related to chloasma can regulate meridians, harmonize qi and blood, resolve blood stasis, and nourish the liver and kidney, and eventually remove pigmentation spots.

Case 3

Cai, female, 27 years old, a student, came for the first visit on April 7, 2004.

Chief complaints: More than 3 years of facial pigmentation and worsened in the recent six months. Previous treatment: varieties of externally-applied medications got recurrent symptoms. Accompanying symptoms and signs include: fatigue or lassitude, poor memory, a poor appetite with loose stool, scanty menstruation in light color, a pale tongue with white coating and a deep and thready pulse. Diagnosis: chloasma. Physical examination showed: bilateral facial pigmentation sized $2 - 4$ cm^2, in light-deep striated color. Method: The local skin lesion area was applied with surrounding puncture by cosmetic needles. The selected body acupoints include Quchi (LI 11), Waiguan (TE 5), Hegu (LI 4), Xuehai (SP 10), Zusanli (ST 36), Sanyinjiao (SP 6), Guanyuan (CV 4), Qihai (CV 6) and Lieque (LU 7). Except for reinforcing manipulation plus moxibustion on Guanyuan (CV 4) and Qihai (CV 6), the other acupoints were punctured with even reinforcing-reducing manipulation. The needles retained for 30 minutes, and the treatment was done once every other day and 10 times make up one treatment course. After one treatment course, the skin lesion area was reduced and the color turned lighter. After three treatment courses, the chloasma basically disappeared. Then another treatment course was applied to consolidate the effect, and the 1-year follow-up didn't find any

汉英对照
Chinese-English Edition of Acupuncture Cosmetology
针灸美容 Part 3 The Typical Case Reports of Acupuncture Cosmetology

按语：美容针能疏通局部气血，改善色斑局部的血液循环，且损伤较小，容易让求美者接受。配合体穴整体调整而获得满意效果。治疗同时嘱咐患者忌食肥甘辛辣，防止日光暴晒，停止使用化妆品，每日温水洗脸，多吃蔬菜瓜果，调整情志也是取效的必要之举。

第二节　痤疮

一、验案 1

刘某，男，28 岁。2001 年 3 月就诊。

主诉：面部痤疮 2 年余。查肤色潮红，额部、面颊痤疮密集，且有脓疱，兼见心烦、便秘、舌尖红、苔薄黄、脉弦数。证属肺经风热型。用针刺大椎、合谷、内庭、足三里配合大椎、耳尖放血，针刺隔日 1 次，10 次为 1 个疗程，共治疗 3 个疗程；耳穴取面颊、额、皮质下、神门、三焦、肺、大肠，以王不留行籽贴压，5～7 d 更换。疗程结束后新皮疹未出现，痤疮炎症逐日减轻，排便正常，至今未复发。

汉英对照

Chinese-English
Edition of
Acupuncture
Cosmetology

针灸美容

下篇 ● 针灸美容典型验案

relapse.

Remarks: Cosmetic needle can regulate local circulation of qi and blood and improve blood flow of the affected area. In addition, it is easily accepted by patients for its small invasive effect. The body acupoints are helpful for the satisfactory results through regulating the whole body. During the treatment, the patient was recommended to avoid sweet, spicy and fatty food, prevent too much sun exposure, stop cosmetics, wash face with warm water every day, take more fruits and vegetables, and keep a peaceful mind.

Section 2　Acne

Case 1

Liu, male, 28 years old, came for the first visit in March 2001.

Chief complaints: More than 2 years of facial acne. Physical examination showed: flush facial color and densely-distributed acnes in forehead and cheeks including pustules. Accompanying symptoms and signs include: restlessness, constipation, a red tongue tip with thin and yellow coating and a wiry and rapid pulse. TCM syndrome pattern: the wind-heat of the lung meridian. Method: to puncture the acupoints Dazhui (GV 14), Hegu (LI 4), Neiting (ST 44) and Zusanli (ST 36) and combine blood letting on Dazhui (GV 14) and ear apex. The acupuncture was done once every other day, 10 times make up one treatment course and 3 courses of treatment were applied to the patient; in addition, to apply cowherb seeds on ear acupoints including cheek, forehead, subcortex, ear-Shenmen, Sanjiao, lung, and large intestine and change the seeds once every 5 - 7 days. After three treatment courses of

按语：大椎是督脉穴位中具有调整整体治疗作用的代表穴，具有疏风解表、泄热降逆作用，三棱针点刺该穴配合耳尖放血可增强泄热功效；配合阳明经的合谷、内庭、足三里达到清热除湿、调理气血及脏腑功能，以消除痤疮的功效。

二、验案 2

高某，女，30 岁。

主诉：面部痤疮反复发作 6 个月。每于食油炸海鲜之品及饮酒后面部出现密集痤疮，大如黄豆，小如粟米，可挤出白色粉状物，个别是脓疱，触诊摸之碍手。伴口干口臭，便秘，舌红，苔黄腻，脉滑数。证属肺胃蕴热，热毒上攻。治以宣肺清热化湿。三棱针点刺大椎、肺俞（双）、心俞（双）、膈俞（双）、胃俞（双）、大肠俞（双），每次取 3～4 个穴位，点刺后，拔火罐 5 min，吸出少许血，每日 1 次，10 次为 1 个疗程。贴压耳穴肺、大肠、心、内分泌、肾上腺、面颊区、额，两耳交替贴压，每日按压 4 次，10 d 为 1 个疗程。经第一个疗程治疗后，痤疮数量减少，大便通畅，治疗 3 个疗程后痤疮全部消失，痊愈。

acupuncture plus ear seeds, no new skin rashes appeared and the acne inflammation relieved day by day, the bowel movement got normal and no relapse until now.

Remarks: Dazhui (GV 14), a representative acupoint of Governor Vessel acupoints in regulating the whole body, can remove wind, clear away heat and down-regulate adverse flow of qi. Pricking this acupoints and blood-letting on ear apex can enhance the heat-clearing effect. In addition, the acupoints Hegu (LI 4), Neiting (ST 44) and Zusanli (ST 36) were combined to clear away heat, remove dampness, regulate qi, blood and function of zang-fu organs and eventually remove acne.

Case 2

Gao, female, 30 years old.

Chief complaints: Six months of recurrent facial acne. Acnes in different sizes (big as soybean and small as millet) always appear after fried seafood or alcohol drinking that can be squeezed white farina, including pustules that feel rough by palpation. Accompanying symptoms and signs include: a dry and foul breath, constipation, a red tongue with yellow and greasy coating and a slippery and rapid pulse. TCM syndrome pattern: the accumulated heat in the lung and stomach and toxic-heat ascending to the face. Therapeutic principle: to promote flow of lung-qi, clear away heat and resolve dampness. Method: Each time 3 - 4 acupoints among Dazhui (GV 14), bilateral Feishu (BL 13), Xinshu (BL 15), Geshu (BL 17), Weishu (BL 21) were selected for pricking and followed by 5 minutes of cupping with a little bit bleeding. The treatment was done once every day and 10 times make up one treatment course. In addition ear seeds were applied to two ears

汉英对照

Chinese-English
Edition of
Acupuncture
Cosmetology

针灸美容

下篇 ◉ 针灸美容典型验案

　　按语：点刺大椎穴是常用的治疗痤疮的方法，能清热解毒、解表解肌。其他诸穴合用能增强驱邪逐瘀、热毒外泄之功效，即"宛陈则除之"。贴压耳穴，尤其是耳穴心，"诸痛痒疮，皆属于心"以泻火止痒，配合诸穴改善面部血液循环，达到消炎退疮的功效。治疗期间嘱咐患者忌食腥腻辛辣之品，多食瓜果蔬菜，防止便秘，注意面部清洁，加强身体锻炼。

　　三、验案3

　　患者，女，26岁。1999年4月就诊。

　　主诉：面部痤疮5年，加重1个月。初起面部少量粉刺，因经常搔抓渐至感染、发红、起脓头，曾用多种中西药治疗，效果不佳。诊见：患者面部大部为红色痤疮，部分紫红色，同时伴数个黄豆大皮下硬结，个别呈脓疱性，舌苔薄黄，脉滑数。耳尖略加按摩，使之充血。用三棱针点刺，挤出5～10滴血，用干棉花擦净。取耳穴肺、胃、面颊、内分泌、肾上腺、皮质下，以王不留行籽贴压，每日按压4～5次，每3～4 d 1换，两耳交替。针刺大椎、肺俞、合谷、膈俞、足三里，毫针泻法，留针30 min，每日或隔日1次，7次为1个疗程。治疗3个疗程，诸疹皆平，结节消失，肤色亮泽晶莹，迄今未复发。

alternately on such auricular acupoints as lung, large intestine, heart, endocrine, adrenal gland, cheek and forehead, 4 times of self-pressure every day, and 10 times make up one treatment course. After one treatment course, the acnes reduced in number and the bowel movement got normal. After three treatment courses, her acnes completely disappeared.

Remarks: Pricking Dazhui (GV 14) is one of the common methods for acne, for this acupoint can clear away heat, remove toxin and relieve the exterior. The combination of other acupoints can enhance the effect of resolving stasis and removing toxic-heat, i. e. , the ancient theory of "stagnant blood has to be removed". Auricular acupoints, especially heart can reduce heart-fire and stop itching on the basis of "pain, itching or ulcers all involve with heart". Other combined acupoints can work together to improve local blood circulation and remove acnes. During the treatment, the patient was recommended to avoid seafood and spicy food, take more fruits and vegetables to prevent constipation, keep face clean and do more physical exercises.

Case 3

One patient, female, 26 years old, came for the first visit in April 1999.

Chief complaints: Five years of facial acne and worsened in recent one month. At first a small number of pimples occurred on the face, however, frequent scratching led to infection, redness and pustules. The patient tried varieties of Chinese and Western medications but didn't get good effect. Physical examination: most acne appeared red, some in purple, and several soybean-sized subcutaneous indurations were visible, including some pustules, thin and yellow coating and a slippery

汉英对照
Chinese-English
Edition of
Acupuncture
Cosmetology

针灸美容

Part 3 The Typical Case Reports of Acupuncture Cosmetology

按语:"耳者,宗脉之所聚也"。通过耳穴贴压能舒畅相应经络,激发机体免疫功能,调节体内性激素水平,降低机体的敏感性,从而达到抑制皮脂腺旺盛分泌并消炎、消肿、散结之目的。嘱咐患者要有充分睡眠,忌食辛辣厚味,切勿挤压,因而取效迅速,疗效显著。且无副作用,患者易于接受。

四、 验案 4

赵某,女,17 岁,学生。2002 年 10 月初诊。

汉英对照

Chinese-English
Edition of
Acupuncture
Cosmetology

针灸美容

下篇 ◉ 针灸美容典型验案

and rapid pulse. Method: To massage ear apex until it is congested and then to prick it with three-edged needle for 5 - 10 drops of blood and clean it with dry cotton; to apply cowherb seeds to two ears alternately on ear acupoints including lung, stomach, cheek, endocrine, adrenal gland and subcortex, 4 - 5 times of self-pressure every day and the seeds were changed once every 3 - 4 days. The body acupoints Dazhui (GV 14), Feishu (BL 13), Hegu (LI 4), Geshu (BL 17) and Zusanli (ST 36) were punctured with reducing manipulation by filiform needle. The needles retained for 30 minutes, once every day or every other day and 7 times make up one treatment course. After three treatment courses, the acne and indurations all disappeared, the patient restored a lustrous complexion and no relapse until now.

Remarks: Based on the theory that "ears are gathering places of meridians", application of ear seeds can regulate the corresponding meridians, activate immune function of the organism, regulate the level of sex hormone, reduce the sensitivity of the body and therefore inhibit the excessive secretion of sebaceous gland and remove inflammation, swelling and indurations. During the treatment, the patient was recommended to have adequate sleep, avoid spicy and fatty food, and prevent squeezing the acne. This therapy is easy to be accepted for its fast and marked effect without adverse reactions.

Case 4

Zhao, female, 17 years old, a student, came for the first visit in October 2002.

Chief complaints: Two years of recurrent facial herpes and worsened in recent days with abscess and pain in nasal tip. She

汉英对照

Chinese-English
Edition of
Acupuncture
Cosmetology

针灸美容

下篇 ● 针灸美容典型验案

主诉：颜面部反复发作疱疹 2 年，近日加重。鼻尖部出现脓肿、疼痛，内服外用多种药物，疗效不佳。月经不调。查：两侧面颊及额头布满红斑丘疹，大如黄豆，小如米粒，部分呈脓疱，鼻尖部有一小脓肿，周围皮肤红肿。颈、背部，尤其是背部，红色丘疹较多。舌苔黄腻，舌质红，脉滑数。诊断：中医：粉刺（湿热蕴结型）；西医诊断：痤疮（Ⅲ度）。采用方法：圆利针，从灵台透至阳（见图 6），每周 1 次，留针 2 h。寻找背部阳性点（小红点），每次 3～5 个，用三棱针挑刺出血，再拔火罐 10 min，隔日 1 次。毫针取大椎、曲池、合谷、足三里、内庭、肩井，行提插泻法，得气后留针 30 min，每 5 min 行针 1 次。治疗 1 个疗程后（10 次），鼻尖部脓肿消失；2 个疗程后，面部痤疮明显减少，继续治疗 2 个疗程，痤疮全部消失，无新痤疮出现，皮肤光滑润泽。随访，无复发。

按语：中医学认为，督脉为"阳脉之海"，总督一身之阳气，其循行过程中与手、足三阳经相交会，能解阳经的热毒，大椎又为所有阳经之会穴，是解诸阳经之热毒的首选穴。古籍又云："灵台主脾热，至阳主肾热"，都能通阳泄热。三棱针加拔罐加强其清泻热毒、理血调气、疏通经络、恢复脏腑功能的作用。治疗期间嘱患者注意改变饮食习惯，忌食辛辣食物，多食蔬菜、水果，保持大便通畅，保持皮肤清洁。防治并进，效果才能满意。

had taken varieties of orally-administered medications but didn't get good effect. She also had irregular menstruation. Physical examination showed: bilateral cheeks and forehead are full of red papules in different sizes (big as soybean and small as millet), some appeared as pustules, and a small abscess on nasal tip with surrounding red and swelling skin, more red papules on the neck and back, especially back, a red tongue with yellow and greasy coating and a slippery and rapid pulse. TCM diagnosis: pimples (accumulation of dampness-heat); Western medicine diagnosis: acne (Ⅲ degree). Method: The round-sharp needle was adopted to puncture from Lingtai (GV 10) toward Zhiyang (GV 9) once every week, 2 hours each time; Each time 3 - 5 positive points (small red spots) on the back were pricked for bleeding and followed by 10 minutes of cupping, once every other day; the body acupoints Dazhui (GV 14), Quchi (LI 11), Hegu (LI 4), Zusanli (ST 36), Neiting (ST 44) and Jianjing (GB 21) were punctured by filiform needles with reducing manipulation through lifting and thrusting. The needles retained for 30 minutes and were manipulated once every 5 minutes. After one treatment course (10 times), the abscess on nasal tip disappeared. After two treatment courses, the facial acne remarkably reduced. After another two treatment courses, the acne completely disappeared and no appearance of new acne. The follow-up didn't show any relapse.

Remarks: TCM holds that Governor Vessel works as the "Sea of all yang meridians" and governs yang-qi of the whole body. It crosses with the three yang-meridians of hand and foot on its running course and therefore can remove toxic-heat of yang meridians. Dazhui (GV 14), a converging acupoint of all

第三节 雀斑

一、验案 1

万某某,女,18 岁,工人。1989 年 8 月 30 日就诊。

主诉:3 年前始,面部生雀斑。雀斑逐渐增多增大,计 26 个,最大者直径 1 mm,经用改造的电热针,即 DRZ-1 型电热针,将其随机携带的特制针具的针尖加大,成为直径 0.8～1 mm 的平头火针,并连接仪器输出线路,按照仪器操作规程,使仪表指针指在 110～140 mA 范围内,将针头对准皮损点烧灼,根据皮损组织的深浅进针,使皮损局部起小水疱或结痂,7～10 d 后痂自行脱落,半月后随访,已脱痂,全部治愈。后随访 1 年余未复发。

yang meridians, is the first choice for toxic-heat of yang meridians. The ancient classic also states that "Lingtai (GV 10) is used to clear spleen-heat and Zhiyang (GV 9) is used to clear kidney-heat", indicating the two acupoints can both activate yang and clear away heat. Pricking by three-edged needle plus cupping can enhance the effect in clearing toxic-heat, regulate qi and blood circulation, dredging meridians and restore functions of zang-fu organs. During the treatment, the patient was recommended to avoid spicy food, take more fruits and vegetables to keep normal bowel movement, and keep skin clean. Satisfactory effect always comes from both treatment and prevention.

Section 3   Freckle

Case 1

Wan, female, 18 years old, a worker, came for treatment on August 30, 1989.

Chief complaints: She started to get freckles on the face 3 years ago, and then the freckles got bigger and increased to 26 ones, and the biggest one was 1 mm in diameter. She was treated with the reworked electric heat needle, i. e. , DRZ-1 type electric heat needle. Method: To increase the needle tip of portable needle into flat-headed fire needle 0. 8 - 1 mm in diameter; next to connect the input circuit of the instrument and make the gage pointer to range of 110 - 140 mA according to the operation procedures; and then to burn the targeted skin lesion spots and insert the needle according to the depth of skin lesion to make local area either blisters or scabs. After 7 - 10 days, the scabs fell off spontaneously. The follow-up after two weeks found a complete recovery and more than one year

汉英对照

Chinese-English
Edition of
Acupuncture
Cosmetology

针灸美容

下篇 ● 针灸美容典型验案

按语：使用改造的电热针是利用电能产生热能，使全部的热效应集中在针具的尖部。治疗时，热辐射直接作用在皮损部位，根据皮损组织的深浅，随意调整电流的强度，使局部达近Ⅱ°的烧伤，结为皮痂，脱痂而愈。注意局部皮痂的保护，让其自行脱落，避免抓掉遗留斑痕。

二、 验案 2

吴某，女，23 岁，宾馆服务员。1986 年 6 月 5 日就诊。

主诉：面部雀斑痣 10 余年。检查：面部以鼻翼两旁为主，皮肤呈褐黄色斑点，形状大小不一，几乎布满整个面部，以手指压迫皮肤有瘾疹，舌淡红，苔少而滑，脉沉细弱。诊断：雀斑（水亏火炽型）。遂用温针烧灼治疗。隔 2 d 1 次，经 3 次烧灼治疗，创面结痂良好，无渗出，无感染，7 d 自行脱落，无浅迹，随访半年无复发。

按语：火针是治疗雀斑的常用的工具和有效方法。治疗中要注意每次烧灼范围不宜过多，注意保护正常组织，结痂应以自行脱落为好。

三、 验案 3

孙某，女，26 岁，工人。1990 年 7 月 17 日就诊。

214

follow-up didn't show any relapses.

Remarks: The reworked electric needle can concentrate all heat effect on tip of the needle. During the treatment, the heat radiation worked on skin lesion directly and the current intensity can be regulated according to the depth of skin lesion to make a nearly $\amalg°$ burns of the local area and subsequently to make scabs and recovery. The patient was asked to protect the local scabs to allow a spontaneous falling off.

Case 2

Wu, female, 23 years old, a hotel waitress, came for the first visit on June 5, 1986.

Chief complaints: more than 10 years of facial freckles. Physical examination: brown-yellow pigmentation spots in different shapes and sizes are scattered almost all over the face, especially the areas on both sides of the nasal wings, hidden rashes with finger pressure, a pale-red tongue with scanty and slippery pulse and a thready and weak pulse. Diagnosis: freckle (the pattern of fire hyperactivity due to water insufficiency). The patient was treated with warm-needle burning therapy once every 3 days. After 3 times of treatment, the wound surface scabbed without oozing or infection. After 7 days, the scabs fell off spontaneously without marks. The six-month follow-up didn't show any relapses.

Remarks: Fire needle is a common and effective tool for freckles. During the treatment one needs to be careful to avoid too large burning areas to protect the normal tissue and allow spontaneous falling off of scabs.

Case 3

Sun, female, 26 years old, a worker, came for the first visit on July 17, 1990.

主诉：面部雀斑 7～8 年。检查：面颊部散在十来个褐色雀斑，形状如小米粒，舌脉正常。遂用火针法治疗，隔 2 d 1 次，经 2 次治疗，雀斑全部结痂，2 周后复诊，结痂已脱落，无浅迹，随访半年，皮肤正常无复发。

按语：治疗时应注意局部勿沾水，并勿用手搔抓。

第四节　神经性皮炎

一、验案 1

朱某，男，48 岁，农民。2001 年 7 月就诊。

主诉：左腰部瘙痒、皮肤粗糙增厚 5 年。患者 5 年前左腰部瘙痒、皮肤粗糙增厚，多方治疗，收效不明显，每逢夏季加重，奇痒难忍。查：左腰部有一 10 cm×12 cm 皮损区，皮肤苔藓化，抓后呈丘疹状，经皮肤科确诊为"神经性皮炎"，故此来治。方法：双侧血海、曲池、足三里。25 号 2 寸毫针直刺，行平补平泻，留针 30 min，同时用七星梅花针叩刺皮损表面，每日 1 次，10 次为 1 个疗程。连续治疗 2 个疗程后，瘙痒完全消失，皮肤变薄变软，色泽恢复正常，追踪 2 年未复发。

汉英对照

Chinese-English
Edition of
Acupuncture
Cosmetology

针灸美容

下篇 ● 针灸美容典型验案

Chief complaints: Facial freckle for 7 – 8 years. Physical examination: about 10 millet-sized brown freckles in the facial cheek and a normal tongue and pulse. She was treated with fire needle therapy once every 3 days. After twice treatments, all freckles scabbed. The return-visit after 2 weeks showed a falling off of scabs without marks. The six-month follow-up didn't show any relapses.

Remarks: During treatment the patient shall avoid wetting the local area and scratching the area with fingers.

Section 4　Neurodermatitis
Case 1

Zhu, male, 48 years old, a farmer, came for the first visit in July 2001.

Chief complaints: Itching sensation in left-sided lumbus with rough and thickened skin for 5 years. Five years ago, the patient got itching sensation in left-sided lumbus with rough and thickened skin. Varieties of therapies didn't work well on his condition. He got intolerable itching in every summer months. Physical examination: an area of skin lesion sized 10 cm × 12 cm in left-sided lumbus with skin lichenification and papules occurred after scratching. Diagnosis of dermatology department: neurodermatitis. Method: Bilateral Xuehai (SP 10), Quchi (LI 11) and Zusanli (ST 36) were punctured perpendicularly with No. 25 2-cun filiform needles by even reinforcing-reducing manipulation. The needles retained for 30 minutes. In addition, the seven-star plum-blossom needle was used to tap the surface of skin lesion once every day and 10 times make up one treatment course. After 2 continuous treatment courses, his itching completely stopped, the skin got

汉英对照
Chinese-English Edition of Acupuncture Cosmetology
针灸美容

Part 3 The Typical Case Reports of Acupuncture Cosmetology

按语：本法运用梅花针叩刺皮部以激发经络之气，疏通经络、调整脏腑功能达到防治疾病的目的。现代研究表明，梅花针通过皮神经的调节作用，促使皮损区微循环加快，抑制介质的合成和释放，增强免疫力，从而达到消炎、镇痛、止痒的功效。配合体穴共奏扶正固本、养血活血、祛风止痒之功。

二、 验案 2

李某，女，28 岁，护士。

主诉：颈项部瘙痒，皮肤苔藓样变 3 年。患者 3 年前出现颈项部瘙痒，肤色灰褐，皮肤苔藓样变，经多种中西药治疗，时轻时重，反复发作，近日加重，瘙痒较剧，难以入睡，伴烦躁易怒。查体：颈项部多处圆形、大小不等皮损，皮肤呈淡褐色，表面有少许鳞屑。舌边尖红，苔薄微黄，脉弦。辨证为肝郁化火。以棉绒灸治，即将消毒干棉球撕成极薄的棉绒，呈蝉翼状，大小及形状刚好覆盖皮损表面，用火迅速点燃，火一接触棉绒即听见"哧"声，约持续 1～2 s。每处灸 3 次，灸后瘙痒立即减轻，继取耳穴坐骨神经、颈割治（用小手术刀轻割，以轻度渗血为度，每周 1 次），之后取合谷、曲池、血海、三阴交、风池、太冲，毫针平补平泻法。2 d 后复诊，自述瘙痒明显减轻，并见皮肤粗糙明显好转，继续针刺及棉绒灸治，1 周后再取对侧耳穴坐骨神经、颈割治。治疗后瘙痒和皮肤苔藓样变逐渐减轻，棉绒灸治改为隔日 1 次，1 个疗程（10 d）后症状基本控制，瘙痒停止，皮肤表面鳞屑减少，情绪平稳，睡眠正常。为巩固疗效共治疗 2 个疗程，随访 1 年未复发。

thinner and softer and the skin color restored normal. The 2-year follow-up didn't found any relapses.

Remarks: Tapping with plum-blossom needle can activate meridian-qi, dredge meridians and regulate zang-fu organs to prevent diseases. Modern research suggested that with regulation through cutaneous nerve, plum-blossom needle can speed up micro-circulation of the skin lesion area, inhibit synthesis and release of medium, enhance immunity and thus achieve the effect of anti-inflammation, analgesia and stopping itching. The combined body acupoints can support anti-pathogenic qi, consolidate the exterior, nourish and circulate blood, and remove wind and stop itching.

Case 2

Li, female, 28 years old, a nurse.

Chief complaints: Itching in neck and nape as well as skin lichenification for 3 years. Three years ago, the patient got itching in her neck and nape area, grey-brown skin color and skin lichenification. She was treated with varieties of Chinese and Western medications, but the condition sometimes got better and sometimes worse with recurrent attack. In recent days, her condition worsened and she couldn't sleep because of the severe itching, as a result she also got restless and irritability. Physical examination: Several round skin lesions in different sizes in neck and nape area with a little scale, a red tongue tip with thin and slightly yellow coating and a wiry pulse. TCM syndrome pattern: liver-qi stagnation transforming into fire. Method: To apply cotton linter moxibustion on the affected area, more specifically, to tear the sterile dry cotton into extremely thin cotton linter that can exactly cover the skin lesion area, and then to light it with fire as fast as possible with

汉英对照

Chinese-English
Edition of
Acupuncture
Cosmetology

针灸美容

下篇 ⊙ 针灸美容典型验案

　　按语：《内经》中有"诸痛痒疮，皆属于心"，应用灸法可"借火助阳"以补虚，又可"开门祛邪"以泻实，"以热引热"使风热、湿热、肝火得泻，即"火郁发之"之义。配合病变部位的割治来调整病损部位的气血，使皮损尽快康复。再结合"治风先治血，血行风自灭"的原则取体穴针刺，是彻底获效的关键。灸法能"借火助阳"以补虚，又可"开门祛邪"以泻实，"以热引热"，采用棉绒灸治使风热、湿热、肝火得泻，即"火郁发之"之义。坐骨神经割治有调整大脑皮质兴奋与抑制，使之平衡而止痒，配合病变部位取穴割治以调整病损部位的气虚，使皮损尽快康复。针刺风池、合谷、曲池、风门，有祛风止痒之效；而血海，取"治风先治血，血行风自灭"之义；大椎祛风散热；阴陵泉、内庭清热利湿；膈俞、三阴交滋阴养血；肝俞、太冲清泄肝火而除烦。

a "Chi..." sound lasting about 1 - 2 seconds, 3 times for each area, and the itching relieved immediately after that; next to incise ear acupoints sciatic nerve and neck (to incise with small scalpel until slight capillary hemorrhage, once a week); and then to puncture Hegu (LI 4), Quchi (LI 11), Xuehai (SP 10), Sanyinjiao (SP 6), Fengchi (GB 20) and Taichong (LR 3) with even reinforcing-reducing manipulation. The patient told the itching got obvious relief in her return-visit after 2 days and her skin roughness also got obvious improvement. Therefore she was continuously treated by the acupuncture and cotton linter moxibustion. One week later the ear acupoints sciatic nerve and neck in the other ear were incised. After that, her itching and skin lichenification were both relieved. Then the cotton linter moxibustion was changed to once every other day. After one treatment course, her symptoms were basically controlled with disappearance of itching, reduction of skin scale, a stable mood and normal sleep. The patient was treated for two courses to consolidate the therapeutic effect. The 1-year follow-up didn't show any relapses.

Remarks: The *Nei Jing* states that "pain, itching and ulcers all involve with heart". Moxibustion can "supplement yang by means of fire" to tonify deficiency, "remove pathogenic factors by means of opening door", and "induce heat by means of heat". The cotton linter moxibustion can remove wind-heat, resolve damp-heat and clear liver-fire, i. e., "fire stagnation needs dissipation"; incision of ear acupoint sciatic nerve can balance excitation and inhibition of cerebral cortex to stop itching, and incision of ear acupoint neck can regulate qi deficiency of the correspondingly affected area to speed up the skin lesion; Needling Fengchi (GB 20), Hegu (LI 4), Quchi

第五节 荨麻疹

一、验案 1

李某,女,23 岁。1997 年 5 月初诊。

主诉:患慢性荨麻疹 5 年。患者于春冬两季多发,发作时四肢及胸部出现大块风团,瘙痒剧烈,午后或夜间加剧,严重影响了工作和生活,曾用糖皮质激素、抗组胺、钙剂及中药等治疗,均未显效,无奈求助于针灸治疗。检查:四肢、胸部有多数散在不规则形、大小不等的淡红色风团,部分皮损融合成大片。诊断为慢性荨麻疹。以针刺配合隔蒜灸治疗,经 1 个疗程后痊愈,至今未复发。方法:主穴:曲池、三阴交、血海;配穴:委中、尺泽、合谷、足三里、大椎、风市,毫针轻刺激,平补平泻,得气后留针 30 min。隔蒜灸,取穴:足三里、血海、曲池、大椎、膈俞、外关、太溪。以新鲜大蒜切成片,厚 0.3～0.4 cm,用针在蒜片上扎 5～10 个小孔,置于穴位上,以艾炷施灸,每穴 7～9 壮,补法。两种方法隔日交替使用,各 5 次为 1 个疗程。

(LI 11) and Fengmen (BL 12) can remove wind and stop itching; Xuehai (SP 10) was selected on the basis of "circulating blood before stopping wind and smooth blood circulation makes wind stop spontaneously"; Dazhui (GV 14) was selected to remove wind and clear away heat; Yinlingquan (SP 9) and Neiting (ST 44) were selected to clear away heat and resolve dampness; Geshu (BL 17) and Sanyinjiao (SP 6) were selected to nourish yin-blood; and Ganshu (BL 18) and Taichong (LR 3) were selected to clear liver-fire and stop restlessness.

Section 5　Urticaria

Case 1

Li, female, 23 years old, came for the first visit in May 1997.

Chief complaints: Five years of chronic urticaria, especially in spring and winter months. With an attack of urticaria, she always gets large wheals in four limbs and chest with severe itching, especially in the afternoon or at night. Her work and life has been greatly affected by this condition. Previous treatment: she was once treated with glucocorticoid, antihistamine, calcium-contained agents and Chinese herbs, but didn't get marked effect, and therefore came for acupuncture treatment. Physical examination: light-pink wheals in irregular shapes and sizes scattered in her four limbs and chest, and some skin lesion merged into large patches. Diagnosis: chronic urticaria. Method: acupuncture plus garlic-partitioned moxibustion. After one treatment course, the patient got recovery and the urticaria didn't reoccur until now. Major acupoints: Quchi (LI 11), Sanyinjiao (SP 6) and Xuehai (SP

按语：本病多由于平素体弱、气血不足或因久病气血耗伤、血虚生风、气虚卫外不固、风邪乘虚而入所致。治疗以养血、活血为主，兼以祛风止痒，针刺阳明、太阴二经。配合隔蒜灸滋阴养血、行气活血、清热解毒、疏散风邪，从而使气血得复，风疹得散。在治疗期间，患者要少食刺激性食物及尽可能减少寒冷刺激等，如患有肠道寄生虫，应先驱虫后治疗。

二、 验案 2

张某某，女，35 岁。2000 年 9 月初诊。

10); adjunct acupoints: Weizhong (BL 40), Chize (LU 5), Hegu (LI 4), Zusanli (ST 36), Dazhui (GV 14) and Fengshi (GB 31). The acupoints were punctured with even reinforcing-reducing manipulation through mild stimulation. The needles retained for 30 minutes. The garlic-partitioned moxibustion: acupoints: Zusanli (ST 36), Xuehai (SP 10), Quchi (LI 11), Dazhui (GV 14), Geshu (BL 17), Waiguan (TE 5) and Taixi (KI 3); application: slices of fresh garlic about 0.3 - 0.4 cm in thickness with 5 - 10 small holes were placed on above acupoints for moxa-cone moxibustion, 7 - 9 zhuang for each acupoint. The two methods were adopted alternately every other day and 5 times of each method make up one treatment course.

Remarks: Urticaria is always caused by congenital weak constitution, qi and blood consumption due to deficiency of qi and blood or chronic disease, blood deficiency stirring wind, and weakness of Wei-defense due to qi deficiency plus an attack of pathogenic wind. Therefore the therapeutic principle shall be to nourish and circulate blood as well as to remove wind and stop itching. The acupoints of Yangming and Taiyin meridians were selected for acupuncture. In addition, garlic-partitioned moxibustion was combined to nourish yin-blood, circulate qi and blood, clear away heat, remove toxic substance, remove wind and subsequently remove skin rashes. During the treatment, the patient was recommended to reduce pungent food and try as best as he can to reduce cold stimulation. In case of intestinal parasites, the parasites shall be treated primarily.

Case 2

Zhang, female, 35 years old, came for the first visit in September 2000.

Chief complaints: Five years of chronic urticaria. In the

主诉：患慢性荨麻疹 5 年。5 年来，每遇春冬季，全身即发大小不等风团，瘙痒剧烈，发作时即服用糖皮质激素，抗组胺药，钙剂或中药等治疗，得以缓解，但病情反复，难以根治。此次又发，皮肤科介绍来诊。体检：全身散在不规则、大小不等的暗红色风团，尤以胸背部为多，部分皮损融合成大片。诊断：慢性荨麻疹。针刺取穴：主穴：膈俞、肺俞；配穴：风池、血海、三阴交、足三里、肝俞、合谷，每次 3～4 穴，采用轻刺激，快速进针，平补平泻，留针 20 min。针刺后，再在患者背部太阳经、督脉循经涂上一层凡士林后，用闪火法快速在肺俞穴上拔火罐，然后循经走罐，上至肺俞下至大肠俞，反复操作 3～4 次，至皮肤红紫色为止。1 个疗程（5 次）痊愈，半年后随访未复发。

按语：《素问·阴阳应象大论》有"阴病取阳"。背部为阳，为太阳经所主，太阳为一身之表，脏腑背俞穴所在，通过走罐自上而下历经数穴，不仅具有祛风散寒、调和营卫、益气固表之功，还有调理脏腑、益气养血活血之效。获得内外兼治，达到根治的目的。

past 5 years, she got wheals in different sizes all over the body in spring and winter months with severe itching. She used to take glucocorticoid, anti-histamine, calcium-contained agents or Chinese herbs to relieve the condition. However, the condition kept reoccurring and this time she came for acupuncture referred by dermatology doctors. Physical examination: irregular dark-red wheals in different sizes were scattered all over the body, especially on the chest and back, and some of them merged into large patches. Diagnosis: Chronic urticaria. Selection of major acupoints: Geshu (BL 17) and Feishu (BL 13); selection of adjunct acupoints: Fengchi (GB 20), Xuehai (SP 10), Sanyinjiao (SP 6), Zusanli (ST 36), Ganshu (BL 18) and Hegu (LI 4). Each time 3 - 4 acupoints were punctured with fast insertion and mild stimulation by even reinforcing-reducing manipulation. The needles retained for 20 minutes. After that, the patient's back along Taiyang meridian and Governor Vessel were applied a layer of Vaseline for flash cupping on Feishu (BL 13), then moving the cup from Feishu (BL 13) to Dachangshu (BL 25) for 3 - 4 times until the skin turned purple red. After one treatment course (5 times), the patient got complete recovery and the six-month follow-up didn't show any relapses.

Remarks: The *Su Wen • Yin Yang Ying Xiang Da Lun* states that "yin disease can be treated from yang". The back of the body is yang and governed by Taiyang meridians. Taiyang meridians govern the exterior of the whole body, and as a result, the back-Shu acupoints of the zang-fu organs, involving several acupoints through moving cupping, can not only remove wind, dissipate cold, harmonize Ying-nutrient and Wei-defense and supplement qi to consolidate the exterior, but also to

汉英对照

Chinese-English
Edition of
Acupuncture
Cosmetology

针灸美容

下篇 ● 针灸美容典型验案

三、 验案 3

王某,女,26 岁。1999 年 7 月初诊。

主诉:腰、腹、上下肢皮肤反复出现瘙痒性风团 6 月余。发作时奇痒难忍,搔抓后风团扩大、增多,相互融合成片,随时发作,影响工作、生活、睡眠。经口服西药抗组胺、静推钙剂、中药汤剂及防风通圣散等治疗后,症状可缓解,但仍反复发作,诊为慢性荨麻疹。取穴风池、合谷、曲池、足三里、尺泽、三阴交,毫针得气后,行平补平泻,留针 30 min。留针时用清艾条施温和灸,以患者局部皮肤感到温热而无灼痛为宜,每穴灸 5～7 min,灸至皮肤红晕为度。肺俞、大椎、风市、血海,用梅花针轻轻叩刺,以局部皮肤潮红,隐隐渗血为宜,选合适玻璃火罐,用闪火法坐罐于叩刺的穴位上,留罐 15 min。两种方法隔日交替使用。经上法治疗 10 d,感瘙痒性风团明显减轻,继续治疗 20 d 后痊愈。为巩固疗效,又治疗 30 d,随访半年无复发。

regulate zang-fu organs, supplement qi, and nourish or circulate blood to eradicate the condition.

Case 3

Wang, female, 26 years old, came for the first visit in July 1999.

Chief complaints: More than 6 months of recurrent itchy wheals in the lumbus, abdomen and upper or lower limbs. She complained that the itching was almost intolerable and scratching may enlarge and increase the wheals into large patches. Actually the frequent attacks of urticaria have affected her work, life and sleep. Previous treatment and result: oral administration of anti-histamine, intravenous injection of calcium-contained agents, Chinese herbal decoction and patterned Chinese herbal product Fang Feng Tong Shen San may relieve the symptoms but cannot stop relapse of urticaria. Diagnosis: chronic urticaria. Selected acupoints: Fengchi (GB 20), Hegu (LI 4), Quchi (LI 11), Zusanli (ST 36), Chize (LU 5), and Sanyinjiao (SP 6). The above acupoints were punctured with even reinforcing-reducing manipulation and the needles retained for 30 minutes. In addition, the moxa-stick moxibustion (the patient may feel warm but not burning pain) was combined during needle retaining, 5 - 7 minutes for each acupoint until the local skin turned red. The acupoints Feishu (BL 13), Dazhui (GV 14), Fengchi (GB 31) and Xuehai (SP 10) were tapped slightly with plum-blossom needle until the local skin turned slightly red with hidden capillary hemorrhage. After that, appropriate glass cups were applied to the tapped acupoints by flash-fire method and the cups retained for 15 minutes. The above two methods were adopted alternately every other day. After 10 days of treatment, the wheals

按语：实验研究证明：针灸可改善血液循环,促进新陈代谢,提高机体免疫能力。通过针刺、艾灸、叩刺、拔罐的综合应用起到疏风清热、调补气血作用,病当自愈。但应注意,在本病的治疗期间忌饮酒及食油腻辛辣之物。

第六节　斑秃

一、　验案 1

邹某,男,33 岁。2000 年 3 月 13 日就诊。

主诉：头后枕部有一 3 cm×3 cm 大小的斑秃,经多种中西药治疗效果不明显。故来求诊。用梅花针叩刺局部直至局部充血后用消毒纱布擦净,用鲜生姜擦拭。3 日 1 次。以 2%利多卡因注射液 3 ml 加山莨菪碱 2 ml,混匀后局部扇形注射,3 日 1 次。两种方法交替使用。3 次为 1 个疗程。疗程结束后,有新发生出,要求再巩固 1 个疗程,半年后随访已痊愈,无复发。

按语：本法具有活血化瘀的作用,以鲜生姜祛风活络,用山莨菪碱可以改善局部血液循环,促使毛发再生。

obviously reduced. After 20 days, the patient got complete recovery. The treatment continued for 30 days to consolidate the therapeutic effect and the six-month follow-up didn't show any relapses.

Remarks: Experimental study has proved that acupuncture can improve blood circulation, boost metabolism and increase immunity. The integration of needling, moxibustion, tapping and cupping can remove wind, clear away heat and tonify qi and blood. However, the patient shall be recommended to stay away from alcohol and avoid greasy and spicy food.

Section 6　Alopecia areata

Case 1

Zou, male, 33 years old, came for the first visit on March 13, 2000.

Chief complaints: Alopecia areata sized 3 cm × 3 cm in the occipital area and varieties of Chinese or Western medications didn't work well. Method: The local area was tapped with plum-blossom needle until local congestion, cleaned with sterile gauze and then applied fresh ginger. The above procedure was done once every 3 days. Or the local scallop injection of mixed 3 ml containing 2% Lidocaine injection and 2 ml 654-2 was done once every 3 days. The above two methods were used alternately. Three times make up one treatment course. After one course, new hair started to grow. Upon the patient's request, another course was adopted for consolidation. The six-month follow-up showed complete recovery and no relapses.

Remarks: This method can circulate blood and resolve stasis, fresh ginger acts to remove wind and clear meridians and 654-2 can improve local blood circulation and promote rebirth

汉英对照

Chinese-English
Edition of
Acupuncture
Cosmetology

针灸美容

Part 3　The Typical Case Reports of Acupuncture Cosmetology

汉英对照

Chinese-English
Edition of
Acupuncture
Cosmetology

针灸美容 下篇 ◉ 针灸美容典型验案

二、 验案 2

刘某,女,31 岁。

主诉:断续片状脱发 2 周。伴头晕、心烦不寐、舌淡、苔薄,脉细弱。检查:6 处秃发,面积大者为 3 cm×3 cm,小者为 1 cm×1 cm。中医诊断:斑秃。治以养血祛风,活血化瘀。针刺百会、风池(双)、太渊(双)、阿是穴。前 3 穴毫针针刺,补泻兼施,得气后留针 30 min,阿是穴(局部斑秃处),用无菌梅花针反复叩刺,每次叩刺 10 min,使局部头皮出现潮红、充血。两种方法均隔日 1 次,10 次为 1 个疗程。经 2 个疗程治疗后,5 处脱发区生长黑色茸毛。4 个疗程后,脱发区全部长出黑色短发。

按语:本病多由于各种原因引起大脑皮质过度紧张,血液循环不畅所致。中医学认为,气血虚弱、虚热生风而致脱发。取百会、风池,疏风解表,温养诸脉,安神健脑。肺主皮毛,取肺之原穴太渊,补法以益气生血,泻法能活血化瘀;梅花针叩刺脱发区能增强头皮的血液循环,增加头皮组织的新陈代谢和营养供应,促进上皮组织增生,刺激毛发生长。通过皮肤—孙脉—络脉—经脉起到通经活络、调理气血、调整脏腑功能,使气血充盛,精气上升于头部,发为血之余,精血足,则毛发生。本病还应注意休息,降低工作强度,缓解精神压力。

of hair.

Case 2

Liu, female, 31 years old.

Chief complaints: Two weeks of intermittent and patchy hair loss. Accompanying symptoms and signs include: dizziness, restlessness, insomnia, a pale tongue with thin coating and a thready and weak pulse. Physical examination showed: Among 6 areas of alopecia areata, the bigger area sized 3 cm × 3 cm and the smaller sized 1 cm × 1 cm. TCM diagnosis: alopecia areata. The therapeutic principle: to nourish blood, remove wind, circulate blood and resolve stasis. Selected acupoints: Baihui (GV 20), bilateral Fengchi (GB 20), bilateral Taiyuan (LU 9) and Ashi points. The first three acupoints were punctured with filiform needles by both reinforcing and reducing manipulation and the needles retained for 30 minutes. The local Ashi points (alopecia areata) was done repeated tapping with sterilized plum-blossom needle for 10 minutes until the local scalp turned slightly red and congested. The two methods were both adopted once every other day, and 10 times make up one treatment course. After two courses, black fuzz appeared in five areas. And after four courses, black hair appeared in all the affected areas.

Remarks: Alopecia areata is caused by over-tension and blocked blood circulation of cerebral cortex due to varieties of reasons. TCM holds that deficiency of qi and blood and wind due to deficient-heat may result in loss of hair. Therefore Baihui (GV 20) and Fengchi (GB 20) were selected to remove wind, relieve the exterior, warm and nourish meridians, calm the mind and refresh the brain. As the lung governs skin and skin hair, Taiyuan (LU 9), the Yuan-primary acupoint of lung

三、 验案 3

朱某某,男,18 岁,学生。2004 年 6 月初诊。

主诉:半个月前出现斑秃,因考试未及时就诊。查见:脑后偏右处有一直径 3.2 cm 圆形脱发区,边界清楚,局部头皮光亮,无其他特殊症状。毫针阿是穴、风池、合谷、三阴交、后溪等,阿是穴针从脱发区边缘向中心平刺,捻转行针,其他穴位直刺,行平补平泻手法,留针 20 min。梅花针在秃发区叩刺,以皮肤潮红或微渗血为度,大椎穴叩刺微出血。每次以清艾条温和灸秃发区 15~20 min,以局部皮肤潮红为度,3 种方法交替,轮流进行,30 d 为 1 个疗程。经采用上述针灸治疗 40 d 后,局部长出肉眼可见的黄白色细小绒毛,2 个月后复诊时局部头发基本正常。

meridian, was punctured to supplement qi and generate blood by reinforcing manipulation and to circulate blood and resolve stasis by reducing manipulation. Tapping the local area with plum-blossom needle can enhance the blood circulation of the scalp, boost metabolism and nutrition supply of the scalp tissue, promote proliferation of epithelial tissue, and stimulate hair growth. The therapeutic effect can be obtained through skin-minute collaterals-collaterals or subcollaterals-meridians to dredge meridians, regulate qi and blood as well as zang-fu organs, and eventually to produce abundant qi and blood and ascend essence-qi to head. As hair is the extension of blood, abundant essence-blood enables hair to grow. During the treatment, the patient was also recommended to take rest, reduce work time and relieve mental stress.

Case 3

Zhu, male, 18 years old, a student, came for the first visit in June 2004.

Chief complaints: Alopecia areata for 2 weeks. Two weeks ago, the patient got alopecia areata and didn't get immediate treatment because of school examination. Physical examination: A round area of alopecia areata 3.2 cm in diameter in occipital area (more right-sided) with clear borders and local shiny scalp but no other special symptoms. Method: The acupoints Ashi, Fengchi (GB 20), Hegu (LI 4), Sanyinjiao (SP 6) and Houxi (SI 3) were punctured with filiform needles. Except for subcutaneous needling from edge of the affected area toward center on Ashi point with manipulation by rotation, the other acupoints were punctured perpendicularly with even reinforcing-reducing manipulation. The needles retained for 20 minutes. Or the plum-blossom

汉英对照

Chinese-English
Edition of
Acupuncture
Cosmetology

针灸美容

Part 3 The Typical Case Reports of Acupuncture Cosmetology

按语：本病发生的原因不明，可能与遗传有关，或是一种自身免疫性疾病，精神创伤可能是诱发因素之一。针灸治疗青少年斑秃，以行气活血、祛风通络为原则。3 种方法交替使用，目的在于加强对斑秃部位的刺激，温通气血，改善营养，促进头发的生长。

第七节　黑痣

一、验案 1

刘某，女，43 岁，工人。

主诉：自幼左眉头处有色痣如小米样，随着年龄增长而增大，但生长缓慢。近几月增长迅速，至 0.8 cm×0.8 cm，并发痒，洗面不当则溃破而求诊。行火针取痣法，10 d 后脱落，无印痕，无色素改变，随访 5 个月无复发。

needle was adopted to tap on the affected area until local skin turned slightly red or slight capillary hemorrhage and on Dazhui (GV 14) for slightly bleeding. Or moxa-stick moxibustion was adopted on the affected area for 15 - 20 minutes until the local skin turned slightly red. The above three methods were used alternately and 30 days make up one treatment course. After 40 days of treatment, yellow-white fuzz in the local area can be seen with naked eyes. The return-visit after 2 months showed basically normal hair in the local area.

Remarks: The etiology of alopecia areata is still unknown, probably related to heredity or autoimmune disease, and mental trauma may contribute to its attack. For alopecia areata of teenagers, acupuncture acts to circulate qi and blood flow, remove wind and clear meridians. The alternate using of above three methods can enhance the stimulation on affected area, warm and regulate qi and blood, improve nutrition and boost hair growth.

Section 7　Black nevus

Case 1

Liu, female, 43 years old, a worker.

Chief complaints: She got a millet-sized pigmented nevus in her left eyebrows since she was young, which turned bigger with increase of ages with a slow growth speed, however, the nevus started to grow fast in the recent months and turned as big as 0.8 cm × 0.8 cm with itching sensation and diabrosis from incorrect way of washing face. She was treated with fire needle therapy. Ten days later, the nevus fell off without left-over marks and pigmentation changes. The 5-month follow-up didn't show any relapses.

按语：火针操作应注意：针刺的深度以不伤害正常组织为度，否则容易留下瘢痕。所刺的针数，以痣的大小而定。注意不要用退火的钢针硬刺。1周内勿接触水，以防感染。结痂待其自行脱落，不可用手抠掉。

二、 验案2

任某，女，35岁，会计。1985年3月25日就诊。

主诉：右上唇外角长一蚕豆大褐色痣，有毛数根，生长35年，日渐增大而求诊。先接通便携式电子火针仪，灯亮后，医者持针柄，手指按下开关，待电子火针头部发热变红后，医者用另一手持镊子夹住痣，将电火针对准病变的根部拉锯式取下，再沿痣中心向外点刺。2个月后随访肤色正常，迄今，痊愈。

按语：治疗前局部应严格消毒。应用电火针烧灼1个黑痣只需几秒钟，但应掌握点刺的深度，避免伤及正常组织而留下瘢痕。

第八节　白癜风

一、 验案1

邓某，女，50岁，教师。

Remarks: Attention: The depth of needle shall be controlled not to damage the normal tissue, otherwise scars may be left. The needles are selected according to the size of nevus. Points to care: avoid puncturing with cooled steel needles; avoid water contact within one week to prevent infection; and avoid scratching the scab with hands but let it fall off spontaneously.

Case 2

Ren, female, 35 years old, an accountant, came for the first visit on March 25, 1985.

Chief complaints: Thirty-five years of a horsebean-sized brown pigmented nevus with several hairs that gradually grew. Method: To connect the portable electric fire needle instrument; then to hold the needle handle after light on and press the switch "on" with fingers; after the needle tip turned red and hot, to pinch the nevus with forceps with the other hand and remove the nevus like dragsaw toward its root part; and finally to apply pricking from the center of nevus to outside area. The 2-month follow-up showed normal color until today.

Remarks: Strict sterilization is required before the treatment. Although burning one black nevus with electric fire needle only takes several seconds, the depth of pricking shall be well-controlled in order not to damage the normal tissue and leave scars.

Section 8   Vitiligo

Case 1

Deng, female, 50 years old, a teacher.

Chief complaints: Two months ago, she found the skin on her left wrist turned white and gradually spread but with no other accompanying symptoms. Physical examination: white

汉英对照
Chinese-English
Edition of
Acupuncture
Cosmetology

针灸美容 Part 3 The Typical Case Reports of Acupuncture Cosmetology

汉英对照

Chinese-English
Edition of
Acupuncture
Cosmetology

针灸美容

下篇◉针灸美容典型验案

主诉：左侧腕部皮肤发白2个月。患者于2个月前发现左侧腕部皮肤发白,逐渐扩大,无其他伴随症状,来我院检查情况：左侧腕部桡动脉上区皮肤呈白色,大约2.5 cm×2.5 cm圆形斑块,病变区知觉存在,分泌及排泄功能正常,无红,无肿,无痛,于皮肤病科诊断：白癜风。曾用维生素类药及外用药治疗无效,病变区仍继续扩大而求诊。以He－Ne激光照射治疗,输出功率15 mW,每日照射1次,每次20 min,照射3次后病变区由白变红,照射10次后,周边区已有黑素生长,继续照射7次后,病变区恢复正常肤色至痊愈。随访半年未见复发。

按语：本病是一种原发性皮肤色素脱失而形成的局限性白色斑片,激光照射病变区能促进局部血液循环,改善供血状态,加强细胞和体液的免疫功能,激活皮肤黑素细胞内的酪氨酸酶将酪氨酸氧化成二羟基苯丙氨酸形成黑素,使肤色恢复正常。

二、 验案2

王某,女,16岁。1984年8月20日初诊。

主诉：皮肤发白2年。患者于1982年先在腹部发现一小块白色的皮肤,1年后逐渐泛发到全身约60%的皮肤,边界不清,多处求医无效而求诊。于1984年夏天采用穴位埋线治疗。1周后病情停止发展,2周后白斑区缩小,边界较清晰,色素增加。又做了32次治疗(共3个月),5 m远外观全身皮肤色泽基本一致,又巩固治疗4次,观察3年,疗效稳定。

skin of the superior area of radial artery of the left-sided wrist with a round patch sized 2.5 cm × 2.5 cm, presence of perception in the affected area, normal secretion and excretory function, and absence of redness, swelling or pain. Diagnosis by dermatology department: vitiligo. The patient once tried vitamins and externally-used medications but didn't get any effect, and the affected area continued to spread, instead. The patient was treated with He-Ne laser radiation (output power: 15 mW), once every day, and 20 minutes each time. After 3 times of radiation, the skin in the affected area turned from whiteness to redness. After 10 times of radiation, melanin started to grow in the surrounding area. After another continuous 7 times of radiation, the skin in the affected area restored to normal color. The six-month follow-up didn't find any relapses.

Remarks: Vitiligo is a type of primary localized white patching resulted from loss of skin pigmentation. Laser radiation on the affected area can promote local blood circulation, improve the blood supply, enhance the immune function of cells and humoral, enable the monophenolase in the melanocytes to oxidate tyrosine into dioxyphenylalanine and form melanin and subsequently restore the normal skin color.

Case 2

Wang, female, 16 years old, came for the first visit on August 20, 1984.

Chief complaints: The whitening of skin for 2 years. She found a small white patch in her abdomen in 1982, which gradually spread to about 60% of the body skin one year later without clear borders. She tried varieties of methods but didn't get any effect. In summer of 1994, she was treated with catgut

按语：穴位埋线能给局部以长久的刺激，加快皮损区的血液循环、细胞新陈代谢，调节皮肤神经、免疫功能，促进黑素细胞的形成，并通过经络的作用，达到疏通气血、激活内在修复系统，恢复正常组织的功能。

三、验案 3

刘某某，男，26 岁，干部。1988 年 4 月 25 日初诊。

主诉：面颊出现白斑 7 个月。自诉于 1987 年 9 月发现面颊有五处白斑，发展较快。与精神、情绪等变化关系密切，曾至大连、沈阳等医院就诊，诊断：白癜风。内服外搽，白斑仅变为粉色。检查：左面颊、鼻旁共五处白斑，小者 0.4 cm×0.5 cm。舌质红、边有齿痕，苔白，脉弦细。先用 75% 乙醇棉球将病灶区清擦后涂抹薄薄一层金银膏，再用艾条熏灸或TDP 热疗 30 min，灸后用手纸揩净局部，每日 1 次，12 次为 1个疗程。经隔药灸 3 次后出现针尖大点色素沉着，继续灸治并加服还原丹（每次 1 丸，每日 3 次，开水送服），19 次时鼻旁处痊愈。21 次时鼻上 2 块痊愈。50 次时带药回家自治。又经 3 个月白斑已基本消退，肤色较正常肤色稍浅。

汉英对照

Chinese-English
Edition of
Acupuncture
Cosmetology

针灸美容

下篇 ◉ 针灸美容典型验案

embedding on acupoints. Her condition stopped progressing one week later, and the white patch shrank two weeks later with clear borders and increased pigmentation. After 32 times (3 months) of treatment, the general skin was seen basically same away from 5 meters. Then she was treated for another 4 times for consolidation of the effects. The 3-year observation showed a stable efficacy.

Remarks: Catgut embedding on acupoints can stimulate the local area for a long time, speed up the blood circulation of the skin lesion area as well as cellular metabolism, regulate the nerve and immune function of the skin and promote the formation of melanocytes. In addition, it can also regulate qi and blood, activate auto-repairing function of the body and restore normal tissue through meridians.

Case 3

Liu, male, 26 years old, a government official, came for the first visit on April 25, 1988.

Chief complaints: White patches on facial cheek for 7 months. He found five white patches on facial cheek in September 1987, which develops fast and closely relates to mental stress or emotional fluctuations. He was once treated in hospitals in Dalian and Shenyang and was diagnosed as vitiligo. Both oral medications and externally-used medications only turned the white patches into pink color. Physical examination: five white patches in left cheek and nasal area, the small ones are sized 0.4 cm × 0.5 cm, a red tongue with teeth marks and white coating and a wiry and thready pulse. Method: The affected area was cleaned with 75% alcohol cotton ball and then applied with a thin layer of Jin Yin Gao (a patterned Chinese herbal paste), followed by 30 minutes of moxa-stick

按语：隔药灸具有活血化瘀祛风的疗效，通过艾条悬灸，使患处皮肤温热红润，血运加快，促进皮肤对药物的吸收，外用药物主要成分有防风、白矾等，配合口服中成药还原丹意在治风先治血、血行风自灭之旨，主要成分为补阴养血、活血祛风通络的药物，如女贞子、丹参、苍耳子、木瓜等。治疗期间注意忌食辛辣、海鲜食物。

汉英对照

Chinese-English
Edition of
Acupuncture
Cosmetology

针灸美容

下篇 ◉ 针灸美容典型验案

moxibustion or TDP thermotherapy and cleaned with tissue after moxibustion. The treatment was done once every day and 12 times make up one treatment course. After 3 times of paste-partitioned moxibustion, pinpoint-sized pigmentation spots started to appear. Then he was treated continuously with moxibustion plus oral administration of Huan Yuan Dan (patterned Chinese herbal pills) (1 pill each time with boiled water, 3 times a day). The patches in the nasal area completely disappeared at the 19th time of treatment and patches on the nose disappeared at the 21st time of treatment. Then he took medications home for self-treatment at the 50th time. After another 3-month treatment, the white patches basically disappeared and appeared slightly lighter color than the normal skin.

Remarks: The drug-partitioned moxibustion acts to circulate blood to resolve stasis and remove wind. Suspending moxibustion with moxa stick can make the affected skin warm and red, speed up blood flow, and promote the skin absorption of the medication. The externally-used medication mainly contains Fang Feng (*Radix Saposhnikoviae*) and Bai Fan (*Alumen*). The patterned Chinese herbal products Huan Yuan Dan mainly contains such herbs of nourishing yin-blood, circulating blood and removing wind as Nü Zhen Zi (*Fructus Ligustri Lucidi*), Dan Shen (*Radix Salviae Miltiorrhizae*), Can Er Zi (*Fructus Xanthii*) and Mu Gua (*Fructus Chaenomelis*), that aim to achieve the goal of "resolving blood stasis before removing wind and smooth blood circulation spontaneously stops wind". During the treatment, the patient was recommended to avoid spicy food and seafood.

第九节 银屑病

一、验案 1

杨某,女,33 岁,干部。1989 年 11 月 20 日初诊。

主诉:周身出现银白色鳞屑性皮损伴剧痒 1 月余。患者无明显原因于双前臂出现红斑,上有鳞屑,伴痒而未介意,近日周身出现广泛性鳞屑、剧痒。检查:广泛性红斑鳞屑性皮损,伴抓痕、血痂、薄膜现象(+)、漏滴现象(+),同形反应存在。诊断:寻常性银屑病(进行期)。取夹脊穴 T_1、T_3、T_5、T_7、T_{11}、L_1、L_3、L_4,左右交替埋线,每次 1 组,7 d 1 次,2 次为 1 个疗程。并取耳穴肺、内分泌,及四肢胸腹相应敏感点,双侧,以王不留行埋籽按压,每日按压 3~4 次,每次 3~5 min,3 d 更换 1 次,之间休息 1 d。1 个疗程后皮损消失达 2/3,症状消失,3 个疗程后皮损全消,随访 1 年未复发。

按语:五脏六腑之经络均有在耳部分布,耳压可刺激经络、调节经络之气,使脏腑气血功能得以恢复。夹脊穴邻近膀胱经与督脉,能调理一身阳气。又位于脊神经分布区域,脊神经通过交通支与交感神经链相连接,后者在远端分布于内脏,并上达脑部,夹脊穴埋线可改善微循环、调节神经功能、改善人体的免疫功能,二者配合,共奏良效。

Section 9   Psoriasis

Case 1

Yang, female, 33 years old, a government official, came for the first visit on November 20, 1989.

Chief complaints: More than 1 month of generalized silver-white scaly skin lesion with severe itching. The patient got scaly and itchy erythema on forearms without unknown reasons and didn't care about it at first but then got generalized scales with severe itching. Physical examination showed: extensive erythematosus and scaly skin lesion with scratched marks, blood crust, filming phenomena (+), dripping phenomena (+), and presence of isomorphic response. Diagnosis: psoriasis vulgaris (progressive). Method: Jiaji (EX-B 2) of T_1, T_3, T_5, T_7, T_{11}, L_1, L_3 and L_4 were applied catgut embedding on both sides alternately. Each time one pair was selected for catgut embedding once every 7 days and twice treatments make up one course. In addition, cowherb seeds were applied on such ear acupoints as lung, endocrine and bilateral corresponding sensitive points of the four limbs, 3 - 4 times of self-pressure every day, and 3 - 5 minutes each time. The seeds were changed once every 3 days with an interval of 1 day in between. After one treatment course, 2/3 of the skin lesion as well as accompanying symptoms disappeared. After 3 treatment courses, the skin lesion completely disappeared and the one-year follow-up didn't find any relapse.

Remarks: The meridians of five-zang and six-fu organs are all distributed in auricular regions, and thus pressing ear acupoints can stimulate meridian-qi and regulate qi and blood as well as functions of zang-fu organs. The Jiaji (EX-B 2) acupoints, adjacent to the bladder meridian and Governor

汉英对照

Chinese-English Edition of Acupuncture Cosmetology

针灸美容 Part 3 The Typical Case Reports of Acupuncture Cosmetology

二、 验案 2

周某某,男,19 岁,工人。1988 年 3 月 16 日初诊。

主诉:患银屑病 1 年 2 个月。1987 年元旦后,四肢部位出现点状红色丘疹,瘙痒,抓后脱屑,面积逐渐扩大,2 个月后扩展到全身。用多种药物治疗,未见好转,无家族发病史。检查:全身满布点滴状红色丘疹,占体表面积 15% 左右,头皮及四肢伸侧部分融合成片,表面覆盖较厚鳞屑,剥后可见点状出血点,可见多次抓痕血痂及皲裂出血。舌质红,苔黄,脉滑。诊断:银屑病(寻常型、进行期、中度)。中医辨证:血热风盛型。用刺血电针法治疗 10～15 次,瘙痒加重,皮疹面积较原来扩大,大部分融合成片,鳞屑增厚。继续治疗 2 个疗程后,瘙痒消除,鳞屑变松容易脱落,皮疹变薄,面积缩小,背部皮疹开始消退。治疗 3 个疗程后,皮疹全部消退而愈。随访到 1992 年 5 月未复发。

汉英对照

Chinese-English
Edition of
Acupuncture
Cosmetology

针灸美容

下篇 ◉ 针灸美容典型验案

Vessel, can regulate yang-qi of the whole body. In addition, Jiaji (EX-B 2) acupoints are located in spinal nerve distribution area; the spinal nerve connects with sympathetic chain through communication branch, and the distal end of sympathetic nerve is distributed in internal organs and reaches brain. As a result catgut embedding in those acupoints can improve microcirculation, regulate nerve function and improve the immune function of the body.

Case 2

Zhou, male, 19 years old, a worker, came for the first visit on March 16, 1988.

Chief complaints: One year and two months of psoriasis. After New Year's day in 1987, the patient got itchy and punctiform red papules in four limbs, desquamated after scratching with a gradually extended area and spread to all over the body two months later. The patient tried varieties of medications but didn't get any effect. The patient had no family history of psoriasis. Physical examination: the punctiform red papules took up about 15% of the body surface, papules merging into patches in scalp and extensor aspects of four limbs, thick scales covering the surface, visible punctiform hemorrhagic spots after peeling off, obvious scratched marks, blood crust and rhagades, a red tongue with yellow coating and a slippery pulse. Diagnosis: psoriasis (vulgaris, progressive and moderate degree). TCM syndrome pattern: blood heat and preponderance of wind. After 10 - 15 times of electric acupuncture following blood-letting, the patient got more severe itching, an more extended area of skin rash, and most papules merged into patches with thickened scales. After another two continuous treatment courses, his itching

按语：应用刺血电针治疗银屑病 158 例，临床近期治愈率 51%，有效率 91%。其中无家族史的青壮年患者，病程短者，疗效显著。本方法有清热解毒、活血化瘀作用，配合火罐、电针能疏通经络、化瘀消斑，调理脏腑阴阳气血，使病变部位血流通畅，皮肤营养充足，从而抑制表皮细胞增生角化过程，加快皮疹消退。

disappeared, the scale loosened and easily fell off, the skin rashes turned thinner, the area of skin rashes shrank and the skin rashes on the back started to disappear. After three treatment courses, the skin rashes completely disappeared. The follow-up until May 1992 didn't find any relapses.

Remarks: Treatment of 158 psoriasis cases with electric acupuncture following blood-letting showed the short-term recovery rate was 51%, the effective rate was 91%, and especially marked effect on those young sufferers with a short duration and without family history. This method can clear away heat, remove toxic substance, and circulate blood to resolve stasis. The combined cupping and electric stimulation can dredge meridians, resolve stasis and remove skin rashes, regulate yin, yang, qi and blood of the zang-fu organs, promote blood circulation of the affected area to provide nutrition for the skin and subsequently inhibit the proliferation and cornification of epidemic cells and speed up removal of skin rashes.

汉英对照

Chinese-English
Edition of
Acupuncture
Cosmetology

针灸美容

Part 3 The Typical Case Reports of Acupuncture Cosmetology

第十一章　五官科病症的典型验案

第一节　麦粒肿

一、验案 1

何某，男，60 岁。2001 年 7 月 15 日初诊。

主诉：双眼上睑红肿，疼痛 2 日，伴头晕、头痛。查：双眼上睑明显发红、肿胀，扪之均有约 0.4 cm×0.5 cm 微硬结节，触之痛甚，体温 38℃，有化脓之势。诊为麦粒肿。方法：将艾条以雀啄灸双侧的后溪穴约 1 min。次日，双眼上睑红肿基本消退，硬结不著，已无头晕、头痛症状，体温降至 36.5℃。依前法再灸，每日 1 次，第 3 日所有症状及眼睑硬结全部消失。

按语：灸法虽可温补，亦可清泻。麦粒肿初起能使其迅速消散，已化脓者促其速溃或吸收，反复发作者可根治。后溪属于手太阳小肠经，其经颊部支脉至目内眦（睛明），与足太阳膀胱经相衔接，且为八脉交会穴之一，通督脉，督脉统领一身之阳气。用灸泻之，可使瘀热邪毒之气发散于外而病获愈。

Chapter 11
The typical case reports of ENT conditions

Section 1   Stye

Case 1

He, male, 60 years old, came for the first visit on July 15, 2001.

Chief complaints: Two days of redness and swelling of upper eyelids with dizziness and headache. Physical examination: obvious redness and swelling of upper eyelids, slightly indurations sized about 0.4 cm×0.5 cm with pressure in both eyes, tenderness, body temperature of 38℃, and a tendency of suppuration. Diagnosis: stye. Method: The sparrow-pecking moxibustion with moxa stick was applied to bilateral Houxi (SI 3) for about 1 minute. In the following day, the redness and swelling basically disappeared, the nodules were not so obvious, symptoms of dizziness and headache disappeared and the body temperature was reduced to 36.5℃. Then the same moxibustion was applied after that, once every day. All the symptoms and nodules completely disappeared on the third time.

Remarks: Moxibustion is always used to warm and tonify, but it can also be used to clear away heat. For early stage of stye, moxibustion can remove it rapidly; for suppurative stye, moxibustion can speed up its diabrosis or absorption and eradicate recurrent stye. The branch of small intestine meridian reaches inner canthus [Jingming (BL 1)] through cheeks and connects with the foot-Taiyang bladder meridian, the acupoint Houxi (SI 3) is also one of the eight confluent acupoint connecting with Governor Vessel that governs yang-qi of the

汉英对照 Chinese-English Edition of Acupuncture Cosmetology

针灸美容 Part 3 The Typical Case Reports of Acupuncture Cosmetology

二、 验案 2

某男,18 岁。2004 年 5 月初诊。

主诉:左眼微痒疼痛 1 日,曾用氯霉素滴眼液滴眼。刻诊:左眼红肿热痛,上睑中部稍外侧有米粒样硬结。舌苔薄白,脉浮稍数。证系脾胃郁热,上攻眼睑。针刺加挑刺法治疗 1 次,红肿消退,肿痛减轻。再治 1 次告愈。方法:取主穴太阳、合谷、曲池;配穴:攒竹、睛明、足三里、内庭等,毫针行泻法,每次 1 次,1 次为 1 个疗程。针刺完后,在患者背部两肩胛间,第 1~7 胸椎两侧探寻反应点(淡红色,比小米粒小,按之不退色),在常规消毒后,用三棱针对准反应点刺入1 mm,挑破皮肤,挤出少量血液,用棉球擦去,可反复挤 3~5次,最后用乙醇棉球压迫局部片刻。每次取 4~6 个反应点。挑治 2 次后,再隔日治疗 1 次。

whole body, and therefore moxibustion on Houxi (SI 3) can remove the stasis and heat and subsequently cure stye.

Case 2

A male patient, 18 years old, came for treatment in May 2004.

Chief complaints: One-day slight itching and pain of his left eye. Previous management: Chloramphenicol eye drops. Present symptoms and signs include: redness, swelling and pain of the left eye, millet-sized indurations on middle part of upper eyelid (slightly lateral aspect), a thin and white tongue coating and a superficial and slightly rapid pulse. TCM syndrome pattern: stagnant heat in the spleen and stomach up-attacking the eyelid. After one treatment with acupuncture plus pricking therapy, the redness and swelling disappeared and pain also relieved. After another treatment, the patient got a total recovery. The method is as follows: Major acupoints: Taiyang (EX-HN 5), Hegu (LI 4) and Quchi (LI 11); adjunct acupoints: Cuanzhu (BL 2), Jingming (BL 1), Zusanli (ST 36) and Neiting (ST 44). The above acupoints were punctured with reducing manipulation by filiform needles, once every day and one treatment can be one treatment course. After acupuncture is done, to sterilize the reaction points (pale-red color, smaller than millet and no color fading on pressure) between two shoulder blades along C_{1-7}, prick 1 mm at these points with three-edged needle and squeeze a little blood and then clean it with cotton ball. This therapy was repeated for 3 – 5 times and finally the local area were pressed with alcoholic cotton ball for a while. Each time 4 – 6 reaction points can be selected. The pricking therapy can be selected once every other day after twice therapies.

按语：本病多属于实热证，针刺应用泻法，以清阳明经实热。然后再挑刺反应点，达到开窍泄热、活血消肿、疏风明目之目的。麦粒肿病程越短临床疗效越佳，因此抓住最佳治疗时机，对症治疗，可提高临床疗效。

第二节　突眼症

验案

项某某，男，61岁，工程师。1999年6月初诊。

主诉：左眼球外突6月余。患者有甲亢病史年余，近半年左眼球逐渐外突。就诊时，测眼球突出度（16～21/100）mm，视力右0.1、左0.12，左眼球向下偏斜、外转、上转受限，左眼球结膜充血（＋），眼睑闭合不全，自觉目胀痛，有异物感，流泪、畏光、视疲劳，舌红，脉细数。证属邪热亢盛，阴液亏耗，气血瘀凝，眼络不畅。治宜滋阴降火，疏通眼络。予以针刺风池、上天柱（天柱上5分）、太阳、阳白、四白、合谷、丰隆、三阴交、行间等穴，每日针刺1次。风池、上天柱针感向前额或眼区扩散，太阳刺后可少量出血，余穴按常规针刺，留针30 min，每隔10 min行针1次；耳压取肝、肾、内分泌、脾、目1、目2穴位，用王不留行籽埋压，两耳交替，3 d 1换。嘱患者按时按压。治后自觉眼部异物感逐渐减轻，流泪明显减少，眼睑松弛，左眼睑已完全闭合，眼球转动灵活，左球结膜红肿消退。9月复查，眼球外突明显改善，测眼球突出度（14～17/100）mm，连续针刺治疗半年，眼部症状已不著，斜视及视力均较前好转，双眼突相差＜1 mm。

Remarks: Stye is usually caused by excessive-heat syndrome and supposed to be treated by acupuncture with reducing manipulation to clear the excessive-heat in Yangming meridians. Pricking on reaction points acts to open orifice, clear away heat, circulate blood to resolve swelling, remove wind and brighten eyes. The shorter duration the stye has, the better the therapeutic effect can be.

Section 2　Exophthalmus

Case

Xiang, male, 61 years old, an engineer, came for the first visit in June 1999.

Chief complaints: More than 6 months of exophthalmus of his left eye. The patient has a history of hyperthyroidism and got a gradual exophthalmus of his left eye in the recent six months. Physical examination: degree of exophthalmus: 16 - 21/100 mm, the right eyesight: 0.1; the left eyesight: 0.12, a downward deviation of his left eyeball with restricted abversion and supervision, conjunctival congestion of his left eyeball (+), hypophasis, distending pain of the eye with foreign body sensation, lacrimation, and photophobia, asthenopia, a red tongue and a thready and rapid pulse. TCM syndrome pattern: hyperactivity of pathogenic-heat, consumption of yin-fluid, stagnation of qi and blood and obstruction of meridians around eyes. The therapeutic principle: to nourish yin, reduce fire and regulate local meridians. Such acupoints as Fengchi (GB 20), Shangtianzhu [Extra: 0.5 cun above Tianzhu (BL 10)], Taiyang (EX-HN 5), Yangbai (GB 14), Hegu (LI 4), Fenglong (ST 40), Sanyinjiao (SP 6) and Xingjian (LR 2) were punctured once every day. The needling sensations on Fengchi

按语：针刺治疗内分泌性突眼症疗效较好，在自觉症状方面，有效率约为 75%，眼球突出度的有效率则为 60%。上法针刺加耳压治疗其眼球突出度总有效率达 81%。治疗疗程宜长，一般来讲，疗程长短与疗效似成正比。

第三节　眼睑瞤动

一、　验案 1

患者，女，50 岁。

(GB 20) and Shangtianzhu (Extra) were radiated to forehead or eye area; a little bleeding can occur upon needling Taiyang (EX-HN 5), and other acupoints were punctured by routine method. The needles retained for 30 minutes and were manipulated once every 10 minutes. In addition, the following ear acupoints were selected for embedding of cowherb seeds in two ears alternately: liver, kidney, endocrine, spleen, eye 1 and eye 2, and the seeds were changed once every 3 days. The patient was asked to press the ear acupoints himself. After the treatment, the patient felt a gradual relief of foreign body sensation in the eye, an obvious reduction of lacrimation, a loosened eyelid, a complete closure of the left eyelid, a flexible oculogyria and disappearance of conjunctival redness and swelling of the left eye. The return-visit in September showed an obvious improvement of exophthalmus with the degree: 14 – 17/100 mm. After continuous treatment with acupuncture for half a year, the eye symptoms were not as obvious as before, and his strabismus and eyesight were better than before with less than 1 mm of the protrusion of the two eyes.

Remarks: Acupuncture works better in endocrine exophthalmus and can get the effective rate of 75% in terms of subjective symptoms and effective rate of 60% in terms of exophthalmus degree. The total effective rate of treating exophthalmus with above needling therapy plus ear-pressure can reach 81%. Generally speaking, the length of treatment course is proportional to the therapeutic efficacy.

Section 3   Twitching of eyelids
Case 1
A female patient, 50 years old.

主诉：眼睑瞤跳 2 月余。患者 2 个月前开始出现眼睑不自主跳动，至某医院神经内科检查无异常，服用谷维素、维生素类药物未见好转，又至眼科就诊未果，求诊针灸科。检查：眼睑时作不自主瞤动，遂取百会、印堂、太阳（双侧）、内关（双侧）、阳陵泉（健侧）、中平（健侧，阳陵泉下 2 寸处）、太冲（双侧）。阳陵泉、中平用轻度提插泻法，余穴平补平泻，留针 30 min。针刺 1 次后即感轻松，跳动次数明显减少，针刺 3 次后基本停止，5 次后瞤跳完全消失，又巩固治疗 1 个疗程（5 次），随访 3 个月无复发。

按语：取穴百会、印堂可镇静安神；内关、太冲有平厥阴风木之动；阳陵泉、中平均位于足少阳经线上，为上病下取之意，风阳之邪常泻之于少阳胆经；配合近取太阳，改善局部气血，疗效显著。需要注意，排除因面瘫失治后遗持续眼肌跳动、癫痫或面肌痉挛引起得眼睑瞤动，后者也可以用本法治疗，但难以根治。

Chief complaints: More than 2 months of eyelid twitching. Two months ago, the patient got involuntary twitching of eyelids. Examination in neurology department of one hospital showed absence of abnormality and she didn't get any effect from oryzanol or vitamins or in ophthalmology, and therefore came for acupuncture treatment. Physical examination showed an involuntary twitching of eyelids. Acupoints of selection: Baihui (GV 20), Yintang (EX-HN 3), bilateral Taiyang (EX-HN 5), bilateral Neiguan (PC 6), healthy-sided Yanglingquan (GB 34), Zhongping [Extra: 2 cun below Yanglingquan (GB 34)] and bilateral Taichong (LR 3). Except for reducing manipulation with mild lifting and thrusting on Yanglingquan (GB 34) and Zhongping (Extra), the other acupoints were punctured with even reinforcing-reducing manipulation. The needles retained for 30 minutes. Only after one treatment, the patient felt improvement with an obvious reduction of twitching. After 3 times of treatment, the twitching basically stopped. After 5 times, the twitching totally disappeared. Another treatment course (5 times) was done to consolidate the effect and the 3-month follow-up didn't show any relapses.

Remarks: The acupoints Baihui (GV 20) and Yintang (EX-HN 3) were selected to tranquilize the mind; Neiguan (PC 6) and Taichong (LR 3) were selected to soothe the liver-wind; Yanglingquan (GB 34) and Zhongping (Extra) were selected on the basis of "treating the problems of upper body with the acupoints in the lower body", as pathogenic wind-yang always affect the foot-Shaoyang gallbladder meridian; and Taiyang (EX-HN 5) was selected to improve the qi and blood circulation of the local area. The above acupoints worked together for the marked effect. Note: the persistent twitching of eyelids due to

汉英对照

Chinese-English
Edition of
Acupuncture
Cosmetology

针灸美容

Part 3 The Typical Case Reports of Acupuncture Cosmetology

汉英对照

Chinese-English
Edition of
Acupuncture
Cosmetology

针灸美容

下篇

●

针灸美容典型验案

二、 验案 2

李某某,女,32 岁。2003 年 10 月初诊。

主诉:右侧上下眼皮跳动明显,不能自主 3 月余,近 3 日加重。经西医治疗,肌肉注射营养神经类药物 1 个月(具体药名不详)无效,特来求治。证见:右侧上下眼睑不时跳动,不能自控,幅度较大,频率快,大约每分钟 55 次左右,眼外观端好,无红、肿、热、痛。治疗取穴:申脉、照海、三阴交、太冲、四白、攒竹,均取右侧。申脉用补法,照海用泻法,其余穴位用平补平泻法。每 10 min 行针 1 次,留针 30 min。经治疗 1 次后,症状明显减轻,治疗 3 次后症状消失。随访 1 年未再复发。

按语:阴、阳蹻脉的功能"司眼睑开合"。申脉、照海为八脉交会穴,申脉通阳蹻脉,照海通阴蹻脉,本案例应用针刺补泻以泻阴补阳,调其经气;取足太阴脾经原穴太白、三阴交补脾以益生化之源;足厥阴肝经原穴太冲以调肝益血熄风;选眼周的穴位来调理眼睑周围的经气,达到疏通经络、调理气血、濡养经筋的作用。该病轻者或偶尔发生者,不必治疗,可以自愈。若跳动过频,久跳不止者则须治疗。

untreated facial paralysis, epilepsy or facial spasm shall be excluded, for they can also be treated with the same therapy but can hardly be eradicated.

Case 2

Li, female, 32 years old, came for the first visit in October 2003.

Chief complaints: More than 3 months of involuntary of right-sided eyelid twitching that worsened in the recent 3 days. Previous treatment: intramuscular injection of nerve-nourishing medications (no specific name of the medications) but no effect. Present symptoms: intermittent twitching of right-sided eyelids in large amplitude and high frequency of about 55 times per minute, normal appearance of the eye and absence of redness, swelling, heat and pain. Selection of acupoints: right-sided Shenmai (BL 62), Zhaohai (Kid 6), Sanyinjiao (SP 6), Taichong (LR 3), Sibai (ST 2), and Cuanzhu (BL 2). Except reinforcing manipulation for Shenmai (BL 62) and reducing manipulation for Zhaohai (KI 6), the other acupoints were punctured with even reinforcing-reducing manipulation. The needles retained for 30 minutes and were manipulated once every 10 minutes. After one treatment, the symptoms were obviously relieved, and after 3 times of treatment, the symptoms disappeared. The 1-year follow-up didn't show any relapses.

Remarks: The Yin-qiao and Yang-qiao meridians govern "opening and closing of eyelids". As two of the eight confluent acupoints, Shenmai (BL 62) connects with Yang-qiao meridian and Zhaohai (KI 6) connects with Yin-qiao meridian. The reinforcing or reducing manipulations were adopted to reduce yin and tonify yang and regulate the meridian-qi; Taibai (SP

患者,男,66 岁,日本人。1999 年 11 月入院。

主诉:阵发性双眼睑痉挛 4 年,加重 1 年。初为右眼睑间断抽动,后发展为双眼,发作时眼睑不自主痉挛,目睁困难,曾就诊于日本多家医院,并接受多种药物治疗和理疗均无效。症见阵发性双眼睑痉挛,以右眼为甚,发作时双眼睑呈痉挛性闭合,睑肌瞤动,目睁困难,精神紧张时痉挛加剧,每日频繁发作,舌红少苔,脉弦细。证属气血亏虚,阴虚阳亢。治以滋阴潜阳,熄风通络。取穴:上睛明、攒竹、丝竹空、瞳子髎、阳白、太阳、鱼腰、四神聪、三阴交、足三里、太冲。针刺得气后加电针,并留针 20 min。阳白、太阳处刺络拔罐,隔日 1 次。经治疗 1 周,症状明显改善,双眼痉挛程度减轻,经治 1 个月左眼诸症消失,右眼发作次数明显减少,眼肌抬举有力。巩固治疗 1 个月,基本痊愈出院。

3), the Yuan-primary acupoint of spleen meridian, and Sanyinjiao (SP 6) were selected to tonify the spleen to supplement the source of generation and transportation; Taichong (LR 3), the Yuan-primary acupoint of the foot-Jueyin liver meridian was adopted to nourish liver-blood and stop wind; the acupoints around the eye were selected to regulate meridian-qi of the local area to harmonize qi and blood and nourish muscles and tendons. The mild condition or intermittent eyelid twitching doesn't have to be treated, for they may recover spontaneously, otherwise high-frequency or persistent twitching have to be treated.

Case 3

A male patient, 66 years old, Japanese, was hospitalized in November 1999.

Chief complaints: Four-year paroxysmal twitching of eyelids (both eyes) that worsened for one year. At first the patient got intermittent eyelid twitching of the right eye, and later eyelid twitching of both eyes with involuntary spasm of eyelids and difficulty in keeping eyes open. Previous treatment: medications and physiotherapies in several hospitals in Japan but no effect. Present symptoms and signs: paroxysmal eyelids spasm of two eyes, especially the right eye, appearing spasmodic closing of two eyes, twitching of eyelids, and difficulty in keeping eyes open, worsened spasm with mental stress, frequent attacks every day, a red tongue with scanty coating and a wiry and thready pulse. TCM syndrome pattern: deficiency of qi and blood and hyperactivity of yang due to yin deficiency. The therapeutic principle: to nourish yin, inhibit yang, stop wind and clear meridians. Selection of acupoints: Shangjingming (Extra), Cuanzhu (BL 2), Sizhukong (TE 23),

按语：本病治疗取手足阳明、少阴、厥阴经中眼睑周围穴位，可疏通经气、舒缓筋急，并通过电针调整神经兴奋性，改善局部营养代谢，加速恢复眼睑部肌肉神经功能。取三阴交、阴陵泉、足三里、太冲以滋阴潜阳、健脾益胃、补后天以治本，兼以平肝柔筋。配合太阳、阳白的刺络拔罐，取"宛陈除之"、"治风先治血"之意，可除瘀血、通经络、祛邪气、止痉挛之功效。

四、 验案 4

　　刘某某，女，63 岁，农民。1998 年 10 月初诊。

Tongziliao (GB 1), Yangbai (GB 14), Taiyang (EX-HN 5), Yuyao (EX-HN 4), Sishencong (EX-HN 1), Sanyinjiao (SP 6), Zusanli (ST 36), and Taichong (LR 3). The electric stimulator was connected to needles upon arrival of qi for 20 minutes. The cupping following blood-letting on Yangbai (GB 14) and Taiyang (EX-HN 5) was done once every other day. After one week of treatment, the patient's symptoms were obviously improved and spasm of two eyes was relieved. After one month of treatment, the symptoms of the left eye disappeared and the attacks of the right eye were obviously reduced with a strong lift-up power of musculi oculi. Then after another month of treatment for consolidation, the patient was discharged from the hospital.

Remarks: Acupoints around the eyes of Yangming, Shaoyin and Jueyin meridians of both hand and foot can dredge meridian-qi and relax muscles and tendons. In addition, electric stimulation can regulate nerve excitability, improve local nutritional metabolism, and speed up the recovery of nerve function of eyelid muscle. The acupoints Sanyinjiao (SP 6), Yinlingquan (SP 9), Zusanli (ST 36) and Taichong (LR 3) act to nourish yin, inhibit yang, strengthen the spleen, benefit the stomach and thus tonify the acquired essence as well as soothe the liver and soften tendons. The cupping following blood-letting on Taiyang (EX-HN 5) and Yangbai (GB 14), based on "chronic blood stagnations shall be removed" or "circulating blood before stopping the wind", can resolve blood stasis, clear meridians, remove pathogenic qi and stop spasm.

Case 4

Liu, female, 63 years old, a farmer, came for the first visit in October 1998.

主诉：左侧眼睑痉挛 2 年。患者于 2 年前左侧眼睑开始轻度痉挛，未予重视，后逐渐加重，曾服用谷维素治疗，疗效不佳。检查：面色㿠白，脉弦细，舌红苔白。取水沟、神庭、头维（患侧）、承泣（患侧）、复溜（双侧）、太冲（双侧），30 号 1 寸毫针速刺入水沟，用雀啄法行针致患者微有眼泪即可。余穴用 1.5 寸毫针，快速进针，行捻转泻法。神庭、神门、承泣、头维、复溜用捻转补法。留针 30 min，每 15 min 捻转 1 次。治疗 15 次后，眼睑痉挛只偶尔发作，巩固治疗 7 次后痊愈。随访半年未复发。

按语：随着人们日常生活步伐加快，该病发病率呈增高趋势。本病治疗应从"神"论治。治宜调气和血，潜阳安神。水沟是治风要穴，功能熄风醒神，且为督脉与手足阳明经的交会穴，手足阳明经与经筋和眼均有重要联系。是治疗本病的主穴。余穴配合，达到标本同治的目的。

Chief complaints: Spasm in the left eyelid for 2 years. Two years ago, the patient got mild spasm in his left eyelid but didn't pay much attention, and then the condition gradually worsened. He was treated with oryzanol but didn't get satisfactory effect. Physical examination: a bright pale complexion, a wiry and thready pulse and a red tongue with white coating. Selection of acupoints: Shuigou (GV 26), Shenting (GV 24), the affected-side Touwei (ST 8) and Chengqi (ST 1), bilateral Fuliu (KI 7) and bilateral Taichong (LR 3). Except for sparrow-pecking method on Shuigou (GV 26) with 1-cun needle No. 30 until slight tears, the other acupoints were punctured with 1. 5 cun filiform needles by fast insertion and reducing manipulation through rotation. Such acupoints were punctured with reinforcing manipulation by rotation as Shenting (GV 44), Shenmen (HT 7), Chengqi (ST 1), Touwei (ST 8) and Fuliu (KI 7). The needles retained for 30 minutes and were manipulated once every 15 minutes. After 15 times of treatment, the spasm of eyelids only occurred occasionally and after another 7 times for consolidation, the patient got a total recovery. The six-month follow-up didn't show any relapses.

Remarks: The incidence of eyelid twitching is on the rise with the increase of modern life pace. According to TCM theory, this condition shall be treated from "heart-mind" with the following principle: to harmonize qi and blood, inhibit yang and calm the mind. Shuigou (GV 26), a key acupoint for stopping wind, acts to stop wind and refresh mind. What's more, it is also a crossing acupoint of Governor Vessel and Yangming meridians of both hand and foot, which closely relate to muscle regions and eyes, and as a result it was selected

第四节 红眼病

一、 验案 1

李某某,男,37岁,干部。1997年7月21日就诊。

主诉:两目红肿涩痛、时有痒感、哆多、流泪、畏光10余日。在当地医院诊断为"急性结膜炎"(红眼病)。经用多种点眼药,并输青霉素、病毒唑等药,均无效,故来求诊。治疗方法:以三棱针点刺双侧太阳、耳尖穴和印堂穴,出血数滴。当时患者自觉涩痛减轻,双目明亮。嘱患者回家后每次小便时,取尿液洗双眼数次。二诊红肿消退,已不涩痒、流泪、畏光,亦无眼哆、视物如常。一次见效,为防复发,再以上法点刺1次,继续用尿液洗双眼数日,随访未曾复发而告愈。

按语:本病早期治疗效果更好,点刺出血或尿液洗患眼后,患者常感局部轻松,双目明亮。在治疗期间忌食辛辣刺激性的食物,治疗好转后要坚持尿洗患眼数日,以防复发。此外,红眼病传染性很强,多由于接触传染而致,需将患者的用具严加消毒和隔离。

as a major acupoint for this condition. The combination of other acupoints worked to treat both the primary cause and symptoms.

Section 4 Conjunctivitis
Case 1

Li, male, 37 years old, a government official, came for the first visit on July 21, 1997.

Chief complaints: More than 10 days of redness, swelling and pain of two eyes, occasional itching, excessive secretion of eyes, lacrimation and photophobia. Previous treatment: the patient was diagnosed in a local hospital as "acute conjunctivitis" (pink eyes) and treated with several eyedrops as well as intravenous injection of penicillin or virazole but didn't get good effect. Method: The bilateral Taiyang (EX-HN 5) and ear apex and Yintang (EX-HN 3) were pricked with three-edged needle for several drops of blood. After that, the patient felt the pain relieved and eyes turned bright. Then he was asked to wash the two eyes several times with his urine each time upon urination. The second visit showed a disappearance of redness and swelling and absence of itching, lacrimation, photophobia, and secretion of eyes and got normal vision. The above pricking method was adopted once more for prevention of recurrence, and he continued to wash his eyes with his urine for several days. The follow-up after that didn't show any relapses.

Remarks: The earlier treatment of this condition may get a better result. The patients always feel relaxed in local area with brightened eyes after pricking therapy plus washing eyes with urine. During the treatment the patients were asked not to take spicy or pungent food and continue to wash eyes with urine for

汉英对照

Chinese-English
Edition of
Acupuncture
Cosmetology

针灸美容

Part 3 The Typical Case Reports of Acupuncture Cosmetology

二、 验案 2

李某,女,35 岁。

主诉:患红眼病数日,服用抗生素仍感疼痛,难以睁眼。诊见双眼结膜充血。治疗方法:取患侧太阳、攒竹、中指端(距爪甲 1 分处)。先揉数下刺血部位使其充血,然后按常规消毒皮肤,用消毒过的三棱针快速刺入,令出血 3～5 滴。次日症状消失而愈。

按语:本方法经济安全、简便易行、无痛苦和副作用。如果 1 次未愈隔日可以再刺 1 次。

第五节　酒皶鼻

一、 验案 1

李某某,男,36 岁,干部。1985 年 3 月 15 日初诊。

主诉:以鼻部为中心红皮肤表面油腻发亮,渐至红斑 3 年余。患者于 3 年前开始鼻尖及鼻翼两侧出现阵发性红斑,继而红斑持久不退,甚至脓疱,瘙痒。常自购外用药涂搽,未见明显效果,近日症状加重,局部增生明显而求诊。检查:鼻尖、鼻翼两侧见红斑,有绿豆大小脓疱,局部毛细血管扩张。诊断:酒皶鼻。取穴素髎、印堂、上星、百会、迎香、合谷、曲池、列缺、支沟,行平补平泻手法,留针 40 min,每 10 min 行针 1 次,每日 1 次,15 次为 1 个疗程,每疗程间隔 10 d,针刺 35 次后,皮疹及自觉症状完全消失,随访半年未发。

several days even after they felt better to prevent recurrence. In addition, the things that the patient touched shall be strictly sterilized and isolated for this condition is very contagious and easily spreads through contact.

Case 2

Li, female, 35 years old.

Chief complaints: Suffering from conjunctivitis for several days, pain even after oral administration of antibiotics and difficulty in keeping her eyes open. Physical examination showed conjunctival congestion of her two eyes. Method: To knead the following acupoints several times to make them congested: the affected-side Taiyang (EX-HN 5), Cuanzhu (BL 2) and Zhongzhiduan (Extra: 0.1 cun away from the nails of the middle finger); next to make routine sterilization; and then to insert rapidly with sterile three-edged needle with 3 - 5 blood drops. The following day, the patient's symptoms disappeared.

Remarks: The above method is safe and simple with low-cost, no pains or side effects. In case one treatment doesn't work well, another treatment can be done one day later.

Section 5 Brandy nose

Case 1

Li, male, 36 years old, a government official, came for the first visit on March 15, 1985.

Chief complaints: More than 3 years of red skin with greasy and shiny surface centered on nasal area that gradually turned too erythema. Three years ago, the patient got paroxysmal erythema in nasal tip and both sides of the nasal wings, and later the erythema became persistent or even

汉英对照

Chinese-English
Edition of
Acupuncture
Cosmetology

针灸美容

下篇 ◎ 针灸美容典型验案

按语:《外科大成》载:"酒皶鼻者,先由肺经血热内蒸,次遇风寒外束,血瘀凝结而成。"针刺取穴局部与辨证循经相配合,清血热、散风寒、通经络、化瘀斑,促进皮损的愈合而达治疗效果。

二、 验案 2

张某,女,39 岁,工人。

主诉:鼻部及面颊部发疹、瘙痒 10 余年。初起经用外用药,未见好转,日渐加重,鼻翼及面部均有散在性之斑片,并有散在性红色绿豆大之丘疹,毛细血管扩张较严重,诊断:酒皶鼻。采用针刺治疗,取穴印堂、素髎、迎香、地仓、承浆、颧髎、合谷、曲池,15 次后毛细血管扩张好转,20 次后红斑及丘疹基本消退,28 次后痊愈,随访未发。

pustules with itching sensation. The patient often applied the self-bought external medication but didn't get obvious effect; however, the condition turned worse with obvious hyperplasia in the local area. Physical examination showed erythema in nasal tip and both sides of the nasal wings, mung bean-sized pustules and local telangiectasis. Diagnosis: brandy nose. Selection of acupoints: Suliao (GV 25), Yintang (EX-HN 3), Shangxing (GV 23), Baihui (GV 20), Yingxiang (LI 20), Hegu (LI 4), Quchi (LI 11), Lieque (LU 7) and Zhigou (TE 6). All above acupoints were punctured with even reinforcing-reducing manipulation by filiform needles. The needles retained for 40 minutes and were manipulated once every 10 minutes. The treatment was done once every day, 15 times make up one treatment course and there is a 10-day interval between two courses. After 35 times of acupuncture treatment, the skin rashes and subjective symptoms totally disappeared. The six-month follow-up didn't show any relapses.

Remarks: The *Wai Ke Da Cheng* (*A complete book of external diseases*) states that "brandy nose is caused by blood-heat of the lung meridian, external contraction of wind-cold and blood stasis". Needling local acupoints as well as acupoints along the running course of meridians based on syndrome differentiation can clear blood-heat, dissipate wind-cold, regulate meridians, resolve stasis spots and speed up recovery of the skin lesion.

Case 2

Zhang, female, 39 years old, a worker.

Chief complaints: More than 10 years of skin rashes in nasal area and facial cheeks. She tried externally-used medications and didn't get any better but worse instead:

按语：本病与情绪紧张、感染、习惯性便秘、月经失调及螨虫寄生等因素有关，针灸治疗的同时，应注意对症处理。同时应嘱咐患者忌食辛辣、酒类等刺激性食物，少饮浓茶，宜保持清淡饮食，保持局部的卫生。

第六节 口舌疮

一、验案1

林某某，女，38岁，干部。1987年6月12日初诊。

主诉：口腔黏膜溃疡反复发作10年余。间隔半个月左右复发1次，每次7～10 d愈合，有灼痛感，进食时加剧。检查：下唇黏膜、舌腹、舌缘等5处溃疡点，呈扁圆形，覆以假膜，周围有红晕，直径为4 mm。诊断：复发性口舌疮。取穴劳宫（双）、涌泉穴，毫针快速刺入0.5寸左右，轻度捻转，行平补平泻，留针30 min，每10 min行针1次，每日针刺1次，针刺4次后症状完全消失。随访3个月未见复发。

scattered patches of erythema in nasal wings and face, mung bean-sized papules in red and relatively severe telangiectasis. Diagnosis: brandy nose. Acupuncture was done on the following acupoints: Yintang (EX-HN 3), Suliao (GV 25), Yingxiang (LI 20), Chengjiang (CV 24), Quanliao (SI 18), Hegu (LI 4) and Quchi (LI 11). After 15 times of treatment, the telangiectasis got improved; after 20 times of treatment, the erythema and papules basically disappeared; and after 28 times of treatment, the patient got a total recovery. The follow-up didn't show any relapses.

Remarks: This condition is related to such factors as emotional stress, infection, habitual constipation, irregular menstruation and mites. In addition to acupuncture treatment, symptom-orientated measures shall also be taken. In the meantime the patients shall be recommended to avoid spicy food and alcohol drink, reduce strong tea, take bland food and keep local area clean.

Section 6   Mouth or tongue ulcer

Case 1

Lin, female, 38 years old, a government official, came for the first visit on June 12, 1987.

Chief complaints: More than 10 years of recurrent ulcer of mouth mucosa. She got one attack every two weeks with burning pain that worsened during food intake, 7 - 10 days each time. Physical examination showed five ulceration areas including lower lip mucosa, ventral aspect of tongue and margin of tongue, the oblate ulcerations were covered with false membrane and peripheral redness and 4 mm in diameter. Diagnosis: recurrent mouth and tongue ulcer. Method: the

按语：中医学认为，本病多由于情志纷扰、思虑过度，虚火上炎、心肾不交所致。劳宫为心包的"荥穴"，涌泉是肾经的"井穴"，二穴相配不仅能清泻心包之火，更能交通心肾，滋水于上，促进溃疡的愈合，达到治本的效果。

二、 验案2

王某某，女，47岁，家庭妇女。于1998年3月27日初诊。

主诉：口腔黏膜溃疡反复发作3年左右，影响进食，灼痛难忍。诊断：复发性口舌疮。取金津、玉液，以三棱针点刺出血，每周2次，配合针刺合谷、曲池、列缺、照海、太溪、太冲，隔日1次，治疗2周后溃疡基本愈合，巩固治疗2周后痊愈。

汉英对照

Chinese-English
Edition of
Acupuncture
Cosmetology

针灸美容

下篇 ● 针灸美容典型验案

278

acupoints Laogong (PC 8) (bilateral) and Yongquan (KI 1) were punctured 0.5 cun with fast insertion and even reinforcing-reducing manipulation through mild rotation. The needles retained for 30 minutes and were manipulated once every 10 minutes. The treatment was done once every day. After 4 times of treatment, the symptoms totally disappeared and the 3-month follow-up didn't show any relapses.

Remarks: TCM holds that this condition is usually caused by emotional disturbance, anxiety, up-flame of deficient fire and disharmony between the heart and kidney. The acupoint Laogong (PC 8) is the Ying-spring acupoint of the pericardium meridian and Yongquan (KI 1) is the Jing-well acupoint of the kidney meridian. The combination of the two acupoints can not only clear pericardium fire but also harmonize the heart-fire and kidney-water and speed up healing of the ulcer.

Case 2

Wang, female, 47 years old, a housewife, came for the first visit on March 27, 1998.

Chief complaints: About three years of recurrent ulcer of mouth mucosa with intolerable burning pain that affected food intake. Diagnosis: recurrent mouth and tongue ulcer. Method: The acupoints Jinjin (EX-HN 12) and Yuye (EX-HN 13) were pricked with three-edged needle for blood letting; and the acupoints Hegu (LI 4), Quchi (LI 11), Lieque (LU 7), Zhaohai (KI 6), Taixi (KI 3) and Taichong (LR 3) were punctured once every other day. After 2 weeks of treatment, the patient's ulcer basically healed; and after another 2 weeks of treatment for consolidation, her ulcer totally healed.

Remarks: Blood letting therapy can clear fire and heat, dredge meridians, promote metabolism of skin mucosa and

汉英对照

Chinese-English
Edition of
Acupuncture
Cosmetology

针灸美容

下篇
⊕
针灸美容典型验案

　　按语：放血疗法能清泻火热、疏通经络，促进皮肤黏膜新陈代谢，加快黏膜愈合。治疗期间嘱患者注意口腔卫生，以盐水漱口。多进食瓜果蔬菜，忌食辛辣，禁烟酒等。

speed up healing of ulcer. During the treatment, the patient was asked to keep oral cavity clean and rinse mouth with saline water, take more fruits and vegetables, and avoid spicy food, cigarettes or alcohol.

汉英对照

Chinese-English
Edition of
Acupuncture
Cosmetology

针灸美容 Part 3 The Typical Case Reports of Acupuncture Cosmetology

第十二章　其他损美性病症的典型验案

第一节　肥胖症

一、验案1

莎拉·塔巴柯娃,女,39岁,文艺工作者。2003年1月初诊。

近5年来,增重显著,身高167 cm,体重由过去的56±1 kg增至76±1 kg,较正常体重超重17 kg。情绪不佳,喜饮酒,吃零食。身倦、少言、嗜睡,且易怒,舌苔白微腻,脉弦滑。查:WC:96 cm,BMI:27.25,TSF:40 mm,SSF:30 mm,F%:42.6%,为Ⅰ度肥胖。方法:取中号火罐(4 cm左右),以闪火法刺激腹部的神阙八阵穴(以神阙为中宫,以神阙至关元穴的长度为半径做一圆周,等分8个点为8个穴位),沿顺时针方向,每穴多次、反复闪罐,直到腹部刺激部位潮红出汗为度,每日治疗1次,每次20～30 min,1周治疗5次,20次为1个疗程。治疗2次后体重即减少1 kg,20次后,体重减少3.5 kg,情绪、精神转佳。随访半年,体重维持在64±1 kg。

Chapter 12
The typical case reports of other beauty-impairing conditions

Section 1   Obesity
Case 1

Sara Tabokov, female, 39 years old, a singer, came for the first visit in January 2003.

Chief complaints: A remarkable weight gain in recent 5 years: with a height of 167 cm, the body weight increased from 56 ± 1 kg to 76 ± 1 kg, 17 kg exceeding the standard body weight. Accompanying symptoms and signs include: mood swings, preference for alcohol drinking and snacks, fatigue, reluctance to talk, drowsiness, irritability, a white and slightly greasy tongue coating and a wiry and slippery pulse. Physical examination: WC: 96 cm; BMI: 27.25; TSF: 40 mm; SSF: 30 mm; and F%: 42.6%. Diagnosis: I°obesity. Method: The Ba-eight acupoints around Shenque (CV 8) (location: to draw a circle by using CV 8 as center and distance from CV 8 to CV 4 as semi-diameter, and then to divide the circle into eight equal parts as eight acupoints) were applied clockwise flash cupping therapy with medium-sized cup (about 4 cm), many times for each acupoints until the local area turned slightly red and sweated. The treatment was done once every day, 20 – 30 minutes each time, 5 times a week, and 20 times make up one treatment course. After twice treatments, the patient's body weight reduced by 1 kg; and after 20 times, the patient's body weight reduced by 3.5 kg with an improved emotional or mental state. The six-month follow-up showed body weight

汉英对照
Chinese-English Edition of Acupuncture Cosmetology
针灸美容 Part 3 The Typical Case Reports of Acupuncture Cosmetology

按语：八阵穴是以一个腧穴为中宫，把中宫到一定距离作为半径，画一个圆，将这个圆分为8等份形成8个穴位，即为八阵穴，是在天地生阴阳、两仪生四象、四象生八卦的基础上形成的。由于阴阳互根，相互转化，故八阵穴也随着阴阳的转化而周流全身。肥胖症主要由于体内津液因脏腑代谢异常而致，本法能调理脾胃功能，促进体内水液代谢而达到减肥功效。

二、 验案2

张某某，女，62岁，退休教师。2001年6月初诊。

主诉：自45岁绝经以后，至今肥胖近30 kg，曾采取运动、医疗器械、按摩等多种方法，疗效不显，而且肥胖呈逐年上升趋势。就诊时体重88 kg，腰围127 cm，身高155 cm，BMI为36.6，食欲旺盛，口臭便秘，面红气粗，舌红苔黄腻，脉数有力。证属中焦火盛，痰热内蕴。取穴：曲池、支沟、大横、天枢、腹结（见图5）、中脘、内庭、足三里、丰隆，选用1.5寸毫针，行泻法，得气后连接G6805电针仪连续波治疗，强度以患者能耐受为度。每日1次，每次60 min，10次为1个疗程。耳穴：口、贲门、食道、胃、大肠、内分泌、渴点、饥点、神门等，用王不留行籽埋穴贴压，每日三餐前30 min揉按，每穴按压50次，4 d 1换。治疗6个疗程后，体重降至59 kg。腰围下降至91 cm，BMI为24.6。

maintenance within 64 ± 1 kg.

Remarks: The Ba-eight zhen acupoints refer to eight acupoints or eight equal parts in a circle drew by using one acupoint as center and certain distance from that acupoint as semi-diameter, which have been based on the ancient theory of "the world produces yin and yang, yin and yang subdivide and produce four images and then the four images produce eight diagrams". Because of yin-yang interdependence and mutual transformation, the Ba-eight zhen acupoints circulate the whole body with yin-yang transformation. Considering that obesity mainly results from abnormal metabolism of body fluids, this method can regulate functions of the spleen and stomach, improve metabolism of body fluids and obtained the effect of weight loss.

Case 2

Zhang, female, 62 years old, a retired teacher, came for the first visit in June 2001.

Chief complaints: nearly 30 kg of weight gain since menopause at 45. She tried varieties of therapies including sports, medical instrument and massage but didn't get marked effect; instead, the obesity seemed to be more and more serious year by year. Physical examination: body weight: 88 kg; WC: 127 cm; height: 155 cm; and BMI: 36.6. Accompanying symptoms and signs include: an extremely good appetite, foul breath with constipation, a red face with fast breath, a red tongue with yellow and greasy coating and a rapid and powerful pulse. TCM syndrome pattern: hyperactivity of fire in middle jiao and internal accumulation of phlegm-heat. Selection of acupoints: Quchi (LI 11), Zhigou (TE 6), Daheng (SP 15), Tianshu (ST 25), Fujie (SP 14), Zhongwan (CV 12), Neiting

按语：针灸减肥疗效显著，反弹率低，部分患者在结束治疗后有体重继续下降至标准体重的趋势。针灸减肥的疗效与年龄和肥胖的时间长短有关。年龄小者优于年龄长者，病程短者优于病程长者。因此，肥胖者应尽早治疗为宜。

三、 验案 3

患者，女，汉族，45 岁。2004 年 3 月初诊。

(ST 44), Zusanli (ST 36) and Fenglong (ST 40). The above acupoints were punctured with reducing manipulation by 1.5 cun filiform needles. The G6805 electric stimulator was connected to needles after arrival of qi with tolerable intensity. The treatment was done once every day, 60 minutes each time and 10 times make up one treatment course. Selection of auricular acupoints: mouth, cardia, esophagus, stomach, large intestine, endocrine, thirst point, hunger point and ear-Shenmen. The ear acupoints were applied embedding of cowherb seeds, self-kneading or pressing 30 minutes before each of the three meals, 50 times for each acupoint. The seeds were changed once every 4 days. After six treatment courses, the patient's body weight reduced to 59 kg, her waistline reduced to 91 cm and her BMI reduced to 24.6.

Remarks: Acupuncture can obtain a marked effect in weight loss with a low rebound rate. Some patients may have the tendency to reduce the body weight to standard body weight after the treatment ended. The therapeutic efficacy of weight loss with acupuncture is associated with the duration of obesity. The younger patients got better results than the older ones, and those with a short duration got better results than those with a long duration. Therefore obesity should be treated as early as possible.

Case 3

A female patient, Han nationality, 45 years old, came for the first visit in March 2004.

Chief complaints: Obesity, heaviness of limbs, fatigue and a poor appetite. As her kid grew up, she felt relaxed. Also as she is an office clerk, she keeps a long-time sitting position during her work. In addition, she likes to watch TV after

汉英对照

Chinese-English
Edition of
Acupuncture
Cosmetology

针灸美容

下篇 ● 针灸美容典型验案

　　主诉：肥胖，肢体困重，疲乏无力，纳差。由于孩子长大，不用操心家事，又是办公室人员，上班久坐不动，晚餐后喜欢靠在床上看电视，2 年后体重急剧上升。未作过任何减肥治疗。身高 160 cm，体重 66 kg。舌质淡红，苔薄腻，脉濡细。诊断：肥胖症（脾虚湿阻型）。治以健脾利湿。采用腹部透刺并用电针，上腹部取太乙透刺下脘（双）（见图 5），下腹部取腹结透刺大巨（双）（见图 5）。毫针刺入太乙、腹结 1 cm 后，再沿皮下 1～2 cm 透刺到同一平面的下脘或大巨。腹结、太乙两侧共 4 穴通电针仪（G6805－2 型），连续波，频率 2.5 Hz，强度以患者能耐受为度。治疗 30 min。配以丰隆、阴陵泉，毫针泻法，得气后留针 30 min，隔日 1 次；耳穴贴压取脾、胃、饥点、口、三焦，每周更换 1 次；神阙灸疗，隔日 1 次。在治疗 3 次后，体重下降 2 kg，经 1 个疗程治疗后（15 次），体重下降 7 kg。

dinner. As a result she got a quick weight gain in recent two years and she was never treated for obesity. Her height: 160 cm, body weight: 66 kg. She got a red tongue with thin and greasy coating and a soft and thready pulse. Diagnosis: obesity (the pattern of dampness obstruction due to spleen deficiency). The therapeutic principle: to strengthen the spleen and resolve dampness. Method: Needling abdominal acupoints from one acupoint toward another one plus electric stimulation. Selection of acupoints: in upper abdomen, Taiyi (ST 23) was punctured toward Xiawan (CV 10) (bilateral) and in lower abdomen, Fujie (SP 14) was punctured toward Daju (ST 27) (bilateral). After inserting 1 cm into the acupoints Taiyi (ST 23) and Fujie (SP 14), the needles were inserted subcutaneously (1 - 2 cm) into Xiawan (CV 10) or Daju (ST 27) in the same surface. Then four acupoints, i. e., bilateral Fujie (SP 14) and Taiyi (ST 23) were connected with electric stimulator (G6805-2) with continuous wave, 2. 5 Hz frequency and tolerable intensity for 30 minutes; the acupoints Fenglong (ST 40) and Yinlingquan (SP 9) were punctured with reducing manipulation. The needles retained for 30 minutes and the treatment was done once every other day; Ear-pressure was also done on such acupoints as spleen, stomach, hunger point, mouth and Sanjiao once every week; moxibustion on Shenque (CV 8) was done once every other day. After 3 times of treatment, the patient's body weight reduced by 2 kg; after one treatment course (15 times), the patient's body weight reduced by 7 kg.

Remarks: Oblique (subcutaneous) puncture on abdomen with elongated needle involves spleen meridian of foot-Taiyin, stomach meridian of foot-Yangming and Conception Vessel and

汉英对照

Chinese-English
Edition of
Acupuncture
Cosmetology

针灸美容

下篇 ◉ 针灸美容典型验案

按语：腹部采用芒针斜（横）次，从足太阴脾经透足阳明胃经，由此又达任脉，一针透多经，可使脏腑、经络、腧穴之间的经气交融贯通，营卫气血疏通畅达，使多经之间同时得气。得气后再运用电针，进一步提高针刺减肥效果。根据全息理论，耳是一个小的整体，取之能宣畅经络，疏通气血，宣肺化浊，利湿降脂，调整脾胃的消化功能，减轻饥饿感，从而达到减肥的目的。神阙居脐中，是全身高级调控系统，借助灸火的温和热力及艾叶的药物作用，通过穴位、经络的传导，起到疏理经络气血，调节肾、脾、胃三脏功能，呵护"精、气、神"，达到阴平阳秘、脏腑协调、气血畅达，促进新陈代谢，实现减肥的效应。在针灸减肥过程中，不过分控制饮食，但要求患者晚餐与睡眠时间要相隔 3～4 h，晚餐 7 分饱，并在餐后不吃零食，可适当吃些水果。在睡前作 20 min 左右的腹式呼吸及揉腹。

第二节　黑变病

验案

胡某，女，28 岁，工人。

enables meridian-qi of zang-fu organs, meridians and acupoints to merge and harmonize Ying-nutrient, Wei-defense, qi and blood and obtain arrival of qi of above meridians simultaneously. The combined electric stimulation can further improve the weight loss effect. Based on the holographic theory, ear can be regarded as a whole, and ear acupoints can dredge meridians, regulate qi and blood, promote the dispersing function of lung, resolve turbidity, remove dampness and reduce fat, regulate digestive function of the spleen and stomach, inhibit hunger sensation and achieve the therapeutic effect. The acupoints Shenque (CV 8) is located in the center of umbilicus, the high-grade regulatory system of the body. Warm or heat sensation from moxibustion and herbal function of moxa wool can dredge qi and blood of meridians through acupoints and regulate the functions of kidney, spleen and stomach and protect "essence, qi and spirit", which in turn to balance yin-yang, harmonize zang-fu organs, regulate qi and blood, promote metabolism and achieve weight loss. During acupuncture treatment, the patient was asked not to over-control her diet, but to keep 3 - 4 hours between dinner and sleep, 70% full for dinner and no snacks after that, but she could take some fruits instead. Also she was asked to do abdominal breathing and knead abdomen about 20 minutes before sleep.

Section 2　Melanosis

Case

Hu, female, 28 years old, a worker.

Chief complaints: In 1980, the patient got gradual Melanosis of her cervical skin without any inducing factors, and

主诉：1980年开始无任何诱因面颈部皮肤逐渐变黑，并相继扩展至四肢、躯干。发病初期皮肤发红奇痒，伴心悸不寐，食少纳差，月经量少，性欲几乎消失。诊断：黑变病。体针取穴：大椎、曲池、血海、三阴交，行平补平泻，留针20 min，隔日1次；耳针取穴：神门、交感、肾上腺、内分泌、子宫、肺，每次每耳取2穴，间断行针加强刺激，留针4 h，隔日1次。穴位注射取穴：肺俞、心俞、肝俞、肾俞，取当归注射液1支，取2对穴位分别注射，隔日1次，10次为1个疗程。经4个疗程治疗，皮肤奇痒明显减轻，饮食大有改善，部分皮肤色素沉着略有减少。半年后，皮肤色素明显减少，兼症基本消失。共治疗27个疗程，肤色恢复正常。

按语：中医学认为本病多为脾肝肾不足、气血亏损、气滞血瘀、肌肤失养所致，通过针灸、耳穴、穴位注射的共同应用，调整脏腑功能，促进气血运行而达治疗效果。由于疗程较长，应与患者进行良好沟通，使之积极配合，坚持治疗。

later the melanosis spread to four limbs and torso. At first, the skin turned red and she felt extremely itching with such accompanying symptoms as palpitations, insomnia, a poor appetite, scanty menstruation volume, and almost no libido at all. Diagnosis: melanosis. Selection of body acupoints: Dazhui (GV 14), Quchi (LI 11), Xuehai (SP 10), and Sanyinjiao (SP 6). The above acupoints were punctured with even reinforcing-reducing manipulation. The needles retained for 20 minutes and the treatment was done once every other day; selection of auricular acupoints: ear-Shenmen, sympathetic nerve, adrenal gland, endocrine, Zigong (uterus), and lung. Each time 2 ear acupoints were selected for needling with intermittent manipulation to intensify stimulation. The needles retained for 4 hours and the treatment was done once every other day; Selection of acupoints for injection: Feishu (BL 13), Xinshu (BL 15), Ganshu (BL 18), and Shenshu (BL 23). One Dang Gui (*Radix Angelicae Sinensis*) injection was injected to two pairs of above acupoints respectively once every other day, and 10 times make up one treatment course. After 4 courses of treatment, the extreme itching of the skin obviously relieved, she got an increased appetite, and some skin pigmentations slightly reduced. After half a year, the pigmentations obviously reduced and her accompanying symptoms basically disappeared. She restored a normal skin color after 27 courses of treatment.

Remarks: TCM holds that this condition is usually caused by insufficiency of the spleen, liver and kidney, deficiency of qi and blood, blood stasis due to qi stagnation and malnutrition of skin. The combined therapy of body acupoints, auricular acupoints and acupoint injection can regulate zang-fu organs and promote qi and blood circulation. Because of the relatively long treatment course,

汉英对照

Chinese-English
Edition of
Acupuncture
Cosmetology

针灸美容

Part 3 The Typical Case Reports of Acupuncture Cosmetology

第三节　皱纹

一、验案 1

赵某,女,47 岁,干部。

主诉:额纹及鱼尾纹,近年明显加剧。伴心慌气短,双下肢酸软,面色萎黄,舌淡苔薄白,脉沉涩。诊断:气血亏虚型。毫针刺阳白、太阳、头临泣、瞳子髎、角孙,中等刺激。沿皱纹走向局部取穴,平刺法重刺激。配以足三里、血海、中脘温针灸,隔日 1 次。共治 40 次后,面色转红润,鱼尾纹基本消失,额纹明显变浅。

按语:针加灸不仅能疏通经络、促进气血运行,更能调整内在脏腑的功能,促进营养物质的吸收。应注意全面合理的营养调配,保持精神愉悦,劳逸结合,避免暴晒等,平时还可自行做面部按摩,从脸部中间向外延伸,每次 5～6 min,更能巩固疗效,延缓衰老的出现。

good communication with the patients and their cooperation are also important for the final result.

Section 3 Wrinkles

Case 1

Zhao, female, 47 years old, a government official.

Chief complaints: Obviously increased forehead wrinkles and crow's feet. Accompanying symptoms and signs include: palpitations, shortness of breath, soreness and weakness of lower limbs, a sallow complexion, a pale tongue with thin and white coating and a deep and hesitant pulse. TCM syndrome pattern: deficiency of qi and blood. Method: The acupoints Yangbai (GB 14), Taiyang (EX-HN 5), Toulinqi (GB 15), Tongziliao (GB 1), and Jiaosun (TE 20) were punctured with moderate stimulation; the local acupoints along the directions of wrinkles were also punctured subcutaneously with heavy stimulation; and the acupoints Zusanli (ST 36), Xuehai (SP 10) and Zhongwan (CV 12) were applied warming needles. The above methods were done once every other day. After 40 times of treatment, the patient got a red and lustrous complexion, the crow's feet basically disappeared and the forehead wrinkles obviously turned shallow.

Remarks: Acupuncture and moxibustion can not only dredge meridians and promote qi and blood flow, but also regulate functions of internal organs and promote absorption of nutrients. Life style recommendations: keep a well-balanced diet and a peaceful mind, balance work and rest, and avoid too much exposure to sun. In addition, self facial massage starting from center of face to outward extension (5 - 6 minutes each time) may consolidate the therapeutic efficacy and delay the

汉英对照
Chinese-English
Edition of
Acupuncture
Cosmetology

针灸美容 Part 3 The Typical Case Reports of Acupuncture Cosmetology

二、 验案 2

刘某,女,56 岁,教师。

主诉:额纹增多 5 年。伴失眠多梦,心烦易怒,口干舌燥,胁肋胀满,舌红脉弦。诊断:阴血不足型。毫针针刺风池、天髎、翳风、扶突、曲池、合谷,中等刺激,天髎、翳风、扶突加低频电针,每次选 2 穴,刺激 4～6 min,以局部感觉微微颤动为度。肝俞、肾俞轻刺激加温针,留针 30 min,隔日 1 次,20 次为 1 个疗程。共治疗 40 次,诸症消失,额纹明显减退,皮肤弹性增加。

按语:针加灸法能疏通经络、调整内脏、疏肝理气、活血化瘀。配合电针,更能促进组织新陈代谢、增强皮肤肌肉的弹性而达到治愈的效应。

第四节 消瘦

一、 验案 1

刘某某,女,24 岁。1997 年 3 月初诊。

aging signs.

Case 2

Liu, female, 56 years old, a teacher.

Chief complaints: Five years of increased forehead wrinkles. Accompanying symptoms and signs include: insomnia, dreaminess, restlessness, irritability, a dry tongue and mouth, hypochondriac distension and fullness, a red tongue and a wiry pulse. TCM syndrome pattern: yin-blood deficiency. Method: The acupoints Fengchi (GB 20), Tianyou (TE 16), Yifeng (TE 17), Futu (LI 18), Quchi (LI 11) and Hegu (LI 4) were punctured by filiform needles with moderate stimulation, and the needles on Tianyou (TE 16), Yifeng (TE 17), and Futu (LI 18) were connected to low-frequency electric stimulator (2 acupoints each time) for 4 - 6 minutes until slight trembling of the local area; the acupoints Ganshu (BL 18) and Shenshu (BL 23) were applied mild-stimulation needling plus warming needles. The needle retained for 30 minutes. The treatment was done once every other day and 20 times make up one treatment course. After 40 times of treatment, all the symptoms disappeared, and the forehead wrinkles obviously reduced with increased skin elasticity.

Remarks: Acupuncture and moxibustion can dredge meridians, regulate functions of internal organs, soothe liver-qi, and circulate blood and resolve stasis. The combined electric stimulation can enhance metabolism of tissues and increase skin or muscle elasticity.

Section 4   Emaciation

Case 1

Liu, female, 24 years old, came for the first visit in March

汉英对照
Chinese-English
Edition of
Acupuncture
Cosmetology
针灸美容

Part 3 The Typical Case Reports of Acupuncture Cosmetology

患者身高 169 cm,体重 45.8 kg,形体消瘦。自述整天无精打采,四肢发凉,不思饮食。毫针足三里、上巨虚、下巨虚、三阴交,直刺,行提插捻转补法,针感上行入腹为佳,留针 30 min。中脘、天枢、关元用长艾条,距皮肤 1 寸,施回旋灸,每个穴位灸 3～5 min,以局部皮肤红润为度。每日 1 次,10 次为 1 个疗程,休息 7 d,再行第二个疗程。脾俞、胃俞用颗粒式皮内针埋针,留针 3～5 d,间隔 3 d,再行第二次埋针。经过上述方法治疗后,第一个疗程增重 1 kg,第二个疗程增重 2 kg,第三个疗程增重 1.5 kg。该患者经过 3 个疗程的治疗,随访半年体重皆在 55～61 kg,现体重为 55.5 kg。

按语:治疗消瘦重在调理脾胃,加强其对饮食受纳、腐熟、消化、吸收、输送的功能,尤其是俞募穴(脾俞、胃俞、中脘、关元、天枢)的配合应用,灸之能温补下元,助脏腑气化,振奋脾胃阳气,气血生化有权,脾胃健运,气机得理,体重增加。但报道也指出,随访病例半年以上,未见持续性发胖或出现肥胖症现象,可见针灸具有双向性的调整作用。

1997.

The patient's height: 169 cm; and body weight: 45.8 kg. She complained of lassitude, cold limbs and no appetite. Method: The acupoints Zusanli (ST 36), Shangjuxu (ST 37), Xiajuxu (ST 39) and Sanyinjiao (SP 6) were punctured perpendicularly with filiform needles by reinforcing manipulation through lifting and thrusting, the needling sensation was supposed to go up to abdomen and the needles retained for 30 minutes; the acupoints Zhongwan (CV 12), Tianshu (ST 25) and Guanyuan (CV 4) were applied circling moxibustion with long moxa stick at 1 cun away from the skin, 3 - 5 minutes each acupoint until the local skin turned red. The treatment was done once every day, 10 times make up one treatment course and there is a 7-day interval between two courses; the acupoints Pishu (BL 20) and Weishu (BL 21) were applied embedding of granule-like intradermal needles once every 3 - 5 days, and there is a 3-day interval between two treatments. Result: the patient got weight gain of 1 kg after one treatment course of above methods; 2 kg after two courses and 1.5 kg after three courses. After 3 treatment courses, the six-month follow-up showed the range of her body weight was from 55 to 61 kg, and the present body weight is 53.5 kg.

Remarks: The key in treating emaciation lies in regulating the spleen and stomach to enhance their function in receive, decompose, digest, absorb and distribute the water and food. Moxibustion on back-Shu and front-Mu acupoints such as Pishu (BL 20), Weishu (BL 21), Zhongwan (CV 12), Guanyuan (CV 4) and Tianshu (ST 25) can warm and tonify Yuan-primordial qi, help qi transformation of zang-fu organs, activate yang-qi of the spleen and stomach, regulate qi activity

汉英对照

Chinese-English
Edition of
Acupuncture
Cosmetology

针灸美容

下篇 ● 针灸美容典型验案

二、 验案 2

张某,女31岁,职员。

主诉:身体消瘦,体重下降2年余。伴倦怠乏力,心慌气短,失眠多梦,纳呆,腹胀便溏,舌淡苔薄白,脉细无力。检查:肝功能、血糖、血色素及心肺均正常,身高163 cm,体重45 kg。诊断:单纯性消瘦。针刺脾俞、胃俞、肝俞、足三里、下巨虚。毫针补法,留针30 min,加艾条悬灸,每穴10 min,每日1次,10次为1个疗程,共治疗25次,形体丰润,体重增至51 kg,诸症消失,随访半年未复发。

按语:针对体重低于标准体重20%以上的消瘦者,可伴有消化系统、内分泌系统及慢性消耗性疾病,治疗时应注意对原发病的坚持与治疗,去除病因。此外,调节情绪、加强营养也是本病取效的关键所在。

and as a result to gain weight. It has also been reported that more than six month of follow-up didn't show persistent obesity or obese signs, indicating acupuncture can have dual regulation.

Case 2

Zhang, female, 31 years old, a clerk.

Chief complaints: Emaciation with more than 2 years of weight loss. Accompanying symptoms and signs: lassitude, palpitations, shortness of breath, insomnia, dreaminess, a poor appetite, abdominal distension with loose stool, a pale tongue with thin and white coating and a thready and weak pulse. Physical examination: hepatic function, blood glucose, hemoglobin, heart and lung function are all normal, height: 163 cm, and body weight: 45 kg. Diagnosis: simple emaciation. Method: The acupoints Pishu (BL 20), Weishu (BL 21), Ganshu (BL 18), Zusanli (ST 36), and Xiajuxu (ST 39) were punctured with reinforcing manipulation by filiform needles, and the needles retained for 30 minutes; in addition, the acupoints were also applied to circling moxibustion with moxa stick, 10 minutes for each acupoint and 10 times make up one treatment course. After 25 times of treatment, the patient's body weight increased to 51 kg, all his symptoms disappeared and six-month follow-up didn't show any relapses.

Remarks: For those with 20% less than the standard body weight and complications of digestive system, endocrine system and chronic consumptive diseases, the treatment shall target on the primary diseases. In addition, emotional regulation and well-balanced nutrition are also keys to the therapeutic efficacy.

第五节　眼袋

一、验案 1

李某,女,49 岁,教师。

主诉:双下眼睑眼袋 10 余年。检查:双下睑皮肤松弛,眼轮匝肌肌力下降。予针刺承泣透目内眦,太阳加电针,次日改承泣透目外眦,太阳加电针,每次 10～20 min,以下眼轮匝肌微微抽动为宜,共治疗 30 次,眼袋基本消失,眼轮匝肌肌力增强。

按语:通过透刺配合电针,加强局部组织的新陈代谢、脂肪组织的吸收,提高肌肉的弹性而达到治疗目的。注意电针刺激的强度应由弱到强,以患者能耐受为度,不宜过强或时间过长,治疗结束后,局部应用干棉球按压,避免出血并注意休息。

二、验案 2

张某,男,55 岁,干部。

主诉:自觉双眼肿胀 2 年,尿常规及肾功能检查均正常。检查:双下睑眼袋,伴面色苍白而浮,乏力气短,失眠,苔薄质淡,脉沉细。将电针的两个电极板接于同一眼袋区内,通电 20 min,以局部肌肉抽动能耐受为度,隔日 1 次。夜间以紫荆皮、白芷、大黄、天南星、大柏皮、赤小豆、寒水石各等份,共研细末,用生地黄汁调成膏,外敷眼袋区。共治疗 28 次,自觉肿胀消失,检查眼袋亦消失。

Section 5   Baggy eyelids

Case 1

Li, female, 49 years old, a teacher.

Chief complaints: More than 10 years of baggy eyelids of the two eyes. Physical examination showed loosened skins of lower eyelids of two eyes and oculi muscle weakness. Method: Needling Chengqi (ST 1) toward the inner canthus, electric stimulation was connected to needle on Taiyang (EX-HN 5); and in the following day, needling Chengqi (ST 1) toward the outer canthus and electric stimulation was connected to needle on Taiyang (EX-HN 5), 10 – 20 minutes each time until slight twitching of the oculi muscle. The treatment was done altogether 30 times. After that, the baggy eyelids basically disappeared and the oculi muscle strength increased.

Remarks: Needling one acupoint toward another one plus electric stimulation can enhance the metabolism of local tissue and absorption of adipose tissue, and increase the muscle elasticity. Note: the intensity of electric acupuncture shall be increased gradually from mild to strong stimulation, up to the patients' tolerance. Over-strong or over-long stimulation shall be avoided. After the treatment, the local area shall be pressed with dry cotton to avoid bleeding and more rest is needed.

Case 2

Zhang, male, 55 years old, a government official.

Chief complaints: More than 2 years of subjective feeling of eyelid swelling of two eyes. The routine urine test and renal function showed normal results. Physical examination showed baggy eyelids of two eyes, a pale complexion with facial puffiness, fatigue, shortness of breath, insomnia, a pale tongue with thin coating, and a deep and thready pulse. Method: To

汉英对照
Chinese-English
Edition of
Acupuncture
Cosmetology

针灸美容   Part 3 The Typical Case Reports of Acupuncture Cosmetology

按语：外敷药每晚贴上，次日晨起去掉，一般 20 次为 1 个疗程，有助于祛瘀通络、除湿消肿。注意应排除其他原发病导致的面目浮肿。

汉英对照

Chinese-English
Edition of
Acupuncture
Cosmetology

针灸美容

下篇 ◉ 针灸美容典型验案

connect the two electrode plates of the electric stimulator to one baggy eyelid for 20 minutes up to the patient's tolerance of local muscle twitching, once every other day. At night, the patient was applied paste made from the fine powder of equal amounts of Zi Jing Pi (*Cortex Cercis Chinensis*), Bai Zhi (*Radix Angelicae Dahuricae*), Tian Nan Xing (*Rhizoma Arisaematis*), Da Huang (*Radix et Rhizoma Rhei*), Da Bai Pi (*Cortex Phellodendri*), Chi Xiao Dou (*Semen Phaseoli*) and Han Shui Shi (*Mirabilitum*) with juice of Sheng Di Huang (*Dried Radix Rehmanniae*). After 28 times of treatment, the patient subjectively felt disappearance of baggy eyelids, which was confirmed by examination.

Remarks: The external application was done at every night and removed in the next early morning, and usually 20 times make up one treatment course. This therapy can resolve stasis, clear meridians, remove dampness and swelling. Note: facial puffiness and edema of eyes due to other primary diseases have to be excluded.

参 考 文 献

1. 李元文,靳琦.美容护肤中医八法.北京：中国中医药出版社,1992.25～31,248～300.

2. 张凤翔.医学整容与美容保健.北京：经济日报出版社,1990.95～154,163～177.

3. 傅杰英.实用经络美容七讲.北京：人民卫生出版社,2004.43～108,115～228.

4. 陈德成.中国针灸美容抗衰全书.北京：中国中医药出版社,2002.12～25,113～191.

5. 张书琴.美容整形临床应用解剖学.北京：中国医药科技出版社,1998.4～9.

6. 李福耀.医学美容解剖学.北京：人民卫生出版社,1999.75～79.

7. 孙国杰.针灸学.北京：中国中医药出版社,1997.25,318～320.

8. http://www.mm616.com/Html/2005111/2005111161918-1.html

9. http://www.acutimes.com/show.asp? lst = 0&classid = 150&id = 1828

10. http://www.mei519.com/jianfei_detail.asp? id = 673

11. http://www.mei519.com/jianfei_detail.asp? id = 674

12. http://www.acutimes.com/show.asp? lst = 0&classid =

References

1. LI Yuan-wen, JIN Qi, Eight TCM Methods of Cosmetology and Skin Protection, Beijing: China Press of Traditional Chinese Medicine, 1992. 25 – 31,248 – 300.

2. ZHANG Feng-xiang, Medical Plastic Surgery and Cosmetic Health-preservation, Beijing: Economic Daily Press, 1990. 95 – 154, 163 – 177.

3. FU Jie-ying, Seven Lectures on Practical Cosmetology through Meridians, Beijing: the People's Medical Publishing House, 2004. 43 – 108, 115 – 228.

4. CHEN De-cheng, Completed Collection of Cosmetology & Anti-aging with Chinese Acupuncture, Beijing: China Press of Traditional Chinese Medicine, 2002. 12 – 25, 113 – 119.

5. ZHANG Shu-qin, Applied Clinical Anatomy of Cosmetic Plastic Surgery, Beijing: China Press of Medical Science & Technology, 1998. 4 – 9.

6. LI Fu-yao, Anatomy on Medical Cosmetology, Beijing: the People's Medical Publishing House, 1999. 75 – 79.

7. SUN Guo-jie, Science of Acupuncture and Moxibustion, Beijing: China Press of Traditional Chinese Medicine. 1997. 25,318 – 320.

8. http://www. mm616. com/Html/2005111/2005111161918-1. html

9. http://www. acutimes. com/show. asp? lst － 0&classid = 150&id = 1828

10. http://www. mei519. com/jianfei_detail. asp? id = 673

11. http://www. mei519. com/jianfei_detail. asp? id = 674

150&id = 1821

13. http://www.51qe.cn/pic/20/17/10/019.htm

14. http://www.51qe.cn/pic/20/17/10/020.htm

15. http://www.51qe.cn/pic/20/17/10/018.htm

16. http://www.acutimes.com/show.asp? lst = 0&classid = 150&id = 1701

17. http://www2.tjutcm.edu.cn/zhentui/list.asp? unid = 173

18. http://www.eshooo.com/online/medinfo/news16379.html

19. http://www.acutimes.com/show.asp? lst = 0&classid = 150&id = 1820

20. http://www.medicenter.cn/data/2005/0921/article _ 75.htm

21. http://www.medicenter.cn/data/2005/0921/article _ 75.htm

22. http://www.medicenter.cn/data/2005/0921/article _ 75.htm

23. http://www.acutimes.com/show.asp? lst = 0&classid = 150&id = 1829

24. http://www.mei519.com/jianfei_detail.asp? id = 667

25. http://www.yszymr.com/zhuanjiadaying11.htm

26. http://health.enorth.com.cn/system/2002/08/01/000387165.shtml

27. http://www.51qe.cn/pic/20/17/10/014.htm

28. http://www.eshooo.com/online/medinfo/news13910.html

12. http://www. acutimes. com/show. asp? lst = 0&classid = 150&id = 1821

13. http://www.51qe.cn/pic/20/17/10/019.htm

14. http://www.51qe.cn/pic/20/17/10/020.htm

15. http://www.51qe.cn/pic/20/17/10/018.htm

16. http://www. acutimes. com/show. asp? lst = 0&classid = 150&id = 1701

17. http://www2. tjutcm. edu. cn/zhentui/list. asp? unid = 173

18. http://www. eshooo. com/online/medinfo/news16379. html

19. http://www. acutimes. com/show. asp? lst = 0&classid = 150&id = 1820

20. http://www. medicenter. cn/data/2005/0921/article _ 75. htm

21. http://www. medicenter. cn/data/2005/0921/article _ 75. htm

22. http://www. medicenter. cn/data/2005/0921/article _ 75. htm

23. http://www. acutimes. com/show. asp? lst = 0&classid = 150&id = 182

24. http://www. mei519. com/jianfei_detail. asp? id = 667

25. http://www. yszymr. com/zhuanjiadaying11. htm

26. http://health. enorth. com. cn/system/2002/08/01/ 000387165. shtml

27. http://www.51qe. cn/pic/20/17/10/014. htm

28. http://www. eshooo. com/online/medinfo/news13910. html

29. http://news. upc. edu. cn/newsupc/news _ jkxx _ bj/ 20060910/081316. shtml

30. http://health. 66wz. com/system/2005/08/18/000007814.

29. http：//news. upc. edu. cn/newsupc/news _ jkxx _ bj/ 20060910/081316. shtml

30. http：//health. 66wz. com/system/2005/08/18/000007814. shtml

31. http：//news. upc. edu. cn/newsupc/news_jkxx_bj/20060910/ 081316. shtml

32. 秦亮.艾条灸后溪穴治疗麦粒肿.中国针灸,2006,26(6)：423.

33. 朴联友,郝广义,段跃武,等.飞腾八法配合刺血拔罐治疗黄褐斑 30 例.中国针灸,2001,21(7)：415～416.

34. 侯蕊莲.叩刺加局部药物注射治疗斑秃 12 例.陕西中医函授,2001,5：28.

35. 田永萍,侯春英.龙文君教授治疗神经性皮炎琐谈.甘肃中医,2005,18(6)：13.

36. 何玲娜,田丰伟,李宁,等.神阙八阵穴闪罐治疗肥胖症临床疗效观察.中国针灸,2004,24(6)：395～397.

37. 王晓燕.体针配合梅花针治疗神经性皮炎.云南中医学院学报,2004,27(3)：52～53.

38. 张红宏.点刺太阳、印堂、耳尖穴配合尿洗治疗红眼病 137 例.实用医技杂志,2001,(7)：48.

shtml

31. http://news. upc. edu. cn/newsupc/news _ jkxx _ bj/ 20060910/081316. shtml

32. QIN Liang, Moxa-stick moxibustion on Houxi (SI 3) and Stye, Chinese acupuncture & moxibustion, 2006, 26 (6): 423.

33. PIAO Lian-you, HAO Guang-yi and DUAN Yue-wu et al, The eight methods of intelligent turtle plus cupping after blood letting and 30 case reports of chloasma, Chinese acupuncture & moxibustion, 2001, 21(7): 415 – 416.

34. HOU Rui-lian, Tapping with dermal needle plus local drug injection and 12 case reports of alopecial areata, Shanxi Correspondence Journal of Traditional Chinese Medicine, 2001, 5: 28.

35. TIAN Yong-ping, HOU Chun-ying, Prof LONG Wen-jun's Experience in Treatment of Neurodermatitis, Gansu Journal of Traditional Chinese Medicine, 2005, 18(6): 13.

36. HE Ling-na, TIAN Feng-wei and LI Ning et al, Clinical efficacy observation on treatment of obesity with flash cupping on Shenque (CV 8)-related eight special areas, Chinese Acupuncture & Moxibustion, 2004, 24(6): 395 – 397.

37. WANG Xiao-yan, Combined body needles plus plum-blossom needle and neurodermatitis, Journal of Yunnan College of Traditional Chinese Medicine, 2004, 27 (3): 52 –53.

38. ZHANG Hong-hong, Pricking Taiyang, Yingtang and ear apex plus urine washing and 137 case reports of conjunctivitis, Journal of Practical Medical Technique, 2001,(7): 48.

汉英对照 Chinese-English Edition of Acupuncture Cosmetology 针灸美容 References

39. 吴百林,江晓俊.针刺放血治疗红眼病.中国民间疗法, 2001,9(6):27.

40. 王为.针刺配合耳穴治疗痤疮 130 例.实用中医药杂志, 2004,20(5):254.

41. 耿萍,田玉华,林兆娟,等.针刺配合隔蒜灸治疗顽固性荨麻疹 46 例疗效观察.针灸临床杂志,2001,17(7): 18~19.

42. 段玲.针刺配合挑刺法治疗麦粒肿 49 例.湖北中医杂志, 2005,27(10):46.

43. 谢衡辉.针刺治疗胞轮振跳 35 例.上海针灸杂志,2003, 22(4):46.

44. 罗明.针刺治疗内分泌突眼症 50 例.针灸临床杂志, 2002,18(2):14~15.

45. 黄琼.针刺治疗眼睑眴动 20 例.四川中医,2005,23(11): 105.

46. 周素琴,韩艾.针刺治疗眼睑痉挛 20 例.中国中医急症, 2006,15(6):665~666.

47. 侯丽,董明栋,吴红新,等.针刺治疗原发性眼睑痉挛 21 例体会.河南实用神经疾病杂志,2003,6(2):94.

48. 袁金兰,张晓萍.针灸、走罐结合治疗慢性荨麻疹 56 例. 针灸临床杂志,2003,19(1):18.

39. WU Bai-lin, JIANG Xiao-jun, Acupuncture plus blood letting and conjunctivitis, China's Naturopathy, 2001, 9 (6): 27.

40. WANG Wei, Acupuncture plus ear points and 130 case reports of acne, Journal of Practical Traditional Chinese Medicine, 2004, 20(5): 254.

41. GENG Ping, TIAN Yu-hua and LIN Zhao-juan et al, Efficacy observation on treatment of 46 urticaria cases with acupuncture plus garlic-partitioned moxibustion, Journal of Clinical Acupuncture & Moxibustion, 2001, 17(7): 18 - 19.

42. DUAN Ling, Acupuncture plus pricking and 49 cases of stye, Hubei Journal of Traditional Chinese Medicine, 2005, 27(10): 46.

43. XIE Heng-hui, Acupuncture and 35 cases of eyelid twitch, Shanghai Journal of Acupuncture & Moxibustion, 2003, 22 (4): 46.

44. LUO Ming, Acupuncture and 50 cases of endocrine Exophthalmus, Journal of Clinical Acupuncture & Moxibustion, 2002, 18(2): 14 - 15.

45. HUANG Qiong, Acupuncture and 20 cases of eyelid twitch, Journal of Sichuan Traditional Chinese Medicine, 2005, 23(11): 105.

46. ZHOU Su-qin, HAN Ai, Acupuncture and 20 cases of eyelid spasm, Journal of Emergency in Traditional Chinese Medicine, 2006, 15(6): 665 - 666.

47. HOU Li, DONG Ming-dong and WU Hong-xin et al, Experience in treatment of 21 cases of primary eyelid spasm with acupuncture, Henan Journal of Practical Nervous Diseases, 2003, 6(2): 94.

48. YUAN Jin-lan, ZHANG Xiao-ping, Acupuncture plus

汉英对照

Chinese-English
Edition of
Acupuncture
Cosmetology

针灸美容

References

49. 徐佳.针灸耳压治疗肥胖症 215 例临床观察.针灸临床杂志,2005,21(4)：13～14.

50. 石奕丽,何立.针灸叩刺拔罐治疗慢性荨麻疹 46 例.陕西中医,2003,24(7)：648.

51. 冯莉.针灸美容验案 4 则.辽宁中医学院学报,2003,5(3)：256～257.

52. 周华青.针灸治疗痤疮 35 例临床观察.吉林中医药,2001,(5)：52.

53. 奚海鸿.针灸治疗单纯性肥胖症 60 例.上海针灸杂志,2005,24(2)：3～4.

54. 贾秀春.针灸治疗青春期痤疮 40 例.辽宁中医杂志,2005,32(4)：358.

55. 周兴明.针灸治疗青少年斑秃 22 例.中医外治法杂志,2005,14(5)：40.

56. 吴超,戴珩.针灸治疗消瘦 17 例.中国针灸杂志,2004,24(5)：314.

57. 李连生.皮肤病针灸疗法.天津：天津科学技术出版社,1993.447～450.

moving cupping and 56 case reports of chronic urticaria, Journal of Clinical Acupuncture & Moxibustion, 2003, 19 (1): 18.

49. XU Jia, Clinical observation on treatment of 215 obesity cases with acupuncture plus ear-pressure, Journal of Clinical Acupuncture & Moxibustion, 2005, 21(4): 13 - 14.

50. SHI Yi-li, HE Li, Acupuncture plus cupping after tapping and 46 case reports of chronic urticaria, Shanxi Journal of Traditional Chinese Medicine, 2003, 24(7): 648.

51. FENG Li, Four experience cases of cosmetic acupuncture, Journal of Liaoning College of Traditional Chinese Medicine, 2003, 5(3): 256 - 257.

52. ZHOU Hua-qing, Clinical observation on treatment of 35 acne cases with acupuncture, Jilin Journal of Traditional Chinese Medicine, 2001,(5): 52.

53. XI Hai-hong, Acupuncture and 60 cases of simple obesity, Shanghai Journal of Acupuncture & Moxibustion, 2005, 24 (2): 3 - 4.

54. JIA Xiu-chun, Acupuncture and 40 cases of puberty acne, Liaoning Journal of Traditional Chinese Medicine, 2005, 32(4): 358.

55. ZHOU Xing-ming, Acupuncture and 22 cases of adolescent alopecia areata, Journal of External Therapy of Traditional Chinese Medicine, 2005, 14(5): 40.

56. WU Chao, DAI Heng, Acupuncture and 17 cases of emaciation, Chinese Acupuncture & Moxibustion, 2004, 24 (5): 314.

57. LI Lian-sheng, Acupuncture therapy on dermatitis, Tianjin, Tianjin Science & Technology Press, 1993, 447 - 450.

汉英对照
Chinese-English
Edition of
Acupuncture
Cosmetology

针灸美容
References

58. 李若辉.中国针灸,1988,8(2)：18～19.

59. 戴玉勤.火针治疗疣、痣58例.中国针灸,1989,2(9)：51.

60. 徐笨人.便携式电子火针治疗皮肤病1268例疗效观察.中国针灸,1988,4(8)：6.

61. 陆健.穴位埋线治疗白癜风147例临床观察.中国针灸,1989,4(9)：13.

62. 魏明丰.隔药灸为主治疗白癜风147例临床观察.中国针灸,1990,(6)：9～10.

63. 来心平.改造电热针治疗面部雀斑196例.中国针灸,1991,11(4)：14.

64. 田永萍,侯春英.龙文君教授治疗神经性皮炎琐谈.甘肃中医,2005,18(6)：12.

65. 胡津丽,傅海扬,蒋彩云,等.美容针结合体针治疗黄褐斑31例.中国针灸,2005,25(10)：698.

66. 裴莉娜.He－Ne激光照射治疗白癜风(附一例报告).激光杂志.1993,14(2)：100.

67. 刘琪.耳压与夹脊埋线治疗银屑病50例.中国针灸,1991,12(11)：513.

68. 梁华梓.放血加电针治疗银屑病158例临床观察.中国针灸,1994,(2)：23～25.

58. LI Ruo-hui, China Acupuncture & Moxibustion, 1988, 8 (2): 18 - 19.

59. DAI Yu-qin, Fire needle and 58 cases of flat wart and nevus, China Acupuncture & Moxibustion, 1989, 2(9): 51.

60. XU Ben-ren, Therapeutic efficacy observation on treatment of 1268 dermatitis cases with portable electric fire needle instrument, China Acupuncture & Moxibustion, 1988, 4(8): 6.

61. LU Jian, Clinical observation on treatment of 147 vitiligo cases with acupoint catgut embedding, China Acupuncture & Moxibustion, 1989, 4(9): 13.

62. WEI Ming-feng, Clinical observation on treatment of 147 vitiligo cases with drug-partitioned moxibustion, China Acupuncture & Moxibustion, 1990,(6): 9 - 10.

63. LAI Xin-ping, Reworked electric heat needle and 196 cases of facial acne, China Acupuncture & Moxibustion, 1991,11 (4): 14.

64. TIAN Yong-ping, HOU Chun-ying, Prof. LONG Wen-jun's experience in treating neurodermatitis, Gansu Journal of Traditional Chinese Medicine, 2005, 18(6): 12.

65. HU Jin-li, FU Hai-yang and JIANG Cai-yun et al, Cosmetic needle and 31 case reports of chloasma, China Acupuncture & Moxibustion, 2005, 25(10): 698.

66. PEI li-na, He-Ne laser radiator and vitiligo (one case report), Laser Journal, 1993, 14(2): 100.

67. LIU Qi, Ear-pressure plus catgut embedding on Jiaji points and 50 cases of psoriasis, China Acupuncture & Moxibustion, 1991, 12(11): 513.

68. LIANG Hua-zi, Blood-letting plus electric acupuncture and clinical observation on 158 psoriasis cases, China

汉英对照

Chinese-English
Edition of
Acupuncture
Cosmetology

针灸美容

References

69. 薛浩. 针刺治疗酒皶鼻. 四川中医, 1988, 6(7): 17.

70. 崔连山. 针刺治疗酒皶鼻. 中医杂志, 1974, (3): 36.

71. 司来林. 针刺治疗口疮 30 例. 中国针灸, 1989, 1(9): 50.

72. 欧阳群. 针刺配合耳穴加穴位注射治疗黑变病 8 例. 新中医, 1984, (10): 26~27.

Acupuncture & Moxibustion, 1994,(2): 23 - 25.

69. XUE Hao, Acupuncture and brandy nose, Journal of Sichuan Traditional Chinese Medicine, 1998, 6(7): 17.

70. CUI Lian-shan, Acupuncture and brandy nose, Journal of Traditional Chinese Medicine, 1974,(3): 36.

71. SI Lai-lin, Acupuncture and 30 cases of mouth ulcer, China Acupuncture & Moxibustion, 1989, 1(9): 50.

72. OU Yang-qun, Acupuncture and ear points plus point injection and 8 cases of Melanosis, New Journal of Traditional Chinese Medicine, 1984,(10): 26 - 27.